T0302463

自然建造2023
ARCHITECTURE
CHINA
AWARD 2023

ARCHITECTURE
CHINA

Trophy design by Qin Xiaowan and Li Hongkai

CONTENTS

Essays

Architecture China Award in Practice

Exploration Award in Technology

Exploration Award for Young Architects

Special Project Award

2023 Architecture China Award

Award Concept

The theme of Architecture China Award, *Building with Nature*, looks at returning to the path of nature in contemporary Chinese architecture, or similar related concepts. Proposed by architects Wang Shu and Lu Wenyu, the theme is well placed in today's over-industrialized context and explores the poetry behind the constructions of the qualifying nominees.

The poetry in "building with nature" is created through a blend of nature, architecture, and the city. Building with Nature – Architecture China Award (the Award) acknowledges (and in that encourages) contemporary manifestations of the "building with nature" concept, while also advocating learning from the countryside—not only on architecture and methods of construction, but also on promoting a way of life that is harmonious with nature. Alongside the exploration and use of traditional materials and construction systems, the Award also promotes the integration of modern technologies. Future architecture, as envisioned based on the theme of the Architecture China Award, will reconnect the city, architecture, and nature with poetry, painting new ways of construction that are inseparable, difficult to classify, and dense.

Award Introduction

In 2016, Wang Shu served as jury chairman for the 4th China Architecture Media Awards sponsored by the Nanfang Media Group and *Southern Metropolis Daily*, and had proposed "building with nature" as a selection criterion for the Award. In 2019, this concept was adopted by the English-language architecture journal, *Architecture China*, as a theme to shape the Architecture China Award. As "building with nature" is the fundamental requisite and core idea of the Award, it was accordingly named the same. *Architecture China* is the first global English-language publication focusing on the development of architectural design in contemporary China, and organizer of the Architecture China Award.

There are four categories in the Award: Architecture China Award in Practice, Exploration Award in Technology, Exploration Award for Young Architects, and Special Project Award, and the review system models the process in major international architecture awards – establish committees for organization, nomination, and evaluation.

Award recipients are selected every two years; in addition to the nominations by the evaluation and nomination committees, both Chinese and foreign architects who have completed two or more high-level works in the Chinese mainland, Taiwan, and Hong Kong can also apply for consideration.

Evaluation Committee

Wang Shu (chair of evaluation committee)
2012 Laureate, Pritzker Architecture Prize
Jury, Pritzker Architecture Prize
Professor and Dean, School of Architecture, China Academy of Art

Cui Kai
Honorary President and Chief Architect, China Architecture Design & Research Group
Academician, Chinese Academy of Engineering

Yung Ho Chang
Former Jury, Pritzker Architecture Prize
Principal, Atelier FCJZ

Li Xiangning
Professor and Dean, College of Architecture and Urban Planning, Tongji University

Ge Ming
Professor and Deputy Dean, School of Architecture, Southeast University

Wang Lu
Professor, School of Architecture, Tsinghua University

Aric Chen
General and Artistic Director, Nieuwe Instituut

Benedetta Tagliabue
Jury, Pritzker Architecture Prize
Principal, Miralles Tagliabue EMBT

Iwan Baan
Architectural photographer

Philip Ursprung
Professor and Chair, History of Art and Architecture, ETH Zurich

Wilfried Wang
Co-founder and Principal Architect, Hoidn Wang Partner

Award Structure

Architecture China Award in Practice

Architecture China Award in Practice is the highest-ranking category in the Architecture China Award. It honors architects who have demonstrated "building with nature" or related concepts in his or her long-term architectural practice and requires that the architects have completed three or more high-quality works in the past ten years.

Three finalists are selected, among which one or two architects are granted the Architecture China Award in Practice. The other/s are granted Shortlisted awards.

Exploration Award in Technology

Exploration Award in Technology focuses on projects with a humanistic spirit and which display continuous innovation with architectural technologies through two or more high-quality works created in recent years. This award also encourages cross-professional and cross-disciplinary exploration.

Two or three finalists are selected, of which one is awarded the Exploration Award in Technology. The remaining finalists are granted Shortlisted awards.

Exploration Award for Young Architects

Exploration Award for Young Architects is granted to young architects under the age of forty-five who have completed two or more high-quality works in recent years. It aims to show professional recognition while encouraging the experimental spirit of young architects.

Five or six finalists are selected, of which three are granted the Exploration Award for Young Architects. The remaining finalists are granted Shortlisted awards.

Special Project Award

The Special Project Award is given to high-quality architectural works completed in recent years that embody the *Building with Nature* concept, or similar concepts. The recipients are nominated and selected by the members of the jury.

Organizing Committee

Nan Dao
Director, *Southern Metropolis Daily*

Lu Wenyu
Professor, Architecture School, China Academy of Art

Li Xiangning
Professor and Dean, College of Architecture and Urban Planning, Tongji University

Ge Ming
Professor and Deputy Dean, School of Architecture, Southeast University

Li Hui
Founder, Shanghai Fengyuzhu Culture Technology Co., Ltd.

Chief Partner

Shanghai Fengyuzhu Culture Technology Co.,Ltd.

Final jury meeting of 2023 Building with Nature—Architecture China Award

May 10, 2023

Final Jury Meeting

The final evaluation meeting of the 2023 Architecture China Award was held in the China National Archives of Publications and Culture in Hangzhou, China. The attending jury members included Wang Shu, Cui Kai, Yung Ho Chang, Li Xiangning, Ge Ming, Wang Lu, and Wilfried Wang. Some jury members joined the meeting virtually (online), and included Aric Chen, Benedetta Tagliabue, Iwan Baan, and Philip Ursprung. The jury discussed the candidates and shortlisted projects in depth. Projects were recognized and appreciated for their characteristics that integrated nature, architecture, and the city. After each category's voting was finalized, the final jury meeting completed the final review.

Jury

Wang Shu (Chair)

Cui Kai

Yung Ho Chang

Li Xiangning

Ge Ming

Wang Lu

Aric Chen

Benedetta Tagliabue

Iwan Baan

Philip Ursprung

Wilfried Wang

Wang Shu

"As the chair of the evaluation committee, I'm very happy to see that everyone has enjoyed the process. I think we had a great discussion today. The Building with Nature – Architecture China Award shows that we share similar sentiments about the way architecture should and will develop in the future. It's really nice that we found a lot of diversity and variety in architecture today. I think this is very good for Chinese architecture. This year, the majority of the winners are very young and this gives us more expectations about the future."

Cui Kai

"I'm very glad to see so many young architects and their wonderful works. I'm looking forward to seeing more of them achieve the completion of great projects. I also hope this award will perhaps lead the development of contemporary Chinese architecture in the future."

Yung Ho Chang

"I think the diversity of the award-winning projects sends a very positive message to architects, especially young architects. It tells the young people that they should pursue their own ideas and ideals because you never know which ideas will actually be developed and accepted by the field, as well as by the society. I think right now, it's a terrible moment for the world, and hopefully, with these awards, we're also sending a humanistic signal to the world."

Li Xiangning

"This is a very special moment in time. We still believe that exchange and communications among different cultures are important in every corner of the world. With this award, we hope to witness the growth of contemporary Chinese architecture in the future."

Ge Ming

"It's my great pleasure to join the jury. For me, 'building with nature' is an idea for architecture, as well as an attitude about architecture, and it also provides a possibility for architects to think and develop design method in their practice."

Wang Lu

"I think the Architecture China Award is a very high-quality and professional award. All the projects are very impressive. I hope, in the future, it will support more architects, especially the young generation."

Aric Chen

"It is really great to be part of this jury. It was a real gift to see so many works that I wasn't aware of and I'm now definitely more interested and eager to see more of such works in the future. I look forward to seeing more works by female architects, architects from outside of the major centers, and more projects by non-Chinese architects."

Benedetta Tagliabue

"It was really enjoyable to be part of this jury. Despite the physical distance, it's really beautiful to go through the ideas, projects, and think about where architecture is going. It was also very enjoyable because we studied the projects and discovered these fantastic architectures with the real desire toward being the best. This was the best surprise for me. Through this jury, there will be the possibility to make these fantastic works and experiments in China today more well-known to the rest of the world."

Iwan Baan

"I was really surprised with the variety of the works, and especially, by a couple of fresh, new projects. It's really nice to see what is being designed in China now."

Philip Ursprung

"It's been an honor to be on this jury. I'm very impressed by the high quality and originality of the projects. I think from an international point of view, it's good that we're reviewing architecture in China instead of Chinese architecture. For the next round, it will be perhaps good to see more female architects."

Wilfried Wang

"A national award jury provides a privileged panorama of the many sincere efforts being made to design and realize lasting pieces of architecture for a range of sites, both rural as well as metropolitan. For me, the best works were those that demonstrated the possibility of creating excellent architecture with frugal use of resources."

Photography:
Aric Chen © Mark Cocksedge
Iwan Baan © Jonas Eriksson
Philip Ursprung © Katalin Deér

The Contemporary Scenery of "Building with Nature"

Li Xiangning
Professor and Dean, College of Architecture and Urban Planning, Tongji University
Yao Weiwei
Lecturer, Shanghai Academy of Fine Arts, Shanghai University

Architecture has a unique presence in the landscape. The concept of "Building with Nature," as expressed in the practice and theoretical thinking of architectural creation, combines the exploration of natural resources and landscapes with philosophical reflection on the integration of nature into architecture. These practices form a complex relationship of joint construction between natural landscapes, architecture, and urban spaces. In the current social context, we first need to understand the multiple meanings of "nature."

The first interpretation of "nature" stems from its traditional context. Many European and American avant-garde architects have been fond of incorporating French painter Henri Rousseau's jungle scenes as architectural backdrops, inspired by Rousseau's idealized portrayal of untamed nature in pre-industrial society. This portrayal evokes a dreamlike image of a pristine and unspoiled natural environment, untouched by the influence of modern activities. Such primitive nature carries a certain primal allure, evoking complex emotions of intimacy, fear, desire, and greed within human beings. Architect Wang Shu frequently draws inspiration from painter Ni Zan's *Rongxi Studio* to express his perception of architectural values and the relationship between architecture and nature. In *Rongxi Studio*, the concept of "nature" takes on a different meaning compared to the primitive nature devoid of human presence. Here, a simple house supported by four pillars becomes a dwelling where humans live peacefully within nature, showcasing the establishment of a connection between humankind and the natural environment through the act of construction.

The second interpretation revolves around artificial nature. Yang Yongliang's series of paintings named *Phantom Landscape* seemingly show a traditional Chinese landscape from a distance. However, upon closer examination, one realizes that the depicted scenes are actually artificial structures constructed from steel and concrete, juxtaposed against natural landscape backgrounds. In this way, Yang Yongliang depicts industrial creations with the illusion of green mountains and flowing water, as if to declare that artificially built scenes have become the "nature" of our time.

The third perspective concerns the notion of excessive "nature." Gong Zizhen, in his book, *My Plum Tree Infirmary,* reflects on how plum trees are deemed beautiful only when they exhibit a bent shape; straightness is considered unattractive. This observation highlights the deliberate selection and modification of the natural appearance of plum trees to cater to certain aesthetic preferences of the literati. Artist Shen Shaomin's artwork, *Bonsai,* accentuates the process of artificially curving plum trees, thereby conveying the irony of this "anti-natural" phenomenon. When architecture purposefully creates and reproduces nature in pursuit of a particular expressive state, it can veer to the extreme. So, the question is: Can we accept the idea that human beings exist within the realm of their own constructed nature, where even reinforced-concrete structures can be viewed as natural as insects' nests?

Within the context of this multifaceted discourse on nature, the Building with Nature: Architecture China Award (Architecture China Award of the Award) aims to inspire contemporary Chinese architects to re-establish their connection with nature through design. The Award seeks to address the fundamental aspects of Chinese building traditions and prompt reflection on the shortcomings resulting from rapid development over the past two to three decades. For instance, in the area of rural architecture, the prize emphasizes not only the integration of locally derived architectural concepts and construction methods, but also a way of life that harmoniously intertwines with nature. Additionally, the Award advocates for the fusion of traditional construction materials with modern technologies and encourages the exploration of traditional techniques throughout the construction process. The overarching vision of the Award is to foster architecture of the future that restores a sense of inseparability among the city, architecture, nature, poetry, and painting through new modes of construction. The selected works for the Architecture China Award exemplify these endeavors and aspirations.

Architecture can shape landscapes. One architectural response to the traditional understanding of nature is the concept of "disappearing architecture," which explores the relationship between building and nature. Zhang Lei (azLa) exemplifies this approach in his design of Ruralation Museum Hot Spring Hotel, Tangshan, by integrating three forcibly imposed axes that establish a dynamic trajectory for human and natural experiences,

1 | 2 | 3

1. Ruralation Museum Hot Spring Hotel, Tangshan by azLa © azLa
2. Dong Lu Yuan by Yinyuan Studio © Ke Yunfeng
3. Dong Lu Yuan by Yinyuan Studio © Wang Dan

guiding and enhancing the spatial rituals within the museum. Upon entering the building's vestibule, visitors are led by the play of light up a staircase, where the space expansively unfolds before their eyes. As they turn toward the east, the entrance porch frames a picturesque mountain vista, seamlessly blending architecture and the natural scenery. This east–west axis extends beyond an infinity pool into the mountains at the west, gradually integrating the building into the natural hues of the surrounding mountain forest. In turn, the building's north–south axis ascends, culminating in a concrete cylinder that opens to the sky, merging the spatial transition with the heavens, and ultimately vanishing into nature. Another approach to the strategy of disappearing architecture is evident in the design of the Jiangsu Garden Expo Treasure Pavilion. Here, Lei skillfully manipulates the landscape, creating overlapping and superimposed spaces, integrating the building into the site to achieve a harmonious unity with the terrain. In this instance, the architecture becomes a fragment of the land, while the folded and intricate roof reconstructs the region's topography.

Traditional Chinese gardens and traditional techniques offer an opportunity for reflection and critical inquiry in the contemporary world. Rooted in a philosophy of closeness and symbiosis with nature, traditional Chinese gardens reflect a way of life that coexists harmoniously with the natural environment. By incorporating elements of gardening into design, architecture can not only recreate miniature versions of nature, but also preserve and extend local architectural culture.

In response to the prevailing indifference of modern architecture toward the connection between architecture and the land, Wang Baozhen (Yinyuan Studio) takes an approach that emphasizes the importance of "seeking inspiration from the earth." Over the course of nearly a decade of design exploration in his Rong Garden, he has developed an architectural language around gardens and courtyards, employing them as the primary organizing principle. Influenced by traditional Chinese landscaping principles, his goal has been to ensure walkability, viewability, inhabitability, and browsability. In the design of his Dong Lu Yuan garden project, Wang ingeniously develops the relationship between space and topography.

By employing modern construction techniques, he seamlessly incorporates the view of the Taihang Mountains into the garden and interior spaces. This approach not only fulfills complex functional requirements but also satisfies people's innate longing for landscapes and nature. Additionally, the deliberate use of local materials, such as rubble, stone slabs, and white plaster reinterprets the wisdom and philosophy inherent in traditional gardens with contemporary materials and techniques, while retaining a modern style. In this garden environment, the poetry of dwelling comes to life.

In response to the current understanding of "nature," architects engage in observation and research, and also in the preservation

1. Xinfan Market by Yanfei Architects © Chen Hao
2. Rice Field Restaurant in Changyangli by Gebie Architects © Xia Zhi

of traditional skills and culture. For example, they recognize that the traditional system of agricultural production is no longer the sole means of survival in rural areas, and they acknowledge the prevalence of collage-like living scenarios in contemporary rural environments. In such settings, architects naturally move into the role of a "builder." Wang Bin's (Gebie Architects) project, Rice Field Restaurant in Changyangli exemplifies the attempt to capture the site's essence using industrialized imagery and its associated strength, enhancing the village's former order that has long since vanished from memory. The space has been crafted using solid, cost-effective materials and a clear structural design. Faced with the complexities of contemporary rural realities, this approach conveys the standpoint of the young architect: one must accept and honor the real status of nature in the present era, and honor the inherent qualities of materials and structures to express ideas.

The Xinfan Market, an old vegetable market that has served the community for over two decades, required urgent reconstruction measures to address structural and sanitary concerns. Architect Shui Yanfei's (Yanfei Architects) design approach focuses on maintaining the layout of the original structure, with the new building largely adhering to the existing contours. By extending its original texture, the design enhances the accessibility and public character of the building. In line with the local architectural heritage of Jinyun (Lishui City, Zhejiang Province, China), also known as "Stone Town," the exterior wall of the vegetable market has been constructed using locally abundant Jinyun tuff. This material not only reflects the historical architectural lineage of the area, but also contributes to the contextual integration of the new building into its surroundings.

Another reproduction of traditional nature can be seen in the project Upper Cloister in Aranya, Golden Mountain (Jinshanling)designed by Liu Yichun (Atelier Deshaus). The Upper Cloister is not an old temple, but it stands in the presence of the ancient Great Wall, a truly awe-inspiring historical marvel. The arrival of the building complex in the mountain valley establishes a new temporal vantage point for observing the surrounding nature. The delicate and accessible zen hall, with a slender and lightweight structure forms a temporal distance to the Great Wall, while simultaneously leaving its mark on

Zen hall, Upper Cloister in Aranya, Golden Mountain (Jinshanling) by Atelier Deshaus © Su Shengliang

the temporality of the secluded valley through human construction activity. Guiding visitors from its upper entrance to the lower meditation hall, through open and closed spatial arrangements, the Upper Cloister also strives to establish an internal temporality. The architect seeks to create a dialog of time and space between the ancient Great Wall and the new complex, as well as to integrate the structure with the topography and wilderness of the valley. From the Upper Cloister, one can enjoy vistas of distant mountains, old beacon towers, cliffs, and the leisurely movement of clouds in the sky; the westward-facing openings that look over the valley frame views of the Great Wall and a natural stone statue. The Buddhist hall, named Omniscience Hall, aims to alleviate worldly troubles; therefore, within the hall, natural rocks that harmonize with the original nature of the site are deliberately exposed.

All these architectural works define "nature" within various contexts. Whether understood as a noun—representing the environment or landscape, or as an adjective—expressing the concept of building "naturally," they embody a perspective on construction that aligns with the principles encouraged by the Building with Nature: Architecture China Award. These works seek to discover the poetic nature of construction in creating spaces, while emphasizing an honest relationship between materials and construction. In doing so, they blur the boundaries between architecture and landscape, creating a harmonious fusion.

Upper Cloister in Aranya, Golden Mountain (Jinshanling) by Atelier Deshaus © Jonathan Leijonhufvud

Concentrated Reflections

Wilfried Wang
Co-founder and Principal Architect, Hoidn Wang Partner

Participating in a jury with both domestic and international colleagues to award prizes for recent architectural works in China has offered a condensed panorama of a nation with an enormous production in construction. Contrasted with decades of memories from earlier visits to China (the first of which was in 1979), it is possible to summarize that architectural design in China is not only matching levels of distinction elsewhere, in some areas it is possible to recognize that new works contribute in an original way to the international architectural discourse.

In the global context of recent urban and architectural construction, much that is built for residential or commercial use is of a normal, if not just of a mediocre quality. Shanghai in 1979 already had hundreds of standardized high rises; the metropolitan expanse was enormous even then. Now, the context in which some of the reviewed work is to be found is as repetitive as it is numbing, both within and between cities. The term landscape or nature can hardly be used for the spaces between the inner cities. The improvement of this broad global settlement phenomenon is a huge challenge for the future. As for the jury's task, we had the luxury of focusing exclusively on the exceptional work by the shortlisted candidates.

Is it possible to deduce some collective qualities in the work in question? Are there issues that are being addressed across the projects?

Given that a few of the selected architects have either studied or worked outside China, such personal experiences, unsurprisingly, have had an effect on design conceptions, sensibilities, and preferences. Thus, an adherence to modernist abstraction and post-modernist reductive configurations, both made with few materials, can be noted, as in the case of Zhang Lei, who studied at the ETH Zurich. In the field of advanced engineering, there are examples of large, elegantly detailed and carefully constructed buildings. Beyond this, Wang Baozhen's work includes locally available materials, together with skilled craft labor. Then, it is also worth noting that the picturesque tradition, either derived directly from Chinese examples of paintings and landscape architecture, or by way of modernist reinterpretations, enjoys a variety of applications and transformations, as seen in the projects of Li Xinggang, Shui Yanfei, and Liu Yichun, just to name three of the shortlisted architects.

In the latter's work, the mastery of picturesque composition techniques plays a powerful role in imbuing the otherwise sterile technical construction elements such as concrete pillars and beams or steel profiles with associative echoes of delicate pavilions or monumental temples of the past. Particularly impressive is the reinterpretation of Louis I. Kahn's Kimbell Art Museum in Fort Worth, Texas, United States of America. In this building, there are only minor picturesque inflections resulting from the three courtyards and the lecture theater. All the exhibition galleries are of the same height and length. The configuration is symmetric, and therefore, classically static. In Liu Yichun's Long Museum (West Bund), a double-cantilevering semi-vault similar to that of Kimbell Art Museum is used, with different heights, and arranged with a seeming casualness that both permits visitors to refresh their attention and allow curators to place works of art of different sizes in a variety of sequences, walls, and space sizes. The Long Museum is minimal in its repetitive use of a basic element. But because the architect has not insisted on laying out this basic element on a simplistic grid, he has innovated the typology of the art museum. This balanced approach of using few elements with such an enriching result is characteristic of Liu's other works, and for this he deserved to receive the 2023 Architecture China Award in Practice. It is an intelligence that has been cultivated within the long tradition of the picturesque, and by this, the knowing creation of a subtle sense of an organic order. This tradition has also been

Jiangsu Garden Expo Treasure Pavilion by azLa © Hou Bowen

Pitaya Yuan by Yinyuan Studio © Wang Baozhen

Lostvilla Boutique I lotel in Yucun by Yanfei Architects © Chen Hao

1. Long Museum (West Bund) by Atelier Deshaus © Su Shengliang
2. Long Museum (West Bund) by Atelier Deshaus © Su Shengliang

a strong source of inspiration in Li Xinggang's work, another contender for this year's Architecture China Award in Practice, and who undoubtedly will remain a strong contender in the future.

Reflecting on the Chinese tradition of the picturesque, and seeing it being cultivated in the work of Amateur Architecture Studio—Wang Shu and Lu Wenyu—the transformation of the picturesque tradition is one of the distinctive forces in contemporary Chinese architecture that raises questions which are no longer asked in other countries: how does contemporary architecture represent a culture and what is the role of tradition?

Given the global building industry's effect in producing regular, repetitive mechanical structures that are practically indistinguishable in terms of identity, place or culture, even when they take the shape of blobs, do people need a sense of cultural identity? Or is it not the case of elite architecture having taken on a course of its own, satisfying its internal discourse? Should topography, climate, site, national, regional and local culture, local materials and crafts play any role at all?

Architecture remains the slowest of all arts. From the client's realization that a construction is needed, to the selection of an architect and finally to the construction's completion, the process can take years. On the other hand, adding a porch or subdividing a room can be accomplished in a few days. The latter can have praiseworthy qualities, though no one would expect to find any in such small "architectures." But why is that the case? A well-chosen rock that has been found by chance in a riverbed or in a field could serve as a stepping-stone to a home, and therefore, would not only be a threshold into an interior, but would also connect the user back to nature, back to some roots. Architecture not only provides spaces for us to gather; it can also carry us to places that we have known or visited, by its power of atmospheric association. Architecture creates identities through associations. Such associations do not come about only through literal images. A building does not have to use the same materials or employ the same form or spaces as the place with which a client or an architect would like to create an association. The re-embodiment of the atmosphere of a precedent can be achieved by using a range of elements that in their synthetic composition create the desired association. Materials, construction details, structural systems, spatial typologies, and configurations are elements that are at the architect's disposal. They can be more or less explicit, more or less literal, more or less abstracted.

Abstraction has been the dominant compositional process in architecture since

"Chongtai"—Winter Olympics Taizicheng Exhibition Hall by Atelier Li Xinggang (used with permission)

the early twentieth century—a century that has seen unprecedented destruction and construction. For many architects and architectural students around the world, this is still the valid form of expression. It is linked to modernization and everything that this process promised. Today's consequence, however, is the disassociation of the architectural form from its construction system, and further, from its place and cultural context, such as it still exists. Unless an architect consciously engages materials and construction details in the realization of a building, there is no visual clue for a user as to what constitutes the building. Abstraction provides both unlimited freedom in the choice of shapes, as well as the convenience in not having to choose a material or to develop any construction details. The software programs show envelopes or surfaces; the contractor completes these with coats of paint. What lies beneath the surface then remains a mystery. To most people, all that matters is that the building stands up, serves its function, and looks somewhat attractive. The last three decades have shown that all formal possibilities in the creation of abstract shapes have been explored. This is a collective global coda to an already exhausted modernism of the second half of the twentieth century. Abstraction, taken to its ultimate logical conclusion, removes not only architecture from a place; it also severs any association that users might have with a place. Today's global dilemma then is the attraction of abstraction as part of a software-driven design process vis-à-vis the waning awareness that architecture, even at a small scale, can connect users to a place, a society, and therefore, to a culture.

Observing contemporary Chinese architecture from this point of view, it is easy to read moments of site and cultural specificity in the shortlisted work for the 2023 Architecture China Award, as well as more general global innovatory contributions. The highest qualitative levels of design—whether in China or elsewhere—transcend the default strictures of simplistic ordering systems. And refreshingly, it is in the small buildings that the selected architects demonstrate the often-neglected fact that a high design quality can exist at all scales, even in the detail. A well-chosen stone may, therefore, not only be a site-specific threshold to a house, it can also be a stepping-stone toward a more profound recognition of quality.

ARCHITECTURE CHINA AWARD IN PRACTICE

Architecture China Award in Practice is the highest-ranking category in the Architecture China Award. It honors architects who have demonstrated "building with nature" or related concepts in his or her long-term architectural practice and requires that the architects have completed three or more high-quality works in the past ten years.

Liu Yichun
Atelier Deshaus

Laureate

Zhang Lei
azLa

Laureate

Li Xinggang
Atelier Li Xinggang

Shortlisted

Liu Yichun

Atelier Deshaus
Co-founder and Principal Architect, Atelier Deshaus
Guest Professor, College of Architecture and Urban Planning, Tongji University
Chartered member, Royal Institute of British Architects
Editorial board member, *The Architect* and *Architectural Journal*

Liu Yichun established Atelier Deshaus with Chen Yifeng and Zhuang Shen in 2001. The works of Atelier Deshaus have participated in a variety of major international architecture and art exhibitions in more than fifteen countries and regions and have been widely published in the professional journals of over twenty-six countries. Liu has been invited to lecture in many universities, such as Harvard Graduate School of Design (United States), University of Hong Kong (Hong Kong, China), Architectural Institute of France (France), and École nationale supérieure des beaux-arts de Lyon (France). The works he directed have won many architectural awards. His representative work, Long Museum (West Bund), has been awarded the 2014 AR Award for "Emerging Architecture" by *Architectural Review*, the Golden Prize for "Public Architecture" in the 2016 ASC Grand Architectural Creation Award, the 2019 Honor Award for "Best in Show for Architecture" by AIA China, and was also the Gold Winner in the "Public Amenity: Social and Cultural Buildings" category in the 2020 ARCASIA Awards for Architecture; Shanghai Modern Art Museum and its Walkways has won the 2021 RIBA International Awards for Excellence. Atelier Deshaus is recognized as one of the 10 Design Vanguards 2011 by *Architectural Record*. Liu was recognized as the Most Influential Designer of China by *Forbes* in 2015 and 2019 Architect of the Year by *UED*.

Selected Works

2022 Upper Cloister in Aranya, Golden Mountain (Jinshanling), Chengde, Hebei Province, China
2021 Qintai Art Museum, Wuhan, Hubei Province, China
2022 Tao Yiqiu Memorial Hall, Kunshan, Jiangsu Province, China
2019 Riverside Passage, Yang Shupu Gasworks Wharf, Shanghai, China
2019 Yunyang Riverfront Visitor Centre, Chongqing, China
2019 Taizhou Contemporary Art Museum, Taizhou, Zhejiang Province, China
2018 House ATO, Beijing, China
2017 Renovation and Reuse of 80,000-ton Silos on Shanghai's Minsheng Wharf, Shanghai, China
2016 Tea House in Li Garden, Shanghai, China
2016 Modern Art Museum and its Walkways, Shanghai, China
2016 Footbridge on Rihui River, Shanghai, China
2015 Atelier Deshaus Office on West Bund, Shanghai, China
2015 Blossom Pavilion, Shanghai, China
2015 Tao Li Yuan School, Shanghai, China
2014 Long Museum (West Bund), Shanghai, China
2014 West Bund Art Centre, Shanghai, China
2014 Artron (Shanghai) Art Centre, Shanghai, China
2012 Qingpu Youth Centre, Shanghai, China
2011 Spiral Gallery I, Shanghai, China
2004 The Dongguan University of Technology, Dongguan, Guangdong Province, China
2002 Tri-house, Jiangsu Province, China

Blossom Pavilion © Zhou Dingqi

Interviewer: *Architecture China*
Interviewee: Liu Yichun (LIU), Chen Yifeng (CHEN)
Editor: Wang Ying

What new insights have you developed on the idea of "Building with Nature"?

LIU: The Chinese word *ziran* is both a noun: "nature," and an adjective: "natural." I tend to prefer its meaning when used as an adjective. "Building with Nature" can refer to the natural environment, but it can also mean architecture built in an appropriate way. "Building with Nature," therefore, means achieving harmony between buildings and their natural surroundings, as well as incorporating them into our daily lives. I think that, as a concept, it helps us take into account more aspects of design that deserve greater attention. Thus, when building with nature, it in fact produces decent architecture. It's a paradigm that emphasizes moderation and balance between different elements.

CHEN: I think that the phrase "building with nature" is really interesting because "nature" can mean so many things. We can interpret it in the context of industrialization, but using natural materials and techniques throughout the design and construction process. We can also interpret it as emphasizing context-specific, customized design in opposition to the trend of mass production. Now, especially in this age of AI-generated content, it has become necessary to reflect on what distinguishes us from robots. I think it's perhaps our emotions. In my opinion, building "naturally" can also be interpreted as allowing architects to give free rein to their emotions.

What direction are you currently exploring in your practice?

LIU: Atelier Deshaus has always attributed much importance to the relationship between humans and nature, as illustrated by our long-term focus on traditional Chinese gardens. Gardens are a type of architectural expression of humans' concern for the environment. So, I think that our architecture is fundamentally a form of expression; it's our way of expressing the relationship between humans and the environment, or humans and their lives. Though many of Atelier Deshaus' buildings are in the city, most are located in natural environments. It, therefore, goes without saying that we pay much attention to a building's relationship with nature. First and foremost, we do our best to minimize its impact on the surrounding ecology. Next, a building must be adapted to local conditions. That includes the local climate, geography, and topography. Based on the principle of minimal intervention, we hope that the building will blend in and form a cohesive whole with nature, rather than stick out.

CHEN: Indeed, there are many ways in which our design practices overlap with the concept of "Building with Nature." We also give much thought to the ties between a building and its region. Of course, that includes not just the construction site itself, but also aspects of the greater region in which a building is located, such as its topography, climate, vegetation, resources, and even cultural traditions. We hope that our buildings will form material, poetic, and spiritual ties with their surroundings.

Atelier Deshaus Office on West Bund © Chen Hao

Tea House in Li Garden © Tian Fangfang

Renovation and Reuse of 80000-ton Silos on Shanghai's Minsheng Wharf © Tian Fangfang

How do you approach the relation between buildings and nature in your architectural practice?

LIU: Any artificial structure is, by definition, at odds with nature. First, we must consider the degree to which humans disturb nature. As the population increases, cities expand, and human beings' material desires grow stronger. Humanity has, in recent years, come to realize that the planet's resources are rapidly depleting. With this awareness, many architects have begun to ask themselves if certain types of buildings are wasteful. I think that's important. We talk so much about low-carbon buildings now, exactly because we are aware of the risks that humans pose to the planet with our existence.

There's an ancient Chinese saying which translates as: "Though man-made, it seems like a product of the heavens." Though this saying originally served to compliment a craftsperson's artistry, I think it can be reinterpreted as an expression of reverence for nature—which I think is something that we should aspire toward in our work today.

If buildings are necessary, then we have no choice but to occupy more of the natural environment. However, in the process, we can find ways of giving back to nature; of finding room for nature in the spaces we occupy. I think that's very important. It's difficult to explain in words how, and to what extent we should give back. That's something that every architect should consider within the context of each individual design. But, regardless of what approach we choose, I think that this process of giving back can only begin once architects recognize that any form of construction disrupts the natural environment. Every architect needs to find their own unique way of ensuring that their buildings will return to nature—that they can be recycled and disassembled, and that their interventions are temporary. Because as time passes, everything returns to its original state—earth to earth, dust to dust.

CHEN: In our designs, we hope that buildings will form a harmonious relationship with the environment, but we oppose the idea of falsifying nature. For us, the buildings themselves shouldn't pretend to be anything other than artificially created monuments. That's a very clear stance we have.

But, in the design process, there are different ways in which we can establish a relationship between the building and its natural surroundings. For example, some buildings appear "embedded" into the natural environment, whereas others seem to grow out of it. No matter what type of relationship it is, we don't want to erase architecture's characteristic of having been "made."

QINTAI ART MUSEUM

Location: Zhiyin Avenue, Hanyang District, Wuhan, Hubei Province, China
Architectural/interior design: (Schematic design, design development, and interior design) Atelier Deshaus
Design team: Liu Yichun, Chen Yu, Wang Longhai, Hu Chenchen, Chen Hao, Shen Wen, Chen Chihhan, Tang Yun, Zhang Xiaoqi, Wu Wenchao, Deng Rui, Liu Xin, Pang Zirui, Wang Jiawen, Cao Ye
Collaboration: (Construction drawing, structure, and M&E) CITIC General Institute of Architectural Design and Research Co., Ltd.
Landscape: Wuhan Institute of Landscape Architectural Design Co., Ltd.
Structural consultant: (during schematic design) AND Office
Gross floor area: 43,080 square meters
Site area: 33,600 square meters
Design period: May 2016–September 2018
Completion: December 2021
Photography: Tian Fangfang

Site plan

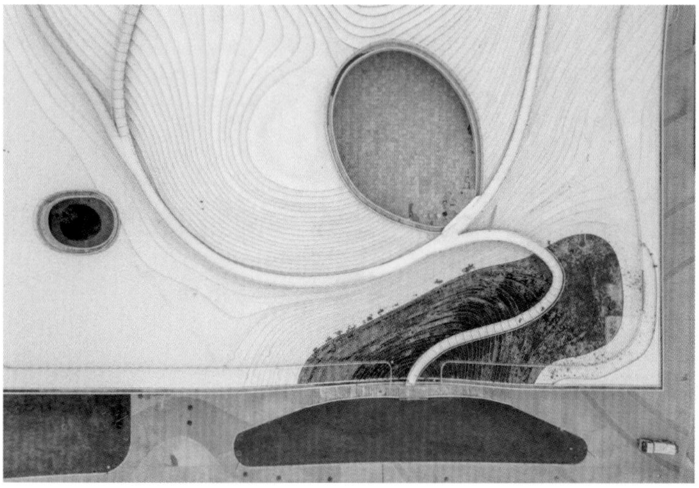

View of the rooftop © Tian Fangfang

Qintai Art Museum is located beside Moon Lake in Wuhan's Hanyang District, facing Meizi Hill situated across the lake to the south. In order to reduce the weight of the architectural mass on the natural surface of the lake, the shape of an undulating natural terrain has been employed for the side facing the lake, while part of the exhibition area has been sunk beneath the ground and also both utilizes the underground space and minimizes the massing on the ground. This contrasts with the side facing the city road, where a vertical façade resolutely upholds the urbanity of the architecture.

The undulating roof is formed by an abstract stepped terrace that follows the topographic contours. The risers of the steps are lined with a silver metallic surface, while the treads are covered with white stones or low vegetation. The roof is scattered with a number of winding, stepped paths for pedestrians, which are entirely open to the public, and which connect Moon Lake with various parts of the museum—such as the exits from museum exhibition spaces, the designated space for public education, the art shop, and the café—and other public spaces. This allows these paths to create a public space framework that is independent of the museum's exhibition spaces. The activities of the public become a part of the architectural surface.

The addition of an art museum has redefined the urban space on the southern shore of Moon Lake. To the west of the museum, the space is reserved for an urban plaza which will be the location of the planned Wuhan Library and Drama Centre. The main entrance to the museum, as well as those functions with strong public associations—such as creative and cultural spaces—are placed on this side, where a subtly inward-curving façade creates a sense of enclosure in conjunction with the location. From the plaza, there are ramped paths linking to the second-floor café and rooftop terrace, establishing a public circulation route that remains accessible after the museum closes. In operational terms, this strengthens the openness of the museum and the urbanity of the architecture.

The combination of the main hall and the undulating roofscape creates a unique venue for exhibitions. The exhibition space uses floating walls, translating the concept of visitors taking a set route around a show. The walls function as surfaces to exhibit art while also providing the structure that supports the undulating roof. The exhibition spaces for contemporary art, modern art, classical art, and special exhibitions display a high degree of functional flexibility and can be independently accessed or sequentially linked.

Bird's-eye view of the roof © Tian Fangfang

Rooftop and walkway © Tian Fangfang

Rooftop backdropped by cityscape © Tian Fangfang

1	
2	3
4	5

1. Cultural and creative space and entrance hall © Tian Fangfang
2. Interior space © Tian Fangfang
3. Exhibition hall © Tian Fangfang
4. Suspended metal grid roof © Tian Fangfang
5. Entrance hall © Tian Fangfang

Rooftop landscape © Tian Fangfang

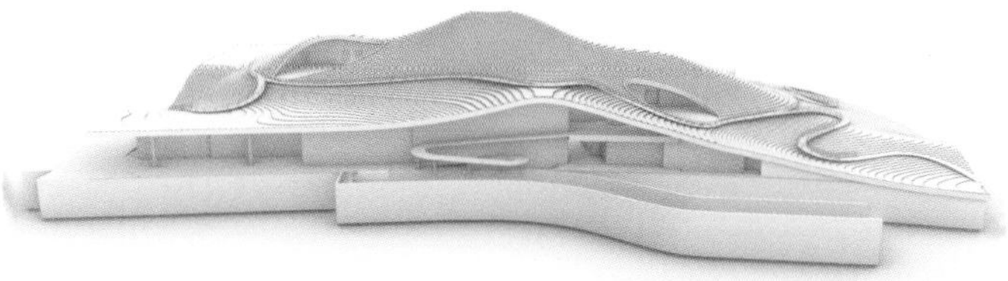

Diagram rendering

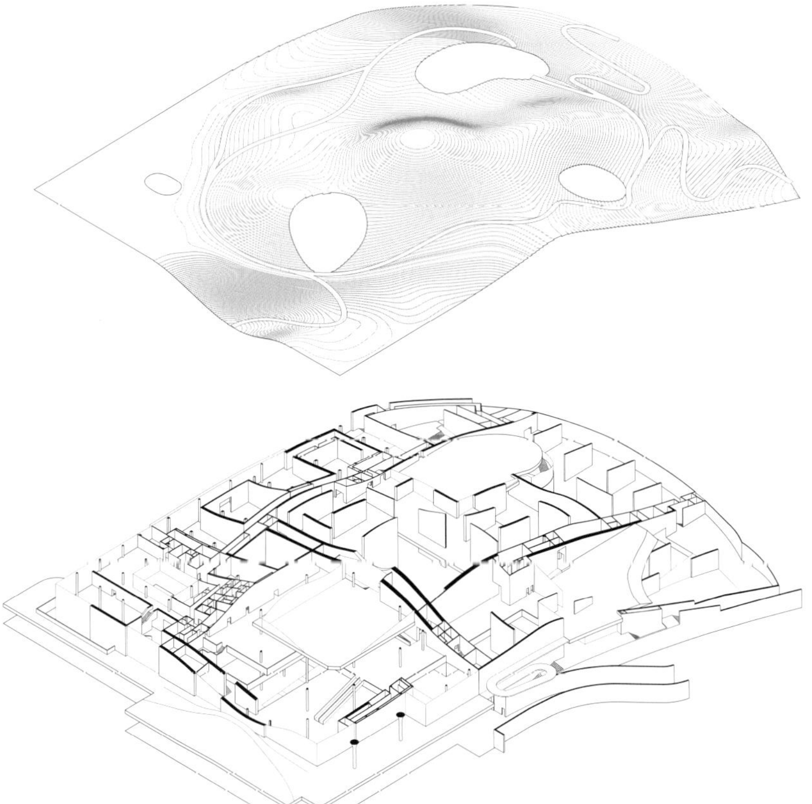

Exploded axonometric diagram

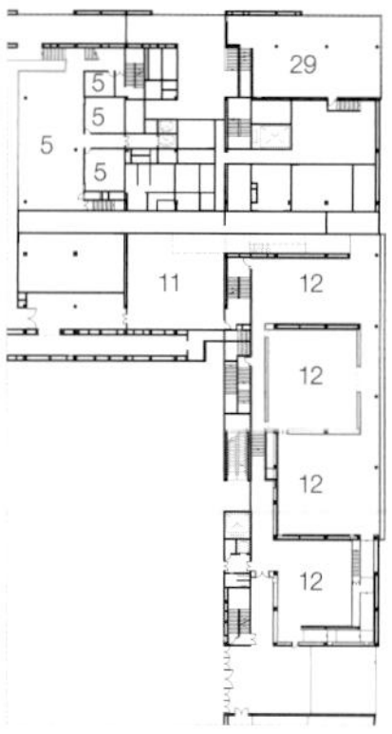

Third-floor plan
(floor height 2.000 m)

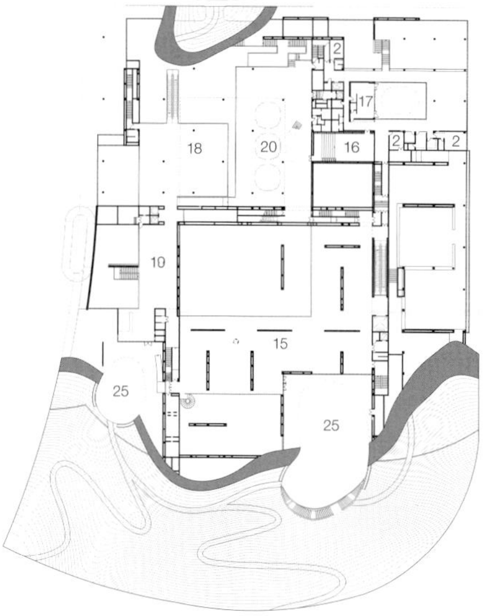

Fourth-floor plan
(floor height 5.500–11.300 m)

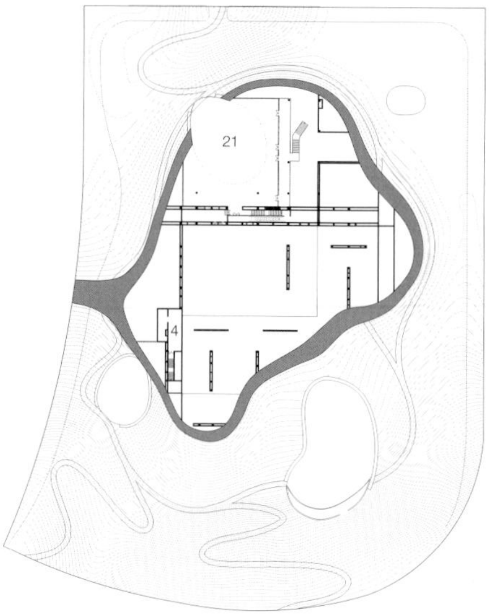

Fifth-floor plan
(floor height 11.300 m–top)

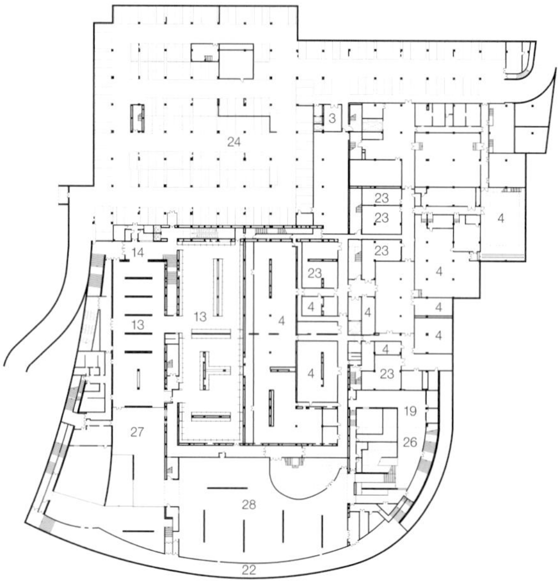

First-floor plan
(floor height -6.600–0.000 m)

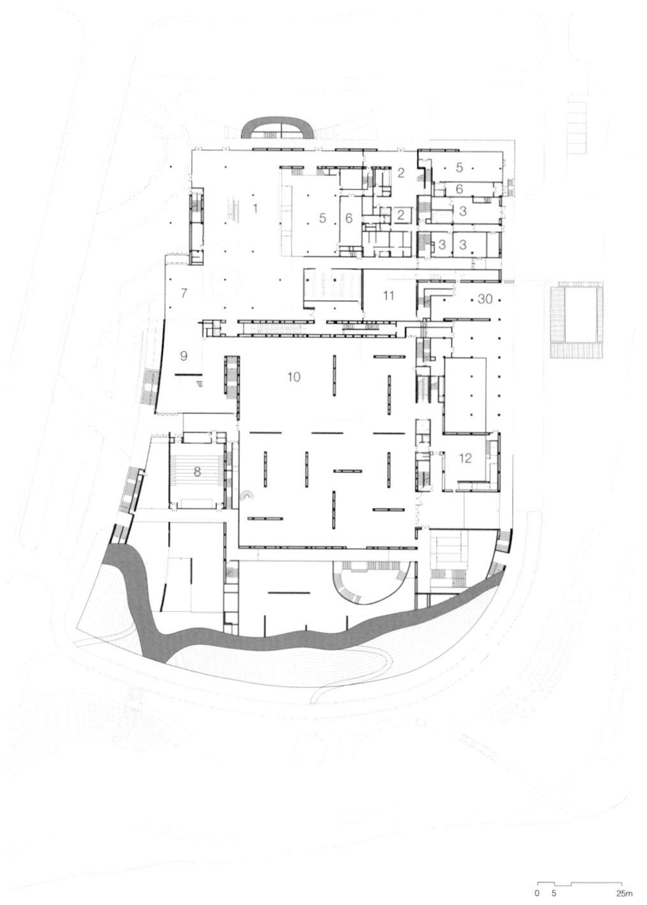

Second-floor plan
(floor height -0.000–5.500 m)

1. Cultural and creative space
2. Office
3. Service
4. Equipment
5. Restaurant
6. Kitchen
7. Entrance hall
8. Auditorium
9. Lobby (Contemporary Art)
10. Temporary exhibition hall (Contemporary Art)
11. Lobby (Modern Art)
12. Temporary exhibition hall (Modern Art)
13. Exhibition hall (Ancient Art)
14. Lobby (Ancient Art)
15. Temporary exhibition hall
16. Multifunction hall
17. VIP room
18. Reading room
19. Café
20. Family activity zone
21. Cultural and creative terrace
22. Exit passageway
23. Underground warehouse
24. Underground parking
25. Terrace
26. East foyer
27. West foyer
28. Underground exhibition hall
29. VIP exhibition hall
30. Outdoor bicycle parking

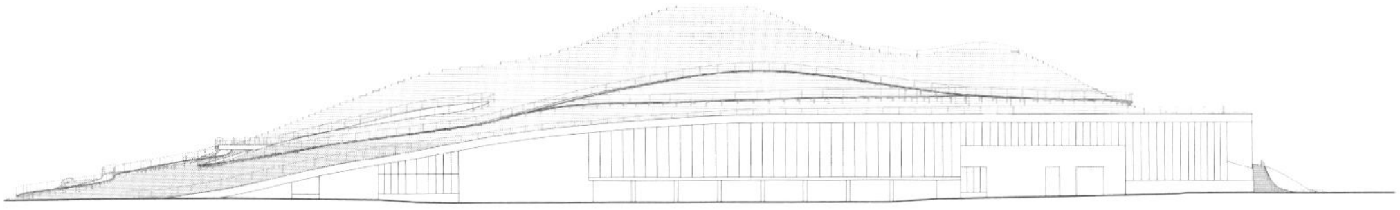

East elevation

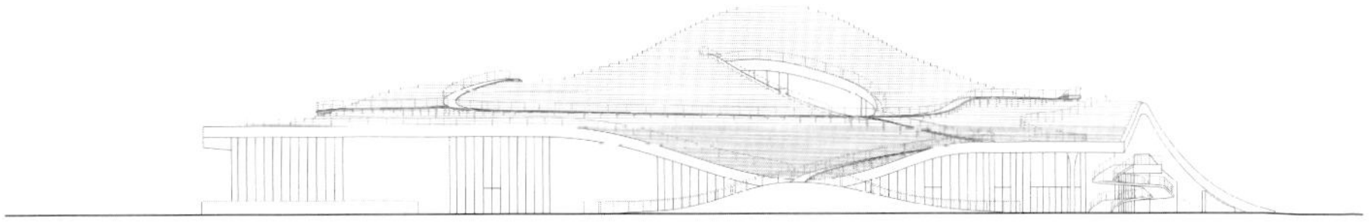

North elevation

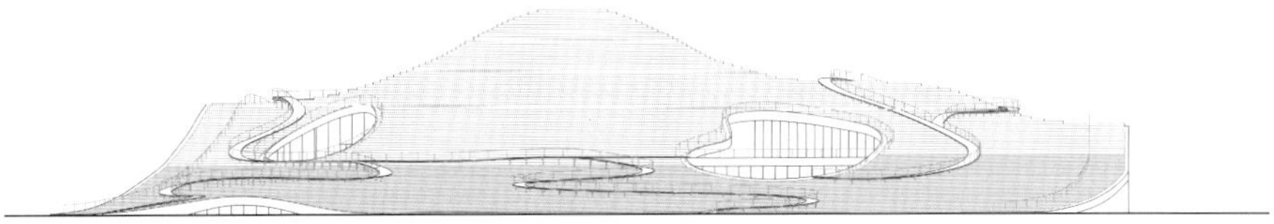

South elevation

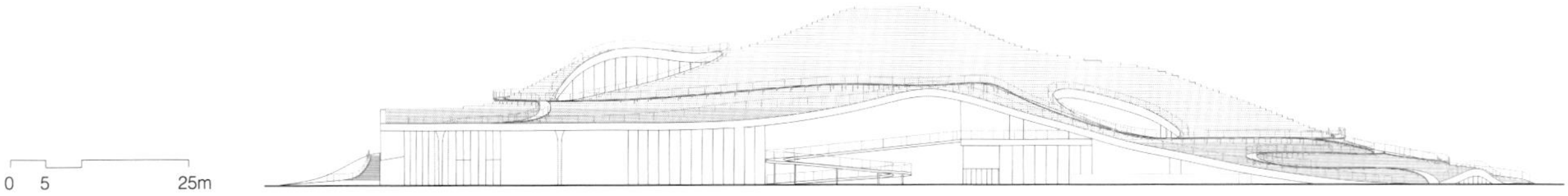

West elevation

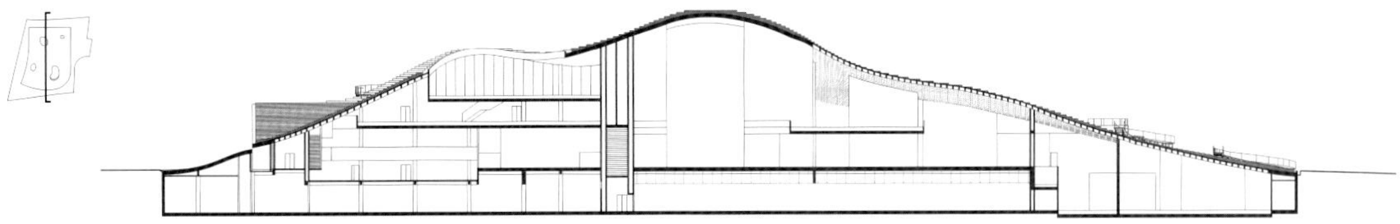

Section A-A

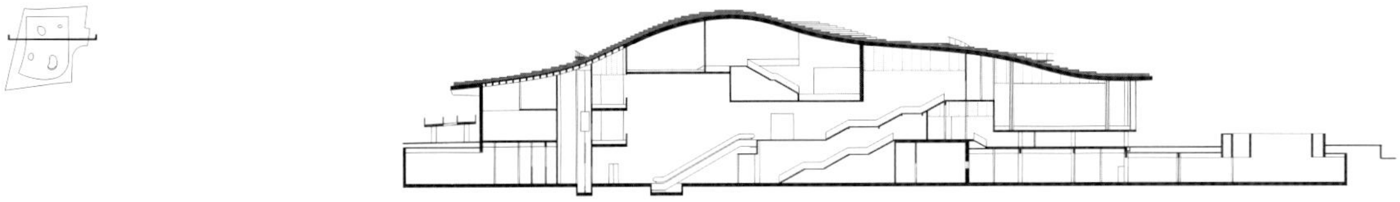

Section B-B

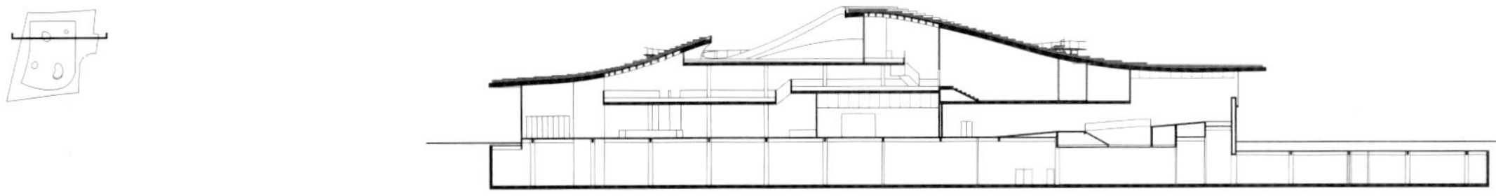

Section C-C

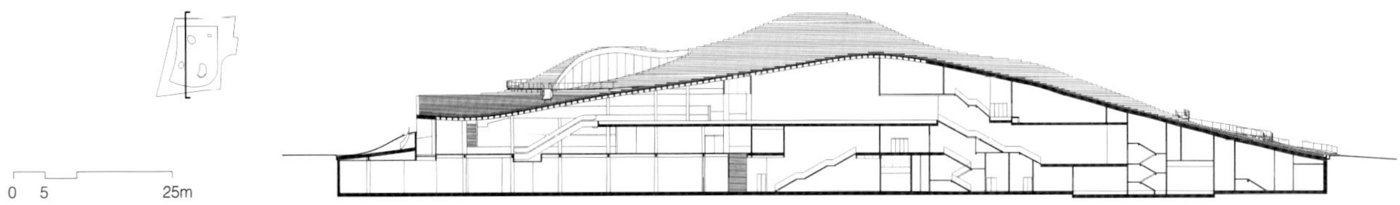

Section D-D

RIVERSIDE PASSAGE

Location: No. 2524 Yangshupu Rd, Yang Shupu Gasworks Wharf, Shanghai, China
Urban design: Atelier Z+, Atelier Liu Yuyang Architects, Atelier Deshaus
Architect: Atelier Deshaus
Construction engineering: AND Office
Team: Liu Yichun, Shen Wen, Chan Hiongai
Project coordination team: Zhang Bin, Wang Weijie, Wang Jiaqi, Guo Yifeng
Landscape consultant: YIYU Design, Laurent Landscape & Architects Firm
Gross floor area: 268 square meters
Design period: March 2018–November 2018
Completion: October 2019
Photography: Atelier Deshaus, Chen Hao, Tian Fangfang

Site plan

Original site © Atelier Deshaus

The wharf after the renovation © Chen Hao

The site of Riverside Passage was once a wharf that was used for unloading coal, as part of the fuel transporting system for the nearby Yangpu Gas Plant. A reinforced-concrete wall was built along the wharf— approximately 90 meters long and 4 meters high—to prevent the unloaded coal from slipping into the river. Since the time the transporting of coal was stopped, the long wall has endured an existence marked by silence and abandonment. Originally, there were two walls, but a long time ago, the one along the river was dismantled. Along the remaining wall, seeds carried in the wind landed in gaps formed by coal debris, broken concrete, and dust, and sprouted and grew into towering trees—the only sign of life embellishing the dilapidated long wall through interruptions of greenery. Together, the trees and the abandoned wall create a special, ruin-like ambiance, which is increasingly vanishing in Shanghai's urban renewal efforts of today that tend to be more delicate and polished.

Now, if a renewal project is to create a waterfront public space out of somewhere that was previously used for an industrial function, then it would be important to preserve the existing ambiance, because it bears witness to the sophisticated industries that have been operating in Shanghai over the past fifty years.

So, the new design sets the long solid concrete wall as a foundation for development—one that has geological meaning. It serves as the basis not only for a sloping bridge connecting the flood-control wall and the gap of the wharf, traversing the wild vegetation, but also as the basis for an elevated open passage and a pavilion where people can rest, observe, and contemplate. A single-pitched roof demarcates the inside and outside of the wall. On the inside, there is a passage at ground level facing a "garden" of ruins in the gap between the wharf and the shore. Outside, there is a cantilevered corridor overlooking the river. Where one is grounded, the other is floating, suggesting the differences in our perception of distance and scale.

The wharf is no longer used for unloading coal, it has been polished so it can function as a roller-skating rink; in conjunction with the cantilevered passage, this establishes a spatial dialog in closer proximity. The ground, the body of the wall, and the inserted structures create a new ensemble. Visitors may linger at will or continue moving through. The former coal wharf has thus become a place for urban flaneurs. The slender post-and-beam steel structures act as a series of frames for the urban views, so that when visitors move through the wharf, they begin to frame the assorted passing epochs: the chimney of the former gas plant, the bright-colored cranes, tide-washed concrete blocks embedded in mud, buildings rising across the river, and bridges in the distance.

Aerial view of the roof © Tian Fangfang

North end © Tian Fangfang

The wharf lit up at dusk © Tian Fangfang

The ramp crossing the gap between the wharf and the flood control wall © Chen Hao

1	2
3	4

1. The passage and the garden © Chen Hao
2. The garden of ruins © Tian Fangfang
3. The elevated walkway with a river view © Tian Fangfang
4. Detail © Chen Hao

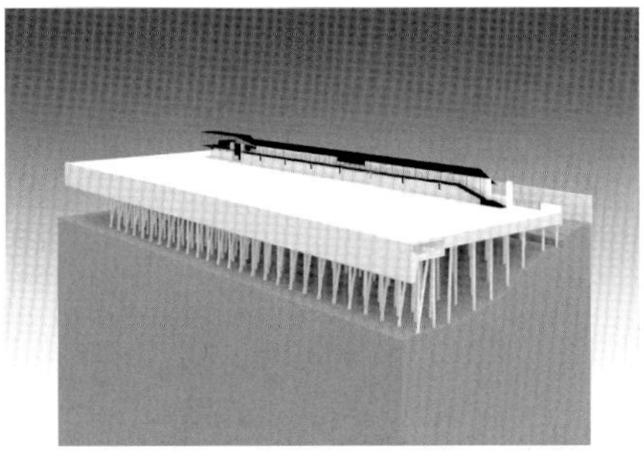

Structure render

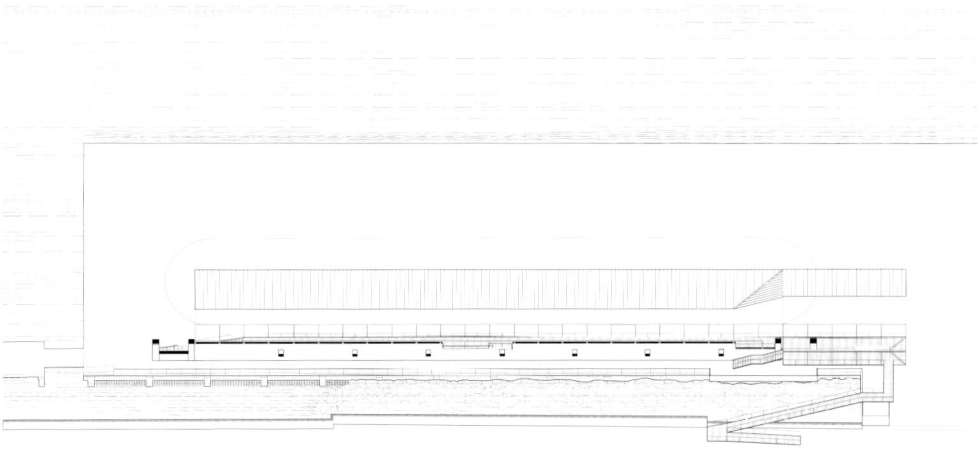

Diagram: frontal oblique

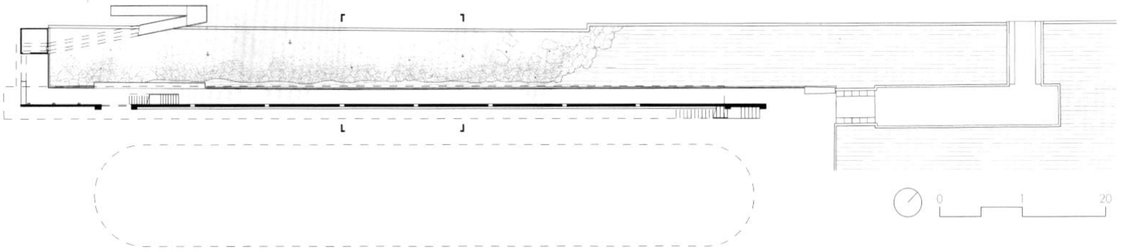

Ground-floor plan

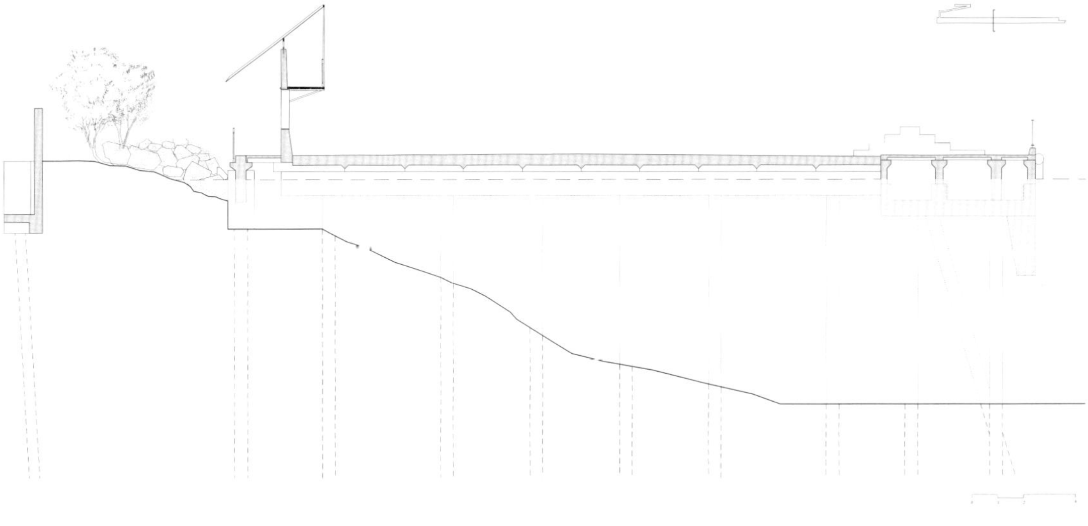

Section

UPPER CLOISTER IN ARANYA, GOLDEN MOUNTAIN (JINSHANLING)

Location: Laowa Village, Luanping, Chengde, Hebei Province, China
Architects: Atelier Deshaus
Design team: Liu Yichun, Shen Wen, Chan Hiongai, Wang Longhai, Gong Yu, Zhang Xiaoqi, Wang Yi, Sun Huizhong, Ji Hongliang; (structure) Zhang Zhun, Zhang Chongchong
Structural consultant: AND Office
Structure and M&E: Beijing Yanhuang International Architecture & Engineering Co., Ltd
Landscape consultants: (Courtyards and gardens) Shunmyo Masuno + Japan Landscape Consultants; (environment) Turenscape
Statue of Buddha: The Jiangs
Design period: November 2016–March 2018
Gross floor area: 615 square meters
Completion: March 2018–September 2022
Photography: Su Shengliang, Wang He, Jonathan Leijonhufvud

Site plan

The zen hall in the valley © Su Shengliang

Snow blankets the valley © Wang He

At the break of dawn I wandered in the ruins of an ancient temple,
On lofty trees of the woods the morning sun cast its rays.
Following a path amongst bamboos, I came to a secluded place,
Hidden deep amidst lush flowery vegetation, it used to be a chamber for meditation.
Birds by nature took delight in mountain scenes,
In the pond, a mind cleansed by the waters a lucid reflection made.
Everything gave way to silence right there and then,
Save for the tolling of bells that resonate.

—Chang Jian, *An Inscription for the Rear Meditation Chamber of a Mountain Temple in Ruins*

1 | 2
3 |
4 | 5

1. The mountains are also a part of the stone courtyard © Su Shengliang
2. View from above © Jonathan Leijonhufvud
3. Looking toward the mountains from the Buddhist hall © Su Shengliang
4. Interior view of the Stone Room © Su Shengliang
5. The zen hall backdropped by autumn colours © Su Shengliang

The upper cloister in Jinshan Mountain, Loawa Village, China, is not an ancient temple, but evokes the sense of a historical monument as it presents like an extension of the ancient Great Wall in the distance, which trails as far as the eye can see.

A light meditation hall (Aranya) touches the ground delicately, as if on tiptoe. Its modern slim and light structure sets the distance in time between the new construction and the ancient Great Wall; the valley has also been relocated over time due to human constructions. From the upper entrance courtyard to the lower open meditation hall, the upper cloister strives to establish an internal time through atmosphere and the opening and closing of space. The new construction not only communicates with the ancient Great Wall in time and space, but also fits into the topography and the wilderness of the valley.

Previously, the valley where the site is located had been developed for both coal mining and terraced farming. Under the weeds, one can still see the terraced arrangement of the retaining walls built by villagers, which have become a topographical landscape in themselves. In addition to the open meditation hall on the lower platform, the new upper cloister is built against the mountain slope and translates the 1.6-meter stepped landscape terrain into the spatial form and scale of the building. It is both terrain and architecture.

The entrance is arranged around an open stone courtyard, with a Buddhist hall to house Buddha statues on one side. The open courtyard conveys the spatial atmosphere of the traditional corridor courtyard with thin steel plates hanging inward and thin steel columns attached to the concrete enclosure wall. The upward opening of the open courtyard frames a view toward the sky. Looking out from the courtyard, one sees views of distant mountains, beacon towers, cliffs, and clouds that drift slowly in the sky. The horizontal opening facing the valley on the west side precisely frames the ancient Great Wall and a natural stone statue. The Buddhist hall is named Omniscience Hall, which denotes the freeing of oneself from troubles with the wisdom of universal knowledge. Natural mountain rocks are left exposed in the Buddhist hall.

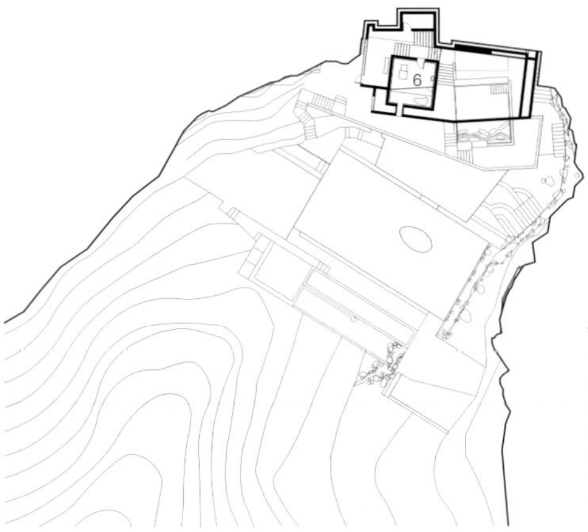

Fourth-floor plan
(floor height -4.800–-6.450m)

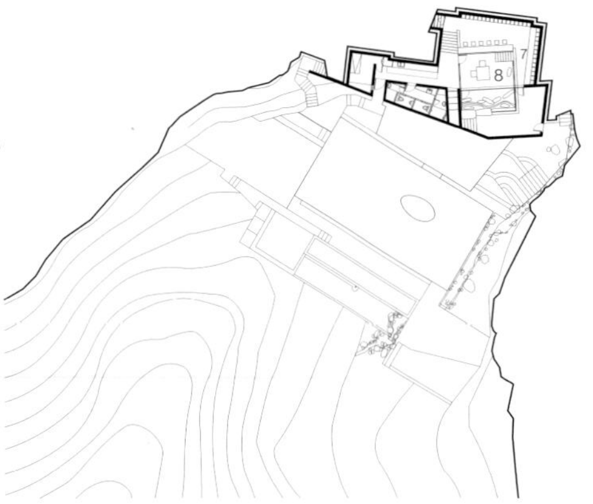

Fifth-floor plan
(floor height -6.450–-7.700 m)

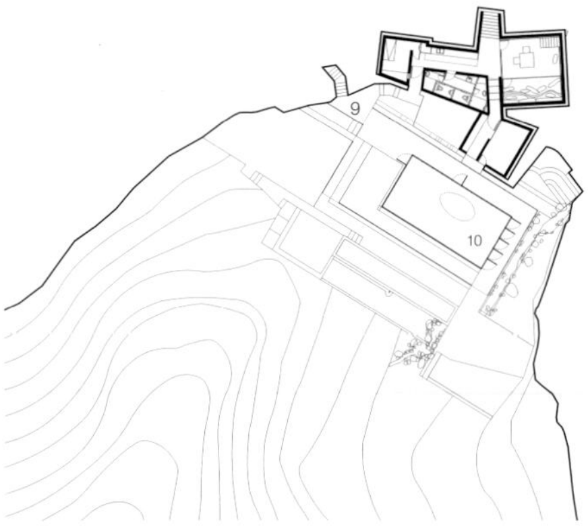

Roof plan
(floor height -7.700–-8.300 m)

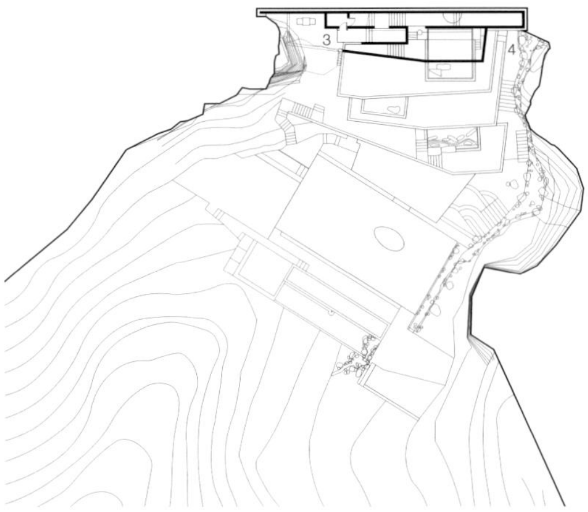

Second-floor plan
(floor height -2.100–-3.800 m)

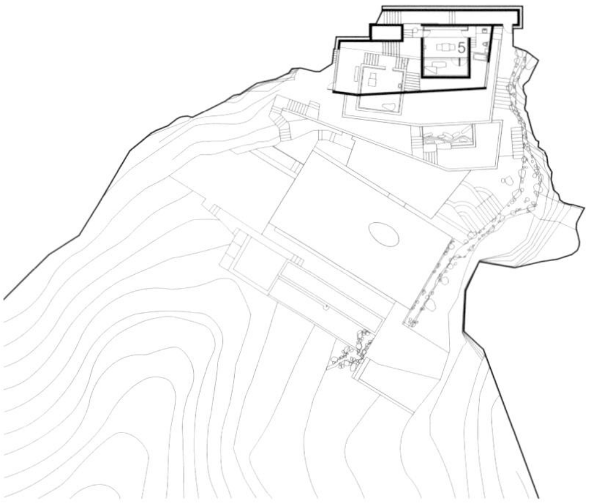

Third-floor plan
(floor height -3.200–-5.700 m)

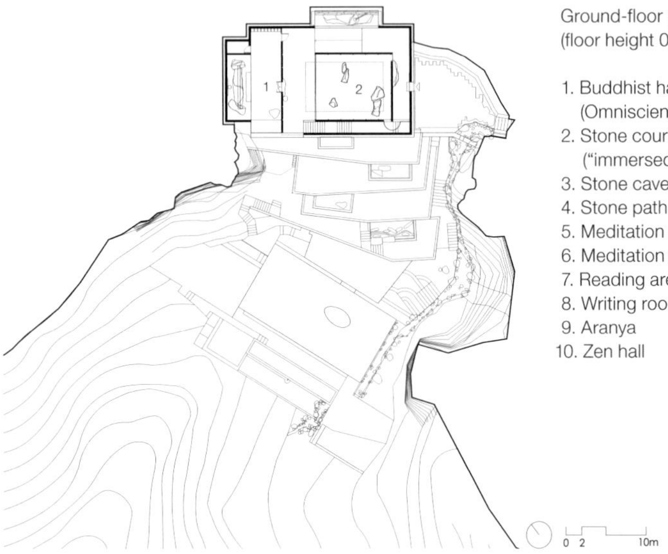

Ground-floor plan
(floor height 0.000–0.600 m)

1. Buddhist hall (Omniscience Hall)
2. Stone courtyard ("immersed in")
3. Stone cave
4. Stone path
5. Meditation room I
6. Meditation room II
7. Reading area
8. Writing room
9. Aranya
10. Zen hall

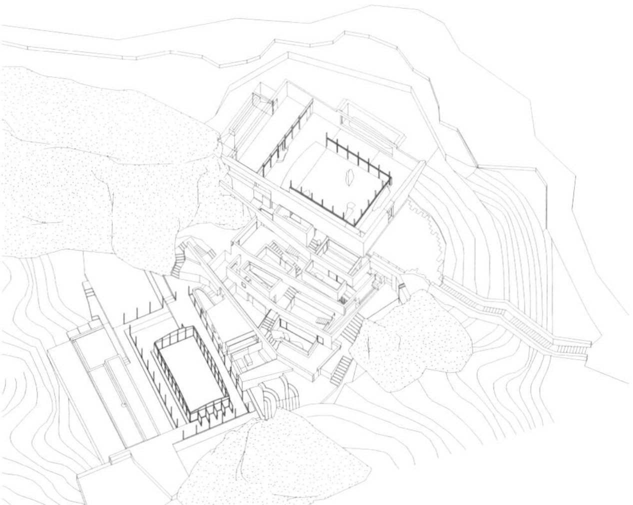

Axonometric diagram

East elevation

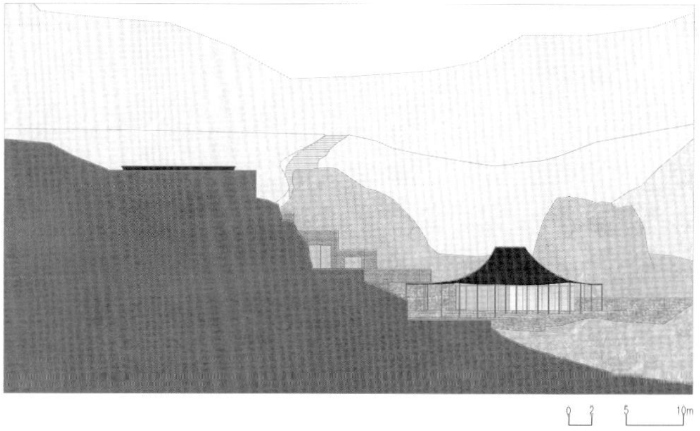

West elevation

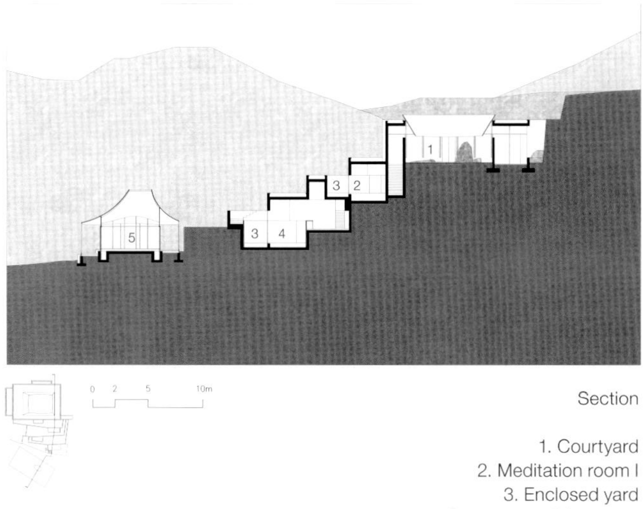

Section

1. Courtyard
2. Meditation room I
3. Enclosed yard
4. Sutra transcribing room
5. Zen hall

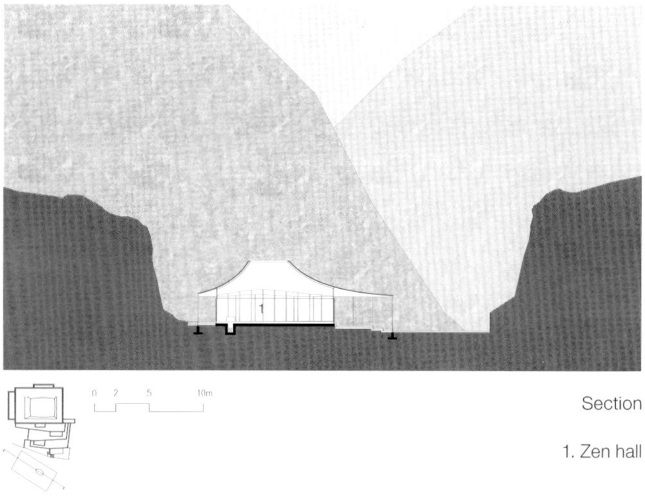

Section

1. Zen hall

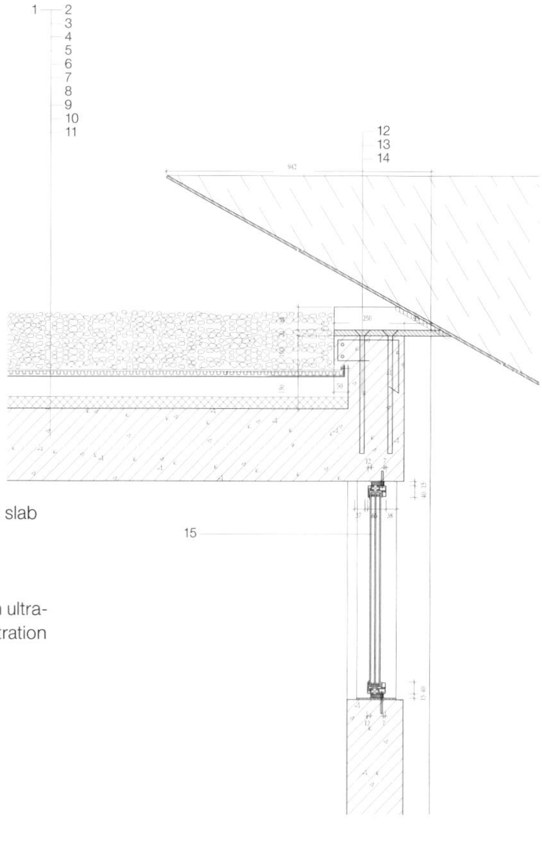

Detail

1. Planting roof with external insulation
2. 200 mm gravel cladding, local stone Φ35-60 mm
3. Geotextile filter layer
4. 12 mm plastic hydrophobic board, nail side up; minimum width 100 mm
5. Impermeable blanket
6. 20 mm 1:3 cement mortar protection layer
7. 4 mm SBS modified asphalt waterproofing membrane (root resistant)
8. 3 mm SBS modified asphalt waterproofing membrane (extra layer at the corner)
9. 30 mm minimum lightweight concrete for both leveling and sloping
10. 40 mm XPS
11. 250 mm in-situ waterproof concrete structural slab
12. 12x80 mm reinforced connection slab
13. 20 mm pre-embedded steel slab
14. D12 anchor bar
15. 5 mm ultra-clear glass + 12 mm argon +5 mm ultra-clear glass + 12 mm argon +5 mm high-penetration tempered laminated glass

Zhang Lei

azLa
Principal Architect, azLa
Professor, School of Architecture and Urban Planning, Nanjing University

Professor Zhang Lei completed both a bachelor's and master's at Southeast University in Nanjing, China, before finishing his postgraduate studies at ETH Zurich Switzerland. In 2001, he co-founded the azLa studio in Nanjing, where he is currently lead architect, in addition to teaching at Nanjing University's School of Architecture and Urban Planning.

In 2021, Professor Zhang was nominated for the Architecture China Award in Practice, and has gone on to clinch the award in 2023. In 2012, he received a nomination for the Swiss Architectural Awards. His studio,azLa, was featured in *Architecture Record's* 2008 Design Vanguard issue.

In recent years, Professor Zhang has been invited to take part in several important international events, such as TUMU—Young Architecture from China Exhibition at the Aedes Architecture Forum in Berlin, Germany, the Contemporary Chinese Art Exhibition at the Centre Pompidou in France, Contemporary Chinese Architecture Exhibition at The Netherlands Architecture Institute in The Netherlands, and "Our Village" exhibit at the 16th Venice Biennale of Architecture.

Selected Works

2023 Citizens' Centre (part of the Kaiping Cultural Complex Initiative), Guangdong Province, China
2023 Wuzhou Zero-Carbon Park Hotel, Inner Mongolia, China
2023 Nanjing Tie Bei Cultural Centre, Jiangsu Province, China
2023 Longjingzhonghe Social Housing Project in Pukou, Jiangsu Province, China
2022 Nanjing Constitution Park, Jiangsu Province, China
2022 Central Culture and Athletics Centre, Gaoxin District, Haining City, Zhejiang Province, China
2022 Shanha Cultural Exchange and Training Centre in Hangzhou, Zhejiang Province, China
2022 Taiping River Urban Exhibition Centre, Shijiazhuang, Hebei Province, China
2022 Renovation of Nanjing Daily Plot in Xi Nan Li, Jiangsu Province, China
2021 Jiangsu Garden Expo Treasure Pavilion, Nanjing, Jiangsu Province, China
2020 Ruralation Museum Hot Spring Hotel, Tangshan, Nanjing, Jiangsu Province, China
2020 Songyang Yunxi MO+ (RURALATION MO+) Shared Vacation Space, Zhejiang Province, China
2019 Bingding Wood Kiln, Jingde Town, Jiangxi Province, China
2017 LEI House, Tonglu, Zhejiang Province, China
2014 Wangjing Garden Chapel, Nanjing, Jiangsu Province, China
2011 CIPEA No. 4 House, Nanjing, Jiangsu Province, China
2011 Zhengdong New District Urban Planning Exhibition Hall, Nanjing, Jiangsu Province, China
2008 Brick House, Zhejiang Province, China
2008 Concrete Slit House, Nanjing, Jiangsu Province, China
2003 Model Animal Genetic Research Center of Nanjing University, Nanjing, Jiangsu Province, China

CIPEA No.4 House © Yao Li

Interviewer: *Architecture China*
Interviewee: Zhang Lei (ZHANG)
Editor: Wang Ying

What new insights have you developed on the idea of "Building with Nature"?

ZHANG: This year is my second time on the panel for the Building with Nature: Architecture China Award. This round, we continually reflected on the relation between architectural practices and the natural environment. I'd say that my new understanding of this theme is "seeking beauty in the ordinary." If buildings are meant to be a reflection of our lives, then they should be ordinary, not stately or grandiose. For that reason, we believe that the value of "building with nature" lies in the small, joyful surprises that pepper our everyday lives. It's about the spontaneous and unexpected things that rules, conventions, logic, and mathematical formulas can't account for.

What direction are you currently exploring in your practice?

ZHANG: In 2019, Lei Xiaohua and I co-founded a new studio: azLa (allied zhang & Lei architects). The direction we're currently exploring is "cultural passcodes." This means, taking the time in every project we undertake to decode what the land wants, what its inhabitants want, and what visitors want. We want to cast a spotlight on the regional specificity of each project, so that we may integrate the local culture into our buildings. Another type of cultural passcode is the unexpected surprises I spoke about, that are unknown to formal institutions, and which can only be discovered in the minutiae of everyday life. In this way, they overlap with our understanding of "building with nature."

Renovation of Nanjing Daily Plot in Xi Nan Li © Qiu Wenjian

LEI House in Tonglu © Yao Li

Brick House © Iwan Baan

Songyang Yunxi MO+ (RURALATION MO+) Shared Vacation Space © Wen Studio

Bingding Wood Kiln in Jingdezhen © Yao Li

In your practice, how do you interpret the relationship between form and sustainable construction?

ZHANG: When it comes to the topic of sustainable development, there are two aspects: the sustainability of culture, and of lifestyles.

In terms of cultural sustainability, I think that we should give more respect to crafts that make use of traditional materials—a concept that I refer to as artisanal architecture. Blending traditional materials and building methods with modern technology can give rise to many joyful surprises.

What opportunities and challenges do you believe China's unique construction practices present to today's architects?

ZHANG: I think that the main challenge is, as I said previously, realizing continuity and sustainability in terms of culture and lifestyles. Our lifestyles will likely continue to become more globalized. Throughout that process, how can we protect our heritage and strike a balance between tradition and modernity? That for me is the biggest challenge.

RURALATION MUSEUM HOT SPRING HOTEL, TANGSHAN

Location: Nanjing, Jiangsu Province, China
Lead architects: Zhang Lei, Lei Xiaohua
Design team: (Architecture) Qi Wei, Wang Liang, Jin Haibo; (Interior) Ma Haiyi, Du Yue, Zhu Wenjian, Huang Rong; (Landscaping) Zhao Min, Jiang Zhiyuan, Chen Juanjuan
Gross floor area: 5,500 square meters
Design period: 2017
Construction period: 2020
Photography: Yao Li, Qiu Wentong, Wen Studio, Qui Wenjian, Dong Suhong, azLa

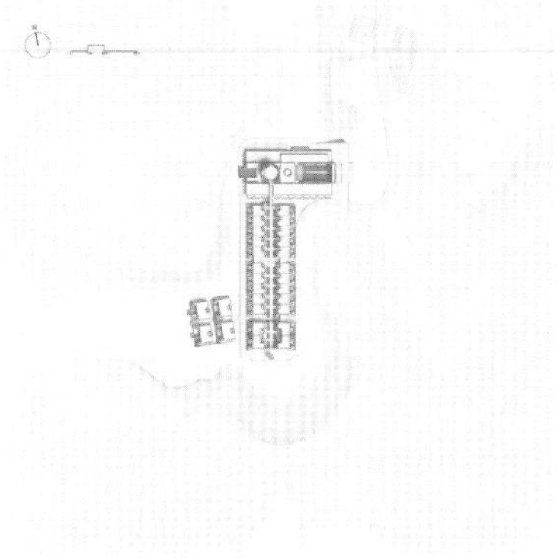

Site plan

Embraced by mountains © Dong Suhong

Hot spring pools outside the courtyards © Yao Li

History of the Earth, History of Humanity

The Ruralation Museum Hot Spring Hotel is located in Tangshan Geopark, to the east of Zijin Mountain on the outskirts of Nanjing, China. Specifically, it's located at the former site of an abandoned quarry, to the southwest of Geopark Museum. In the recent years, pumice stone was gradually removed from the mountain face and nets were laid down to restore the site's ecology and render the terrain safe for construction. The bare walls of the quarry act as a natural barrier on all four sides of the site, and have a pleasingly rough quality.

Tangshan was the site where the Nanjing Man, an early specimen of Homo erectus, the first known human species, was discovered. This association, along with nearby historical sites, such as the ancient Yangshan Quarry and a volcano that was active during the Neogene period, attach a type of solemn, historical reverence to the area. Tangshan District is defined by an abundance of exposed rock face that gives it a unique aesthetic identity. The materials used in the hotel's construction—a combination of stones sourced through local excavation and preparation of the terrain, as well as white cement—serve to emphasize this identity, while also conforming to the principles of sustainable architecture. Taking inspiration from Tangshan's association to the dawn of humankind and the primordial earth, it was decided that the appearance of Ruralation Museum should create the impression of ruins from the future, evoking the transformation of nature over millions of years into the future. As visitors navigate this space that connects the origins of human history and prototypical architecture, they gain an intuitive sense of how time continually breaks and repairs spaces.

Linear Journeys

The Ruralation Museum imposes three immersive linear trajectories on its visitors, each of which follows its own axis and which emphasizes the relationship between humans, architecture, and nature. At the conclusion of each journey, the structure "disappears" in different ways into its natural surroundings.

Hotel rooms facing the mountain valley to the west © Qiu Wentong

The central axis © Wen Studio

Cave-like main entrance to the lobby © Qiu Wenjian

The east–west axis leads down a slope from the front courtyard, crosses over a body of water and guides visitors through the cave-like main entrance to the circular lobby, where they return to the mysterious origins of our primitive ancestors. They then follow rays of natural light upstairs into the spacious main hall, where their view is directed back east. From there, the atmospheric corridor forms a kind of natural frame that proffers a beautiful view of the mountain. A spiral staircase at one end of the main hall takes visitors into a multifunctional shared space. The axis leads further west over an expansive swimming pool into the mountain forest grove, completing visitors' first journey from human-made structures into the wilderness.

The next axis stretches uninterrupted from the mouth of the quarry in the south to the concrete cylinders in the north. These cylinders come together to form a meditative space. They're empty, but pure. From there, the space leads upward, signifying the union between human beings and nature to complete the second "disappearance" into nature.

The third guiding axis of Ruralation Museum leads westward once more, between the stone townhouses and family villas. At the museum complex's westernmost point, visitors can admire the sun setting behind the mountain; yet again, they are whisked away from an artificially created environment to a completely natural one.

Curated Experiences

The Bauhaus movement, which originated in 1919, aimed to integrate design across various disciplines, with architecture at its core. A hundred years later, in the Ruralation Museum Hotel, we harness this holistic view of design to curate spaces that enable dream lifestyles, while showcasing the profound geological and human history of Tangshan. The sense of ritualism that the space evokes through its gallery-like design complements the pace of life typical of a resort setting, creating a thoroughly immersive and romantic ambiance in which visitors gain a much-needed respite from the outside world.

To create a parallel with what the Nanjing Man's cave might have been like, the furniture, walls and platforms in the hotel guestrooms all feature white cement surfaces. They create a minimalist, bohemian atmosphere in which guests feel free to sit on the ground and laze about, in contrast to their everyday lives.

The Shape of Time

The Ruralation Museum Hotel's spatial curation and immersive experiences amply demonstrate an approach to design that centers on the relationship between people and spaces, materials and construction, and sites and settings. The choice of concrete, stone, and water as the central elements of the hotel pays homage to the quarry's surrounding natural terrain. The consideration for the environment has been subtly incorporated into the entire immersive experience through the adoption of sustainable building practices and materials, such as reusing abandoned stones from the quarry, incorporating decorative and functional woven elements made with hemp rope and wicker, tailoring independently designed items made with Tyvek, as well as guesthouse embellishments built using special cement.

Tangshan's profound ties to the history of the earth and humanity are powerfully expressed and experienced through the language of design. Time's restoration of spaces, as well as the unity between content and form are both represented through the museum's minimalist, organic construction. While maintaining deep ties to Tangshan, Ruralation Museum Hotel also has a universal appeal.

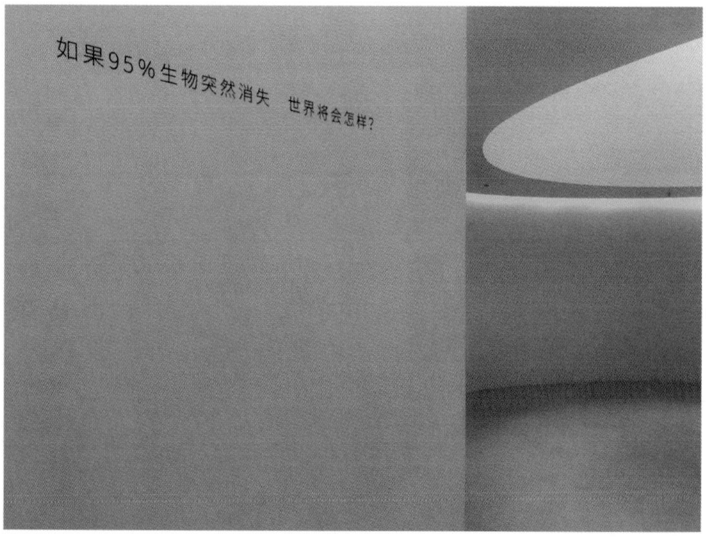

The hotel is also a museum © azLa

Façade made of white stones and fair-faced concrete © Wen Studio

Suspended ceiling with hemp string decor © Wen Studio

Northern view of the hotel's villa-style family rooms © Dong Suhong

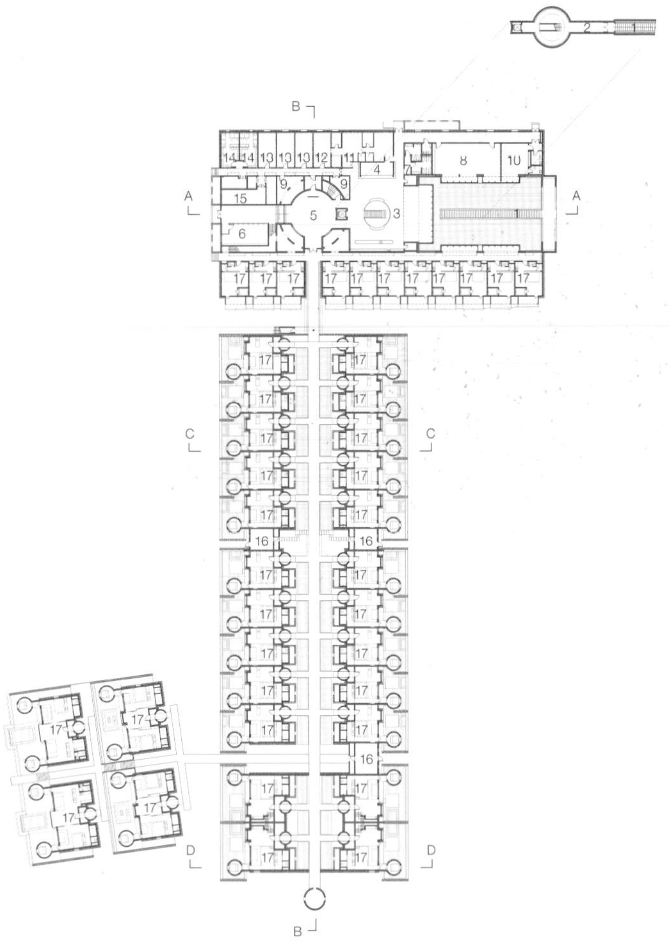

Ground-floor plan

1. Downslope entrance
2. Entrance hall
3. Lobby/restaurant
4. Open kitchen
5. Library
6. Studio
7. Restroom
8. Chinese restaurant
9. Storeroom
10. KTV room
11. Kitchen
12. Staff canteen
13. Staff dormitory
14. Staff changing room
15. Equipment room
16. Linen room
17. Guestroom

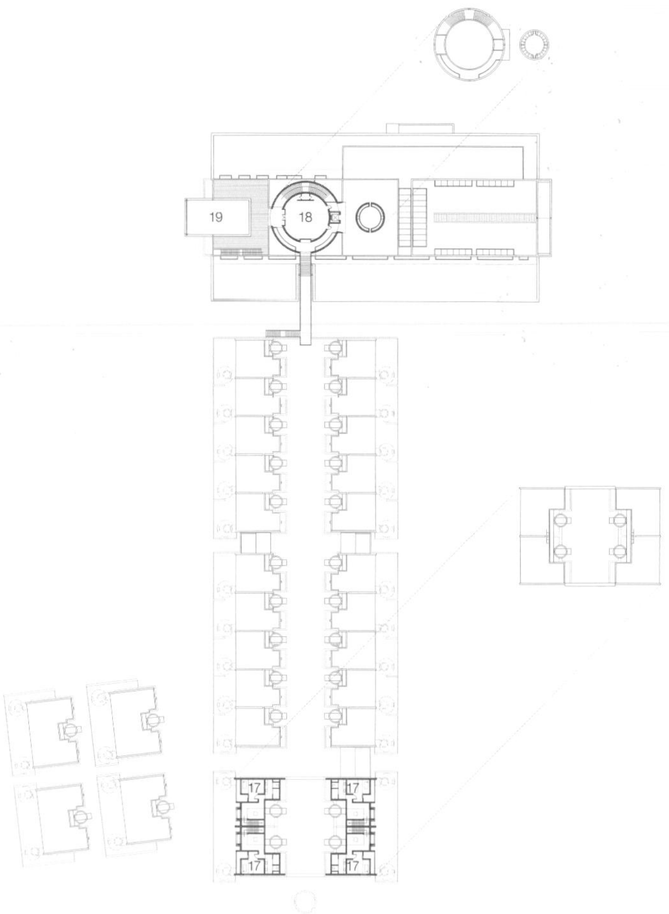

Second-floor plan

17. Guestroom
18. Meeting room
19. Outdoor swimming pool

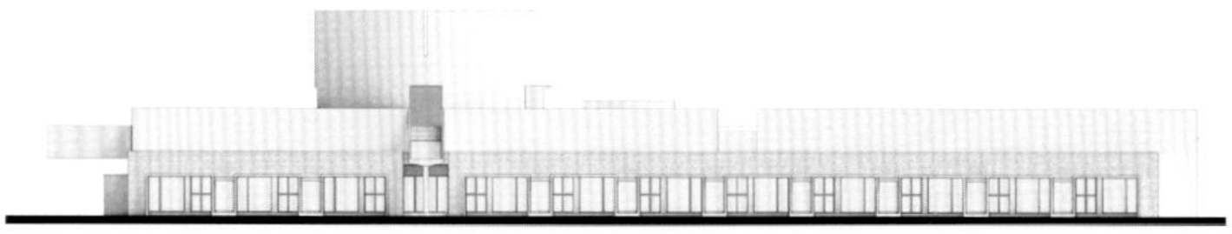

South elevation

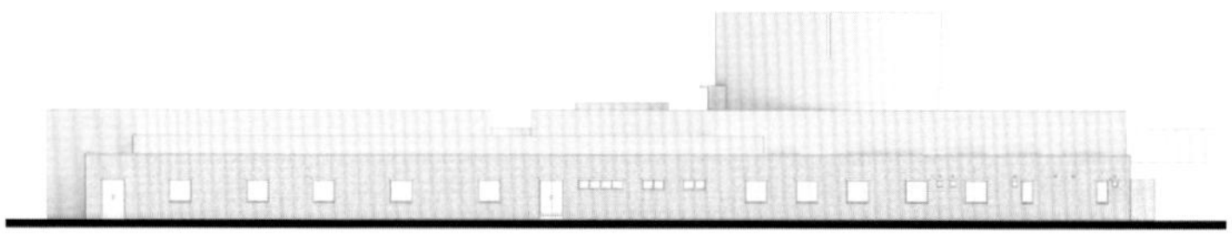

North elevation

West elevation

East elevation

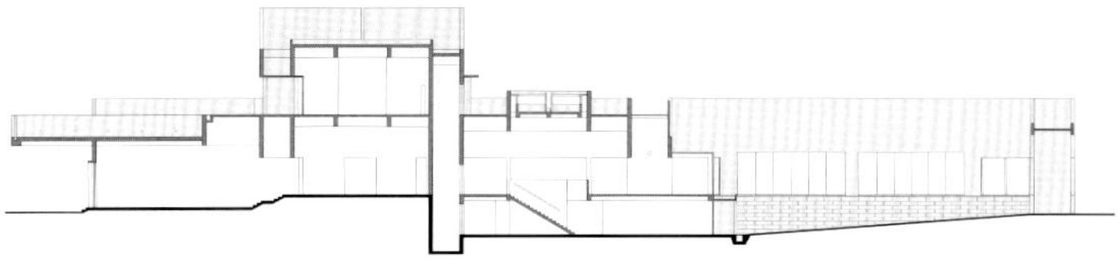

Section A-A

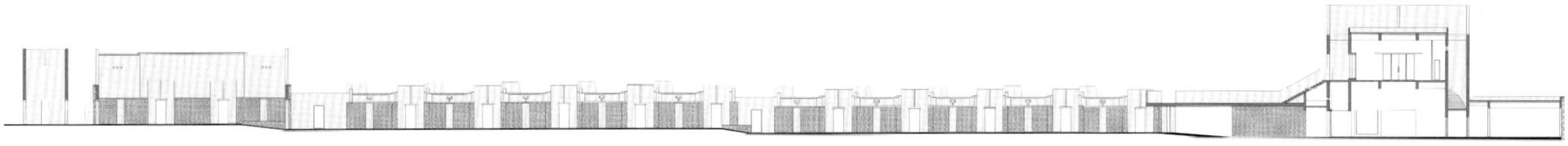

Section B-B

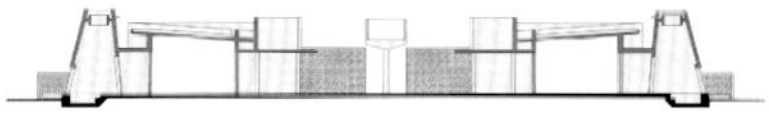

Section C-C

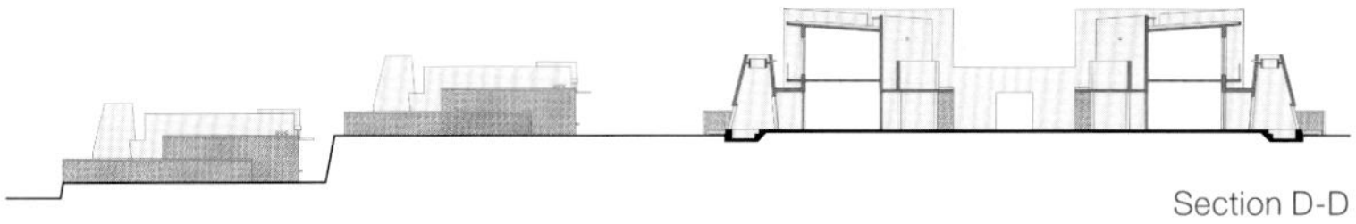

Section D-D

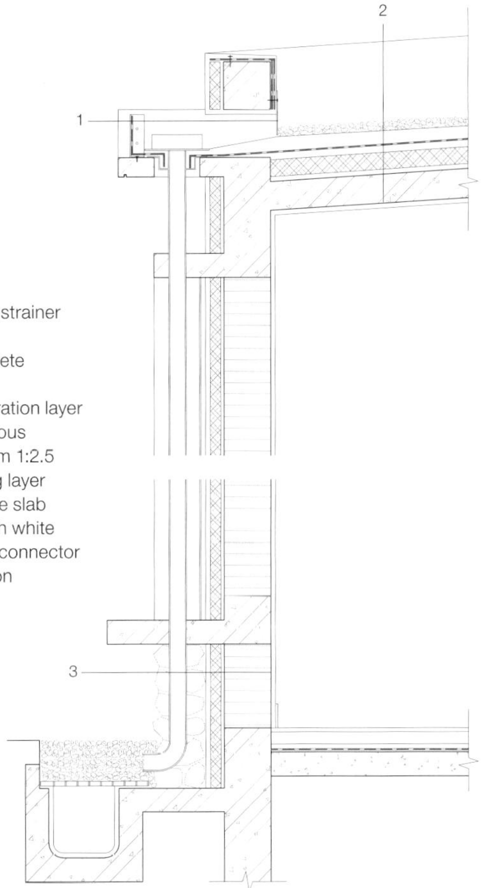

Detail

1. 5 mm metal flashing
   87 type metal rain bucket
   5 mm metal rain downspout strainer
2. 30 mm bed of gravel
   60 mm C30 fine stone concrete protective layer
   10 mm 1:4 lime mortar separation layer
   4 mm SBS modified bituminous waterproof membrane 20 mm 1:2.5 cement mortar slope making layer structural reinforced concrete slab
3. 300 mm rubble masonry with white painting finish Φ6 mm rebar connector
   40 mm XPS thermal insulation
   200 mm masonry

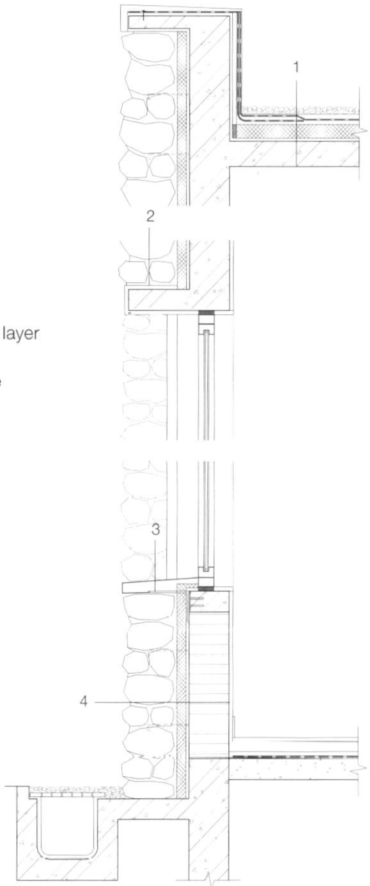

Detail

1. 30 mm bed of gravel
   60 mm C30 fine stone concrete protective layer
   10 mm 1:4 lime mortar separation layer
   4 mm SBS modified bituminous waterproof membrane 30 mm fine stone concrete screed
   60 mm XPS thermal insulation
   20 mm 1:2.5 cement mortar slope making layer structural reinforced concrete slab
2. 300 mm rubble masonry with white painting finish 100 mm concrete lintel
3. 5 mm metal flashing
   150x100x6 mm angle steel fitting
   300 mm rubble masonry with white painting finish
4. 300 mm rubble masonry with white painting finish Φ6 mm rebar connector
   40 mm XPS thermal insulation
   200 mm masonry

CONCRETE SLIT HOUSE

Location: Nanjing, Jiangsu Province, China
Chief architect: Zhang Lei
Design team: Meng Fanhao, Cai Menglei, Lu Yuan, Tang Xiaoxin
Gross floor area: 270 square meters
Design period: 2005
Construction period: 2008
Photography: Iwan Baan

Site plan

Street view © Iwan Baan

Building façade © Iwan Baan

The structural logic of Concrete Slit House can be summarized as follows: A balance between interior design elements; a coherence between space and function; a transparency creating a connection between exterior and interior; textures that mimic and complement those in the building's surroundings; and the relation between the building and the ground.

By bringing the part of the exterior corresponding to the indoor staircase inward and rendering it transparent, the staircase is transformed into an independent space that acts as a kind of partition, splitting the house lengthways using natural light. The slit allows for distinct interior designs in each half of the house, which features different levels of elevation: The living room spans two floors; the dining room occupies one and a half floors; and the three bedrooms and top floor study are each the height of one floor but arranged in a staggered formation with half a floor of displacement between them. The recessed walls have windows that allow occupants to look from one part of the house into the other, and vice versa. The shape of the slit, which creates extensions on each side of the house, as well as the differences in elevation between rooms, produce an unexpected visual effect, such that the layout appears to move in a circular formation.

Nestled within a Republic-era conservation zone alongside a century-old Western-style brick houses, Concrete Slit House—which displays an exterior that was produced using a mold—has a texture that at once contrasts with and pays homage to its surroundings. The seamless connection between the cast-in-place walls and prefabricated rooftop directs the gaze to the division between the two halves of the house and accentuates the slit's significance. This new design language enables a degree of expressivity that was in the past hindered by rigid architectural paradigms, and in doing so, calls those paradigms into question, undermining their authority. The "dark energy" of the slit defines the relationship between the space and the lifestyles of its occupants, as well as creates a definitive opposition between the structure's exterior and its surroundings.

View from the southeast © Iwan Baan

Slit seen from inside © Iwan Baan

Section of the eastern façade © Iwan Baan

Living room © Iwan Baan

Staircase © Iwan Baan

Old and new © Iwan Baan

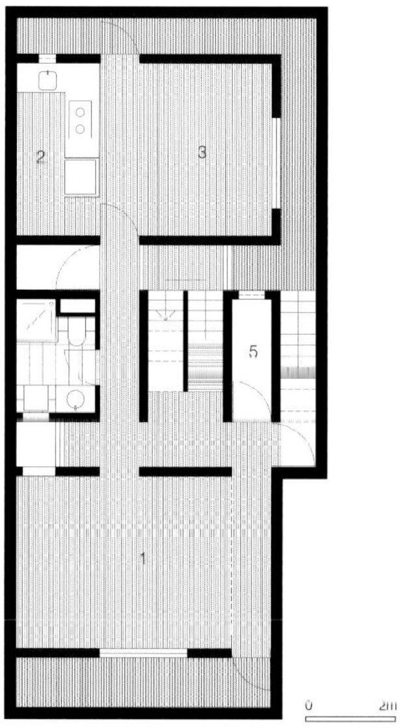

Basement-floor plan

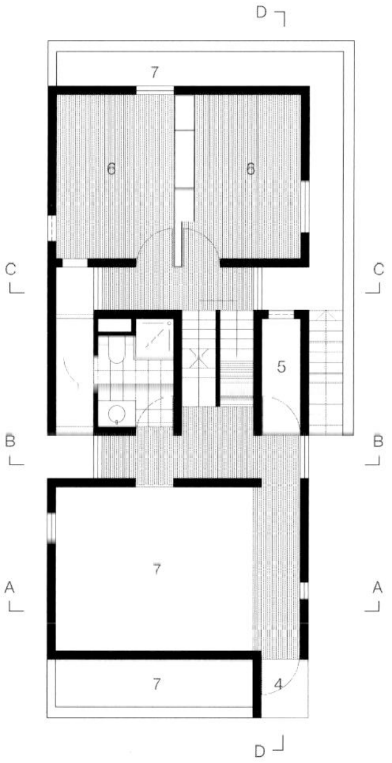

Ground-floor plan

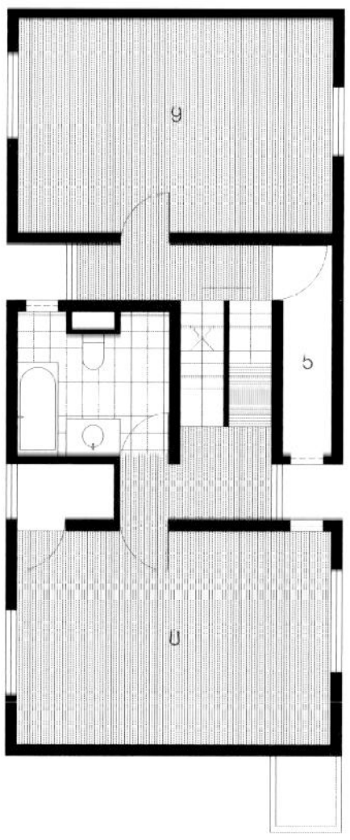

First-floor plan

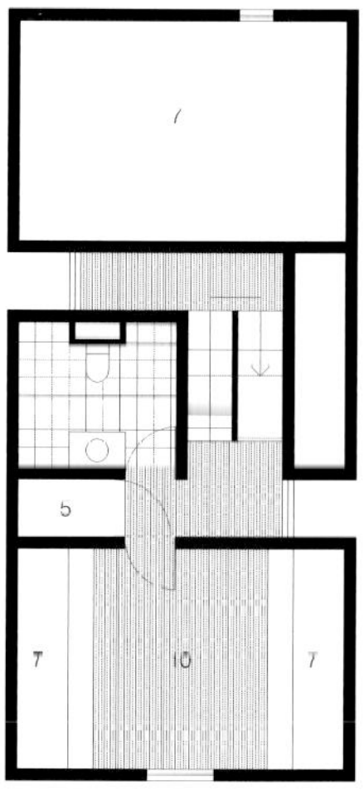

Second-floor plan

1. Living room
2. Kitchen
3. Dining
4. Entrance
5. Storage
6. Guest bedroom
7. Void
8. Main bedroom
9. Family activity room
10. Study

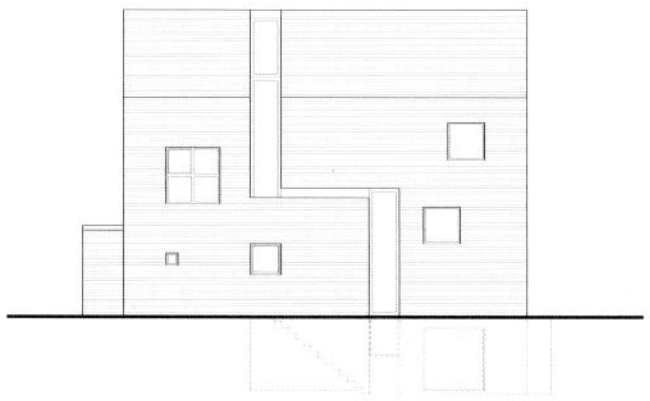

East elevation

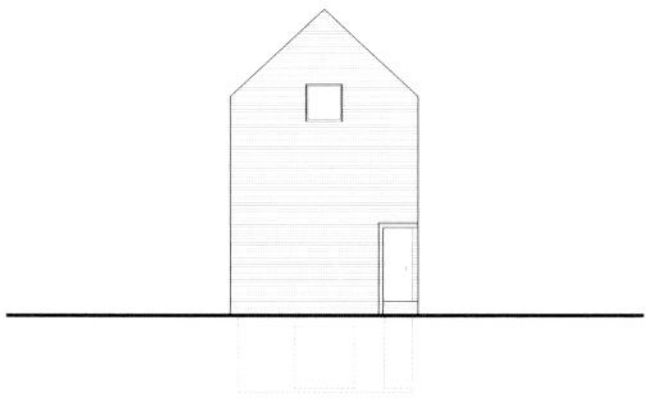

South elevation

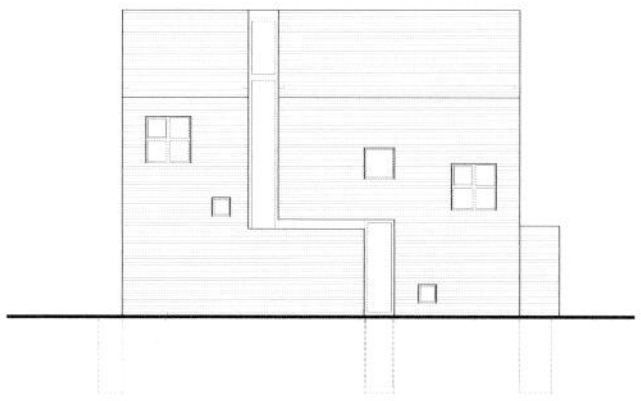

West elevation

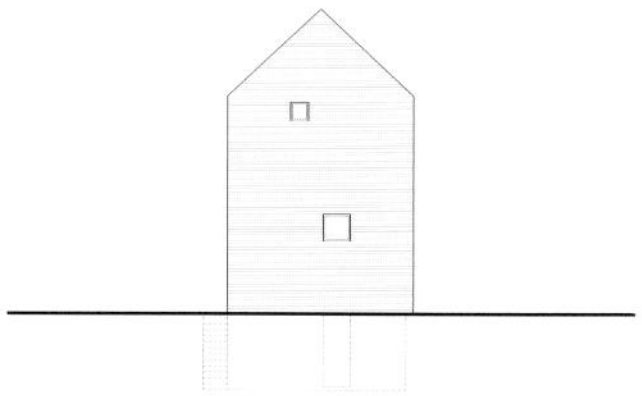

North elevation

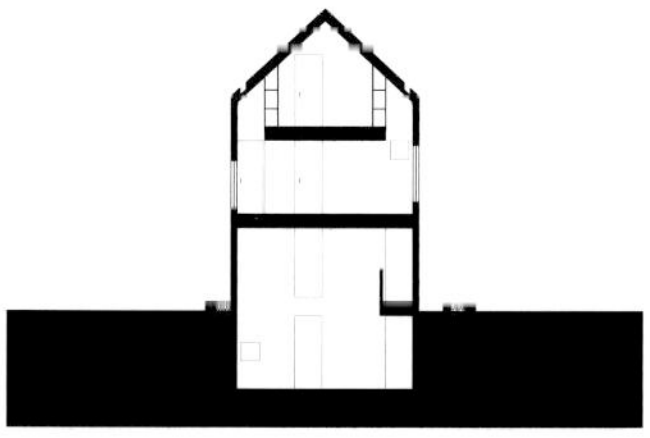

Section A-A

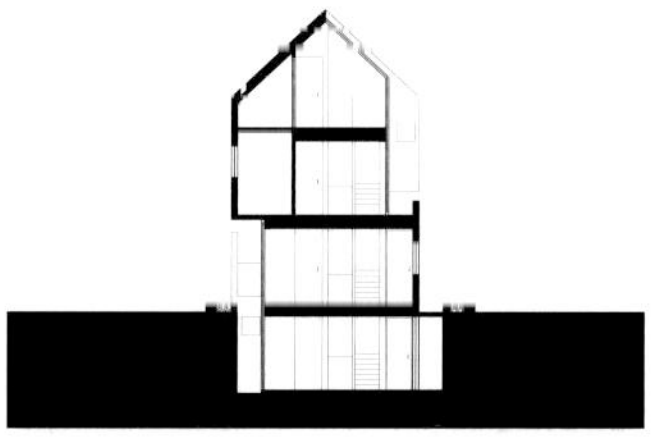

Section B-B

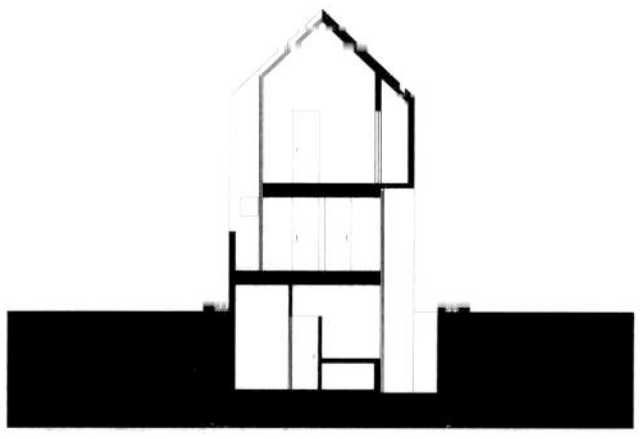

Section C-C

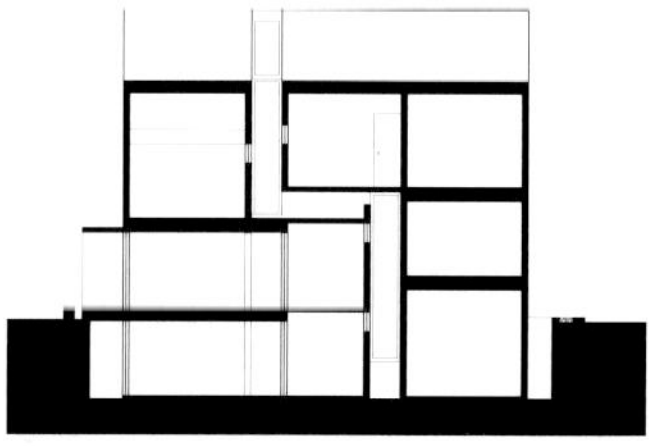

Section D-D

JIANGSU GARDEN EXPO TREASURE PAVILION

Location: Nanjing, Jiangsu Province, China
Lead architects: Zhang Lei, Qi Wei, Li Chenxing
Design team: (Architecture) Wang Liang, Zhang Cheng; (interior) Ma Haiyi, Cao Yi, Huang Rong, Chen Yingjie, Peng Mingxing, Pu Sirui, Luo Tiantian; (landscaping) Zhao Min, Jiang Zhiyuan, Lian Hao
Gross floor area: 15,500 square meters
Design period: 2020
Construction period: 2021
Photography: Hou Bowen

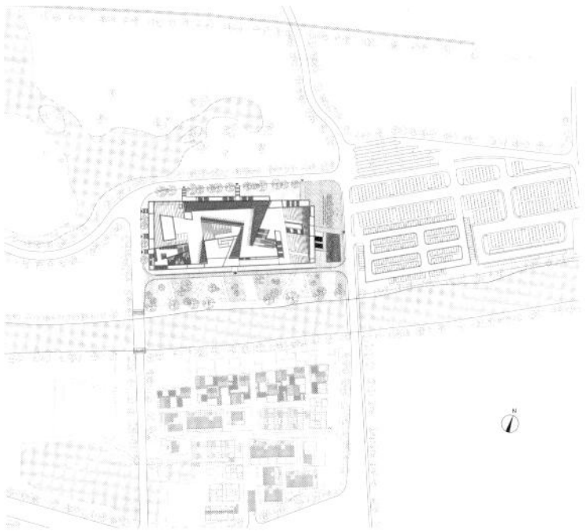

Site plan

Treasure Pavilion and the resort on the south side © Hou Bowen

Bird's-eye view of the main entrance © Hou Bowen

The Treasure Pavilion is located at the northern end of the Jiangsu Garden Expo, close to the No. 2 entrance. It serves primarily as an exhibition space for traditional folk art and handicrafts, and occupies a 15,000-square-meter site, with a total gross floor area of 15,500 square meters. The surroundings of the pavilion are steeped with contradictions and conflicting elements: The northern side of the park borders the Shanghai-Beijing high speed railway, along which trains constantly shuttle back and forth; the southern side, however, is far more tranquil, with a river that separates pavilion from an apartment-style hotel resembling a small village community. In this peripheral area of the city, urbanity and rurality clash and intersect.

An overlapping of space creates order and echoes the region's unique topography. By superposing flat, rectangular structures, the architects have created a striking landscape rich in local affinities that serves two separate functions: indoor artistic exhibition and leisurely rooftop strolling.

The site of the project is a long, narrow strip of vegetation between the mountain range and the high-speed railway. Its planned surface area was 190 meters long and 75 meters wide, with a height limit of 8 meters.

Facing a challenging terrain and design restrictions, a strategy of "heaviness" was adopted, sinking the building into the site to merge it with the land. At the same time, a "folding" concept allows surfaces to at once act as roofs and floors. Broken lines divide the space from east to west into three interlocking parts of different heights. The eastern and western extremities are slightly raised; footpaths enter these upturned structures from different directions while a zigzagging path in the center connects the front courtyard with the rooftop garden. The main part of the exhibition hall is located one floor underground in a spacious sunken courtyard. Curved walls and landscaped steps take the visitor down to this space from the ground floor. Meanwhile, openings of different sizes in the ground floor's outer walls allow visitors to appreciate the building's surroundings from inside the space, creating a sense of continuity between interior and exterior.

The movement of the earth's crust has created exposed rock strata which makes for an interesting feature in the Garden Expo's park. The main hues of pale yellow and green, with hints of deep purple and dusty red welcome visitors with a kaleidoscope of tones. Having been weathered by the elements over countless millennia, the red hues aren't particularly

Ground-level view of the main entrance © Hou Bowen

bold, but nonetheless are still alluring and impactful. They form a visual parallel with the folding layers of the building, reminding visitors of the passage of time. The Garden Expo was formerly a quarry and an industrial building and these industrial ruins constitute the unique memories of the site, forming a juxtaposition of a contemporary construction with natural features, like the rock face—which has inspired the structure of the Garden Expo to display unique materials and textures that reflect the site's layers of historical significance.

Materials are vessels encapsulating time, and as the Corten steel panels rust, they will give the pavilion's façade a rough, industrial texture and a red-brown hue that will complement the surrounding rock face. In that sense, they have an organic quality that recalls at once the past and the future.

Main entrance © Hou Bowen

Connection between interior and exterior spaces © Hou Bowen

Inner courtyard © Hou Bowen

Bird's-eye view of the western rooftop © Hou Bowen

Ramp within the sunken courtyard © Hou Bowen

Detail drawing

1. Base wall body—basic wall cleaning and processing with machine applied plaster
2. 20 mm 1:3 cement mortar leveling, mixed with 5% waterproofing agent
3. Wiping and leveling of the adhesive cement, as well as pressing an alkali-resistant fiberglass mesh into the mass
4. 180x180x10 mm hot-dip galvanized steel plates @ 2,500–3,000 mm
5. 80x60x4 mm hot-dip galvanized steel columns
6. Partial welding of batten bars
7. 1.5 mm steel plate groove
8. Weather-resistant steel curtain wall
9. Coping
10. Metal grid
11. Metal grid steel frame
12. Sleeper wall with stilts
13. Minimum 30 mm C25 fine gravel concrete layer, sloping toward the drainage ditch
14. 1.5 mm JS waterproofing coating, reaching 300 mm up the finished surface of the structure
15. Self-waterproof reinforced-concrete base plate, impermeability grade not less than P6

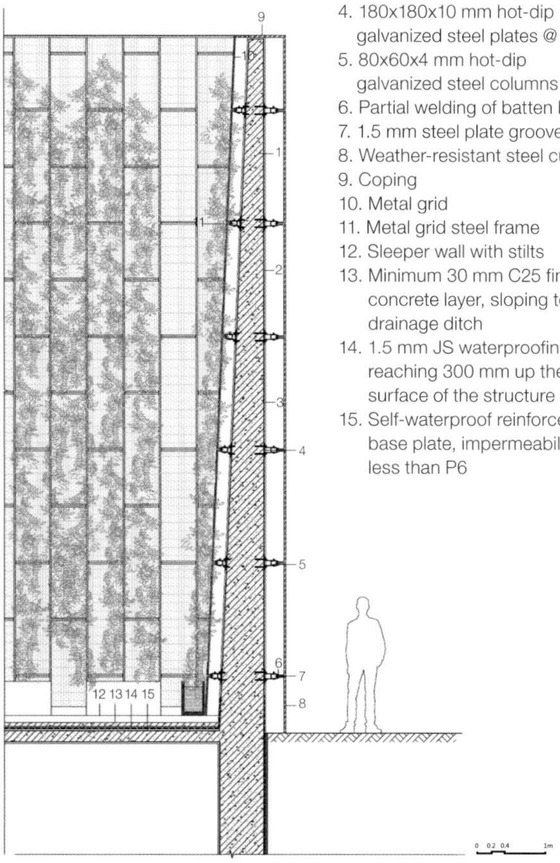

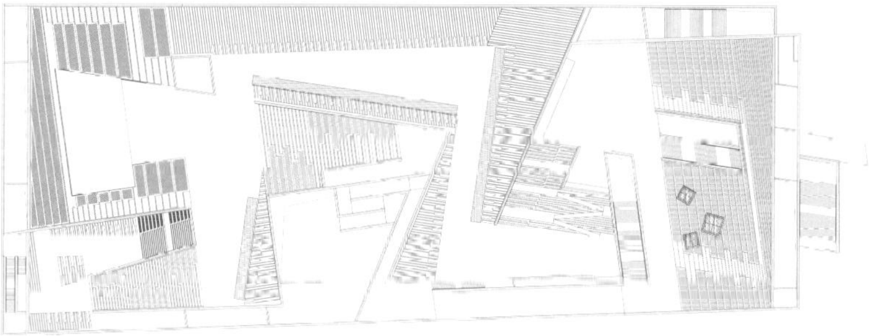

Roof plan

Ground floor plan

1. Lobby
2. Exhibition hall
3. Corridor
4. Café
5. Reception room
6. Restroom
7. Craft shop
8. Office

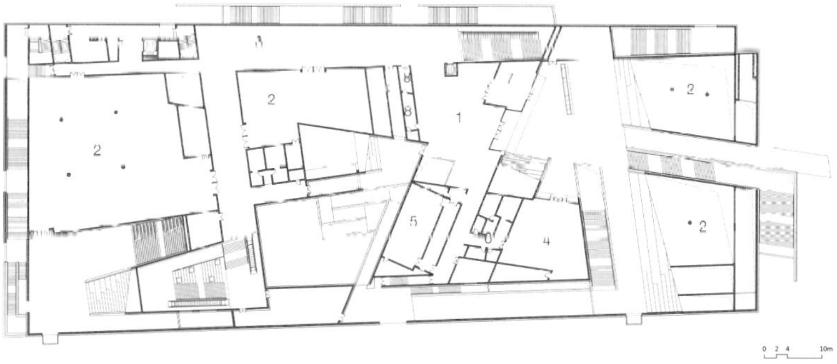

Underground floor plan

1. Courtyard
2. Exhibition hall
3. Corridor
4. Air-conditioning plant
5. Fire pump room
6. Restroom
7. Switching house
8. Storeroom

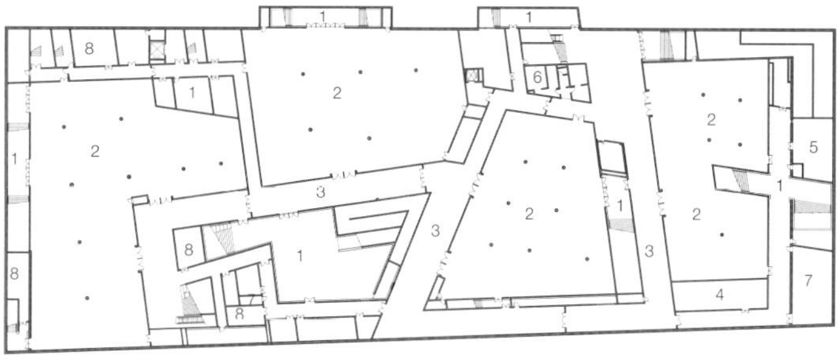

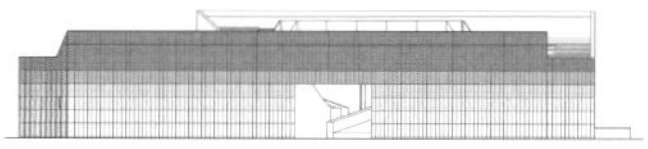

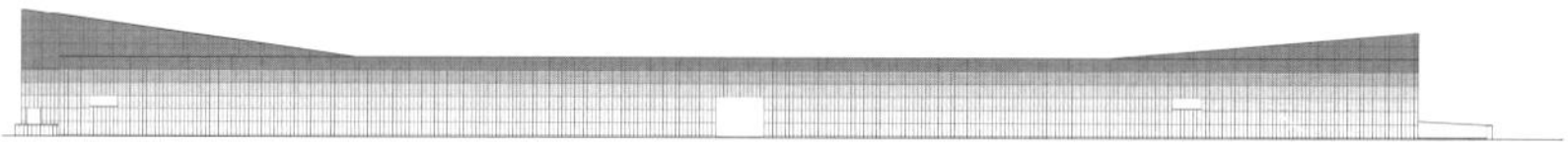

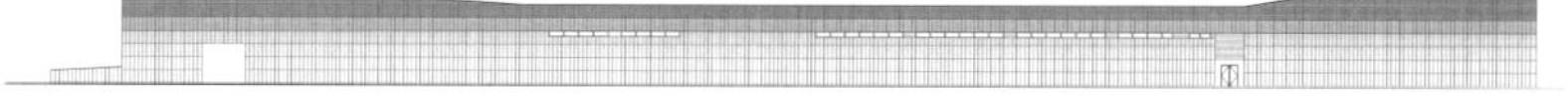

1. Exhibition hall
2. Corridor
3. Lobby
4. Entrance
5. Tank room
6. Pump room
7. Courtyard

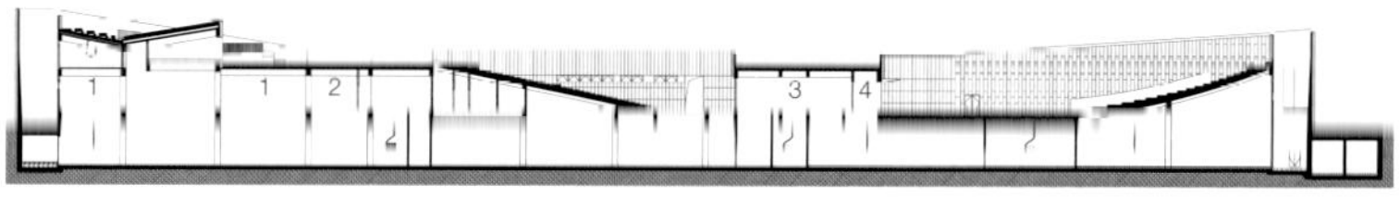

Section A-A

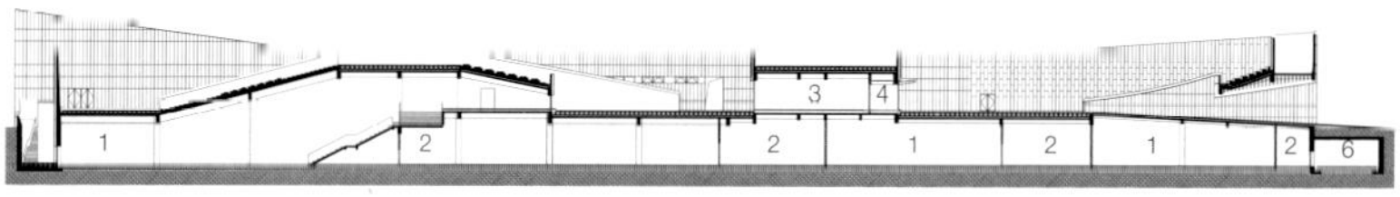

Section B-B

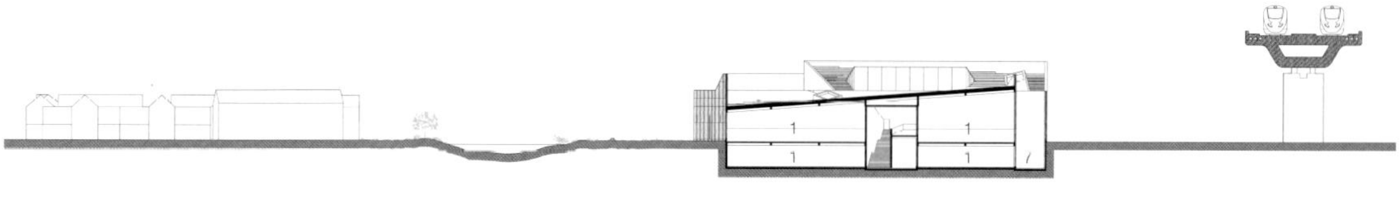

Section C-C

Li Xinggang

Atelier Li Xinggang
Founder and Principal Architect, Atelier Li Xinggang

Li Xinggang is a distinguished architect renowned for his exceptional achievements in the field. He holds the titles "Winner of the National Engineering Survey and Design Master," "Winner of the 10th Liang Sicheng Architecture Prize," and is a member of the Jiusan Society. Presently, he serves as the chief architect of the renowned China Architecture Design & Research Group. He also holds the following positions: professor-level senior architect, director (China Construction Technology Group Large-scale Complex Architecture Research Center), doctoral tutor (Tianjin University), design tutor (Tsinghua University's School of Architecture), and part-time professor (Shanghai Jiaotong University), as well as positions in other esteemed institutions.

Throughout his career, Li Xinggang has dedicated himself to the study and practice of large-scale complex architectural designs. He has developed his own contemporary complex architectural design theory, methodology, and technical system, which is centered around the principles of "integrated geometry and poetic scenery" and "engineering-integrated architecture." Under his guidance, numerous significant national engineering and design projects have been successfully completed. He has also presided over the creation of iconic venues for the 2022 Beijing Winter Olympics and 2022 Beijing Paralympic Games, like the "Bird's Nest" National Stadium, the Yanqing Competition Area of the Beijing Winter Olympics, the National Sliding Center, and the National Alpine Ski Center. His portfolio also includes outstanding works like Museum for Site of Xanadu, Jixi Museum, Gymnasium of New Campus of Tianjin University, The THIRD SPACE in Tangshan, and the innovative "Silo Pavilion" at the Holiday Inn Express Beijing Shougang. These projects collectively exemplify Li's unique and groundbreaking approach to contemporary architecture, which embraces Chinese characteristics while fostering innovation.

Li Xinggang's exceptional contributions to the field and fraternity have garnered him numerous accolades and awards. He has been honored with the China Youth Science and Technology Award, Architecture Gold Award from Asian Association of Architects, the National Excellent Engineering and Design Gold and Silver Awards, National Most Beautiful Scientific and Technological Work Award, National Candidate for Millions of Talents Award, and the National May 1st Labor Medal. He also received commendation from the CPC Central Committee and the State Council for outstanding contributions made to the 2022 Beijing Winter Olympics and 2022 Beijing Paralympics, as well as a special merit with the Beijing Olympics' Engineering Award. He has also had the privilege of serving as a torchbearer for both the 2008 Beijing Olympics and 2022 Beijing Winter Olympic Games.

Selected Works

2022 2022 Beijing Winter Olympic Games, Yanqing Zone, Beijing, China
2021 "Chongtai"—Winter Olympics Taizicheng Exhibition Hall, Hebei Province, China
2021 Yuhuan Museum and Library, Taizhou, Zhejiang Province, China
2021 Anren Great Craftsman Culture Center, Sichuan Province, China
2019 Mountain Garden Cultural Center for the Horticulture Village in Yanqing, Beijing, China
2018 "Silo Pavilion," Holiday Inn Express Beijing Shougang, Beijing, China
2017 "Miniature Beijing"—Renovation of No. 28 Dayuan Hutong, Beijing, China
2015 The THIRD SPACE in Tangshan, Tangshan, Hebei Province, China
2015 Gymnasium of New Campus of Tianjin University, Tianjin, China
2013 Jixi Museum, Anhui Province, China
2011 Museum for Site of Xanadu, Inner Mongolia, China
2008 National Stadium—Main Stadium for 2008 Olympic Games, Beijing, China

Museum for Site of Xanadu © Zhang Guangyuan

The THIRD SPACE in Tangshan © Zhang Guangyuan

Interviewer: *Architecture China*
Interviewee: Li Xinggang (LI)
Editor: Wang Ying

What new insights have you developed on the idea of "Building with Nature"?

LI: If you break it down, "Building with Nature" can mean using natural materials and construction methods, but it can also mean taking a more spontaneous approach to the creative process.

I also personally interpret "Building with Nature" as an on-going dialog between buildings and their natural environment that we, as architects, need to facilitate. Architects should help create a symbiotic relationship between artificial structures and their natural settings. That's my understanding.

"Building with Nature" emphasizes that construction needs to consider more than our own human interests—it also needs to account for the natural environment. It requires an awareness of our place in the natural world and our dependence on nature for survival. This, in my opinion, is the fundamental value at the heart of this concept.

The Building with Nature: Architecture China Award upholds the harmony between artificially constructed buildings and their natural settings—a theme that is reflected in certain aspects of traditional Chinese culture. The Awards are motivated by a clear set of values. I hope that it will continue to be organized long into the future, boosting architects and works that embody these values, promoting Chinese culture and traditions while also proving to the world that Chinese architects can offer answers to both present and future realities.

What direction are you currently exploring in your practice?

LI: My reflection and practice emphasize two points. The first is the creation of a mutual relationship between buildings and the environment. This is one of the main principles and objectives behind my work. The other is to connect and integrate technical and artistic ways of expression.

In essence, this means bridging the gap between the technologies necessary to architectural construction and the poetic experiences of everyday life that people can experience. This is the particular design approach and direction that I'm currently devoting my research to. This approach serves to realize my ideal and objective of "poetic construction," which means connecting and combining technical and poetic forms of expression in order to create a mutual relationship between architecture and nature. Because the term "building with nature" implies an artificial representation of nature, we hope that humans will coexist harmoniously and engage in a dialog with the environment.

ANREN GREAT CRAFTSMAN CULTURE CENTER

Location: Dayi, Sichuan Province, China
Lead architect: Li Xinggang, Liu Zhen
Architecture: (schematic design of the interior and landscaping) Chen Yimin, Guo Wenjia, Wang Han
Structure: He Xiangyu, Chen Xiaoqing
Master plan: Gao Zhi, Zhou Qingzhao
Structural consultant: Dong Yue
Landscaping: Li Li, Kong Weiyi, Cao Lei, Zhang Li, Li Jia, Zhang Yubin
Gross floor area: 7,682 square meters
Design period: March 2017
Completion: October 2021
Photography: Su Shengliang

Site plan

Aerial view from southeast

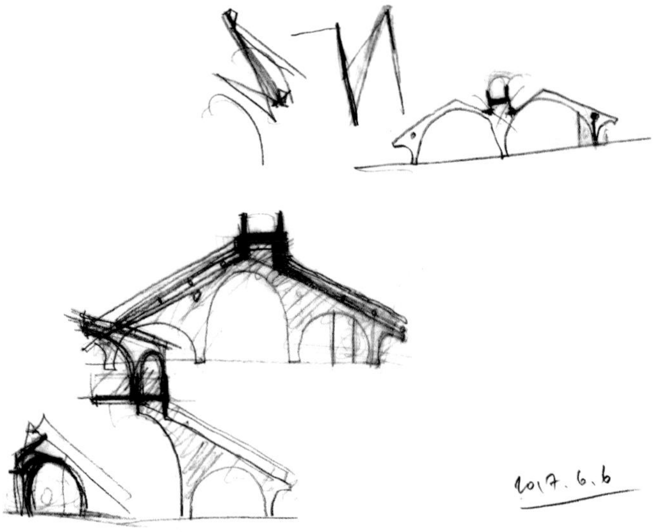

Sketch

The Anren Great Craftsman Culture Center was initially designed in March 2017 and successfully completed and inaugurated in October 2021. Situated at the southern end of Shuren Street in the historic Anren Old Town of Dayi County, Chengdu, Sichuan Province, China, the culture center draws inspiration from the distinctive mansion architecture prevalent in Anren. Taking cues from the texture and scale of the former residence of Chen Yuesheng located on the west side of the culture center, the building embraces a series of sloping roofs that gradually ascend from west to east, resembling a set of mountains.

This design approach creates an expansive courtyard within the cultural center that extends eastward from the southern courtyard of Chen Yuesheng's former residence. A well-planned plank road system has been integrated into the design, allowing visitors to ascend the structure. The elevated plank road system not only illuminates the indoor exhibition hall at the roof ridge through high side windows, but also invites visitors to traverse pathways amid rockeries and over-the-roof valleys, enhancing the immersive mountainous terrain experience. Upon reaching the pavilion at the highest point, visitors are treated to a panoramic view of the cascading roofs of the cultural center, the old residence, and the ancient streets in the distance. This vantage point establishes a visual connection with the water tower—the highest point of the ancient town—uniting the entirety of Anren Old Town within the observer's gaze. The dynamic building volume and the undulating roof forms emulate rolling hills, imparting a sense of continuous transformation.

The design also incorporates concrete arch structures by abstracting the eclectic architectural style seen in the entrances and gables of Anren Old Town and combines them with Chinese and Western decorative elements. Wooden roof trusses have been skillfully utilized in the roof construction, creating a spatial atmosphere that harmoniously blends local and contemporary styles.

Aerial view from northwest

1 | 2 | 3

1. Plank roads shuttle across the sloping roof
2. Aerial view from southwest
3. Aerial view from north (partial)

Lu ting (Lu Pavilion)

Ya ting (Ya Pavilion)

View of the building's courtyard from west to north

Multifunction room and lounge for temporary exhibitions

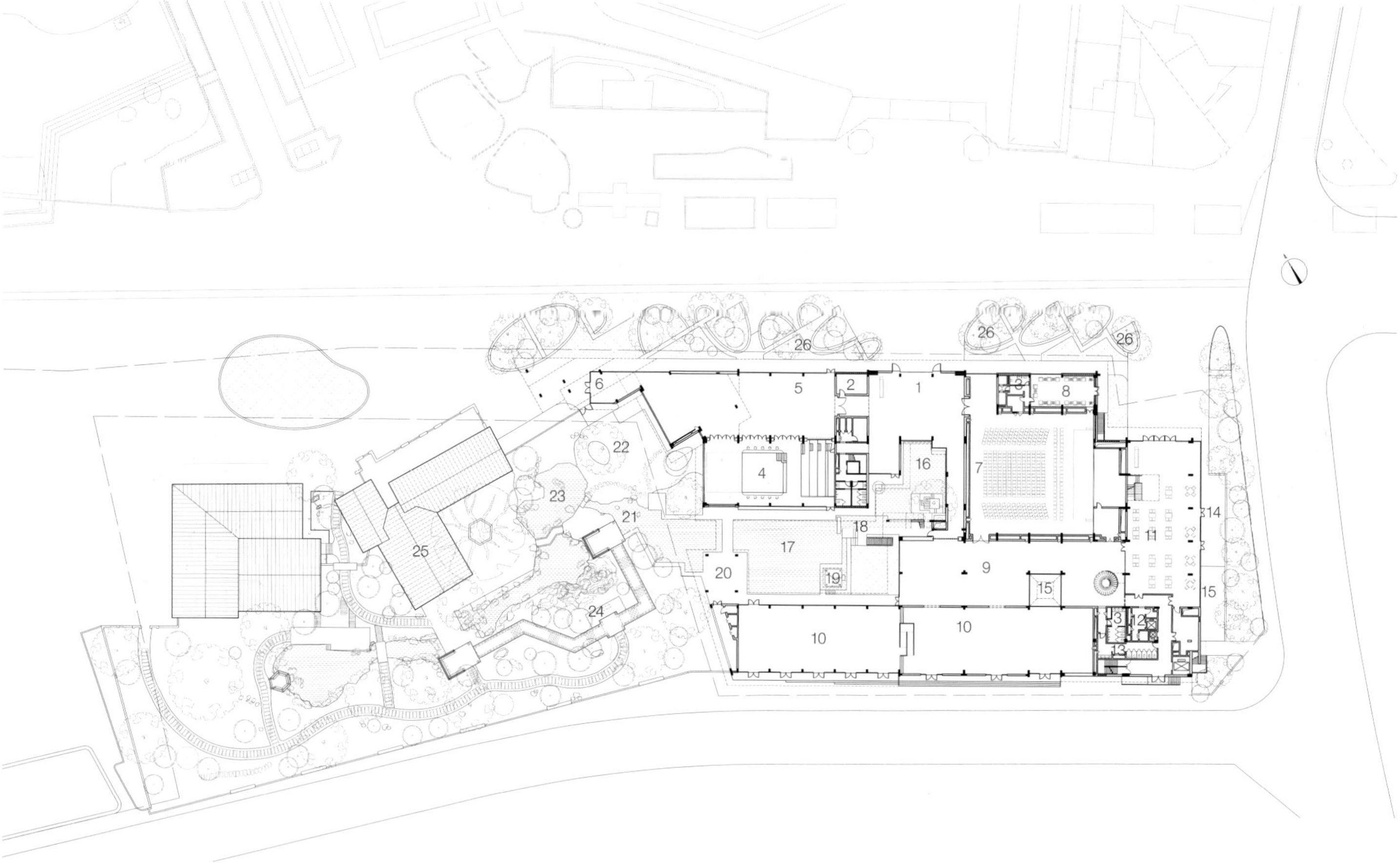

Ground-floor plan

1. Main entrance hall
2. Management room
3. Restroom
4. Concert hall
5. Concert hall lounge
6. Secondary entrance hall
7. Multifunction room
8. VIP room
9. Multifunction room lounge
10. Exhibition room
11. Dining room
12. Pantry
13. Logistics entrance hall
14. Outdoor terrace
15. Sunken courtyard S
16. Yaoyue Pavilion
17. Xiaojing Lake
18. Bamboo grove
19. *"Lu ting"* (Lu Pavilion)
20. Semi-outdoor rest area
21. Ruyi Lake
22. *Karesansui* courtyard
23. Existing lake
24. Existing corridor
25. Existing former residence of Chen Yuesheng
26. Arched tree pool

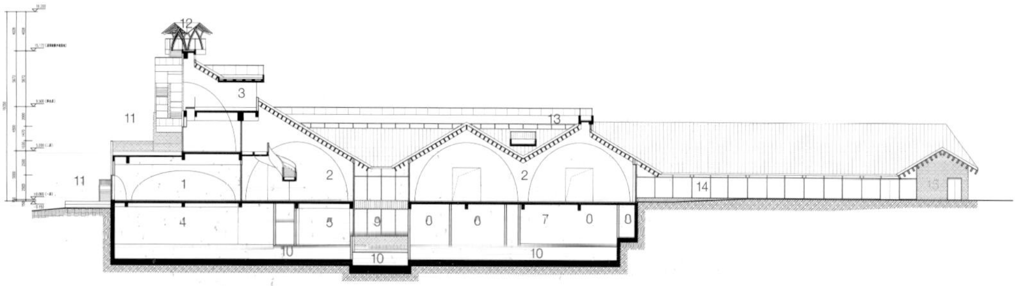

Section

1. Dining room
2. Multifunction room lounge
3. Semi-outdoor balcony
4. Kitchen
5. Office
6. Equipment room
7. Corridor
8. Equipment pipe rack
9. Sunken courtyard
10. Anti-floating weight backfill concrete
11. Outdoor terrace
12. *"Ya ting"* (Ya Pavilion)
13. Roof plank road
14. Road underneath the roof
15. Outdoor rest area

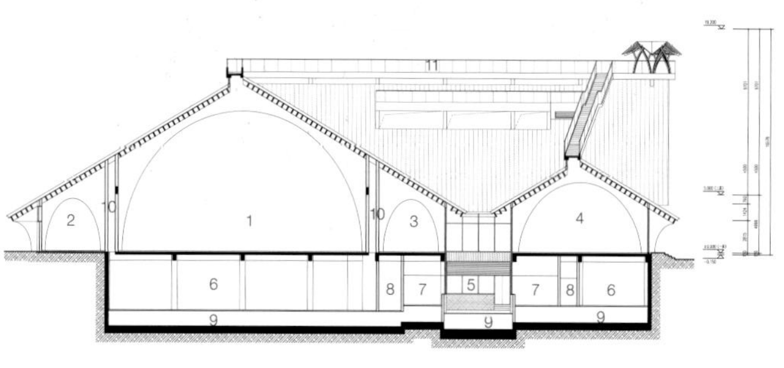

Section

1. Multifunction room
2. VIP room
3. Multifunction room lounge
4. Exhibition room
5. Sunken courtyard
6. Equipment room
7. Office
8. Corridor
9. Anti-floating weight backfill concrete
10. Cavity wall for equipment
11. Roof plank road

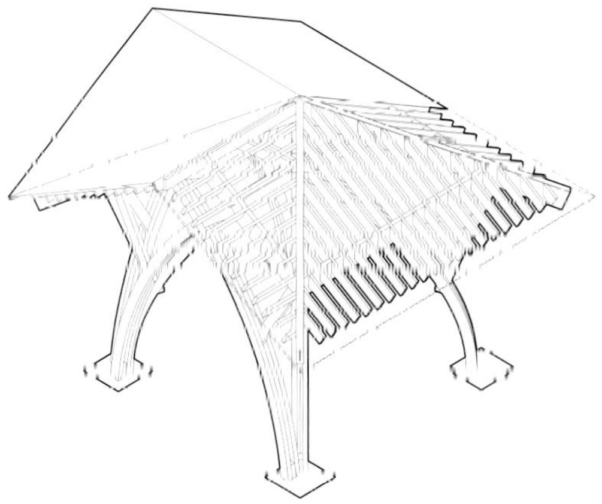

"Lu ting"—axonometric diagram

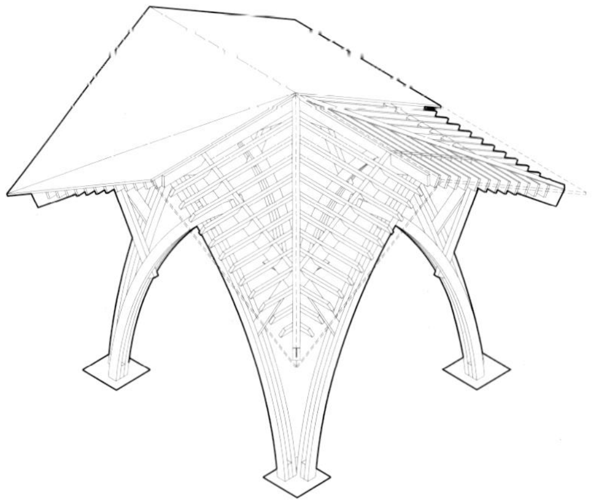

"Ya ting"—axonometric diagram

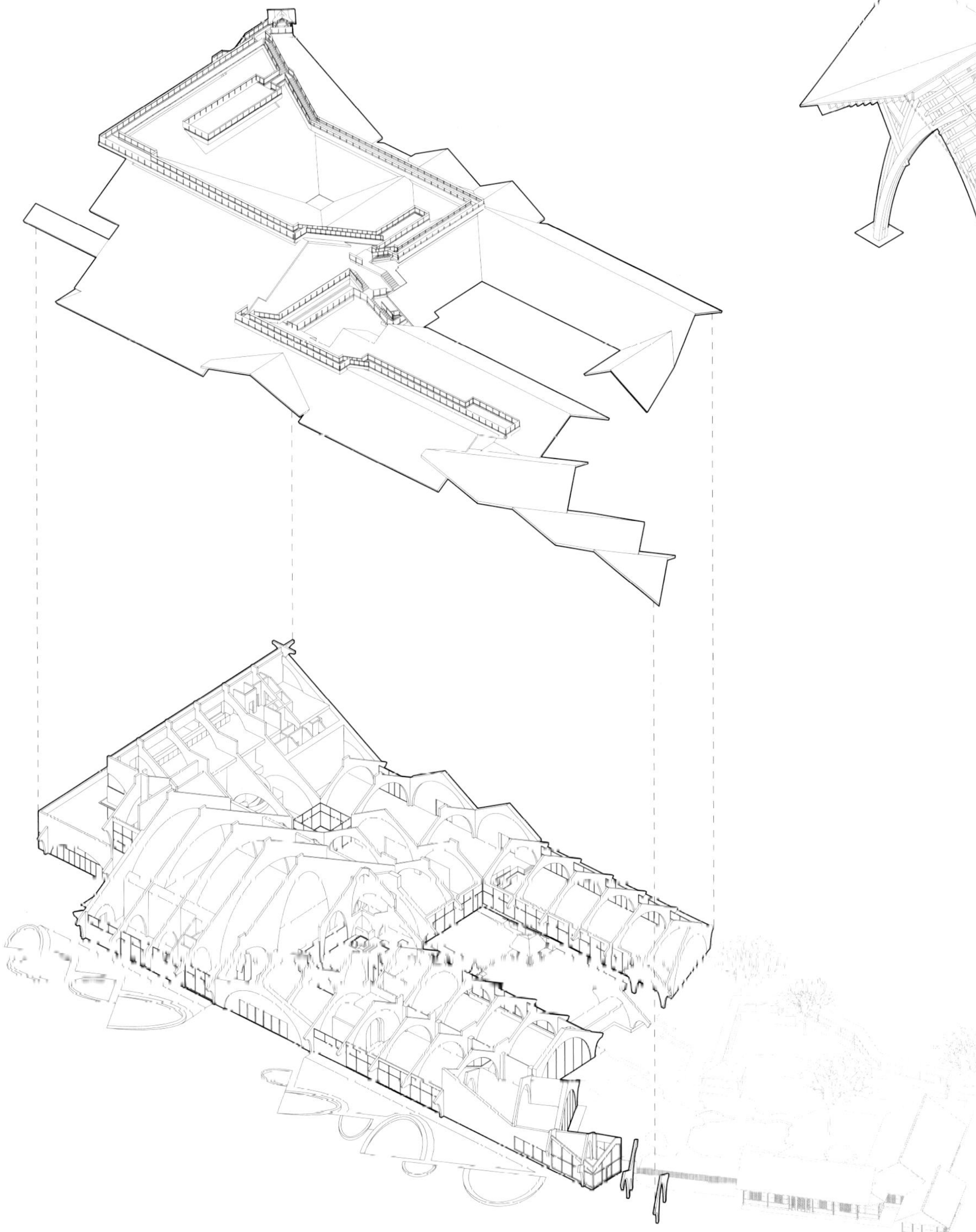

Axonometric diagram

MOUNTAIN GARDEN CULTURAL CENTER FOR THE HORTICULTURE VILLAGE IN YANQING

Location: Yanqing District, Beijing, China
Lead architects: Li Xinggang, Jiang Wenlin
Architecture: Tan Zeyang, Yuan Zhimin, Tan Zhou
Structure: Ren Qingying, Liu Wenting, Yang Songlin
Gross floor area: 2,310 square meters
Design period: October 2018
Construction period: April 2019
Photography: Zhang Guangyuan, Jiang Wenlin, Li Weina

Site plan

Aerial view from the northeast

Sketch

The Mountain Garden Cultural Center for the Horticulture Village in Yanqing District, Beijing, China, was originally designed in May 2017 ; it was completed and opened to the public in March 2019. Situated in the southwest of the park designated for the International Horticultural Exhibition 2019 in Yanqing, the site is in close proximity to traditional sights of the region, such as a characteristic small town and flower fields located to the northeast, and the modern Botanical Hall in the south. The center aims to offer both open and enclosed public spaces for hosting cultural and creative activities, as well as industry experiences typical of such a horticulture exhibition.

The building is composed of two L-shaped volumes, each formed by the combination of two single-slope roofs. These volumes are separated by an internal pathway, but connected through their shared half-height base. Public entrances and exits are located in the northwest and southeast corners of the inner walkway, integrating the building into the expo/fair infrastructure system of the horticultural park. From the inner pathway, visitors can also access a sightseeing platform on the upper floor and roof, where they can enjoy views of the distant landscapes. Independent entrances and exits for functional spaces are situated in the southwest, northeast, and southeast corners.

The southwestern building volume houses cultural and creative service spaces like exhibition halls, lecture halls, and a book bar, while the northeastern building volume contains production workshops, a souvenir shop, and other exhibition appropriate spaces. Management offices and artist studios are located at the base, providing convenient connections to the service and industrial areas. Each space group can function separately or cohesively. During the expo, the building's spaces were used separately, but can be integrated to be operated together after the exhibition.

In addition to its openness, the center also aims to express an internal narrative, maintaining a suitable distance from the artificial scenic

Aerial view from the south

Section model

buildings and landscapes in the surrounding environment. By applying the concept "building houses that imitate mountains," the project aims to create a specific landscape experience. For this purpose, the single-slope roof provides a clear direction and identity to the two main buildings. Within the design concept, "mountains"—represented by natural elements—and "houses"—represented by artificial objects—interconnect and interact with each other. The northeastern building represents the "house," which finds a contrasting backdrop with the "mountain" structure in the southwest of the plot. The "mountain" in the southwest is simultaneously connected to the base of the "house" in the northwest.

The distinct sloping roof defines two interior spaces with different characteristics: the seemingly crouching "mountain" volume creates a cave-like ambiance, while the "house" structure is more defined, symbolizing the spatial characteristics of traditional buildings. The half-height base platform separates and connects the "mountain" and the "house." When viewed from the "house" (in the northeast), the southwestern roof resembles an artificial "mountain." Combined, the "mountain" and the "house," as well as the colonnade, the eave porch, the attic on the upper floor, and the pavilion on the "mountain" roof collectively form a three-dimensional visual system that has been named Mountain Garden.

The "mountain" section of the center makes use of full cast-in-situ fair-faced concrete walls to support the inclined roof and enhance the spatial characteristics of a "mountain cave." The "house" section utilizes a composite structural system consisting of reinforced concrete and wooden roof frames that echo traditional wooden roof structures. The wooden framework in the "house" adopts orthogonal wooden trusses, connecting wooden components with the same cross section through prefabricated multidirectional steel components, which results in a modern and efficient composite joint system that pays homage to traditional mortise and tenon timber structures.

View from the book bar, looking out to the exhibition hall

Northern view from the platform underneath a wooden frame

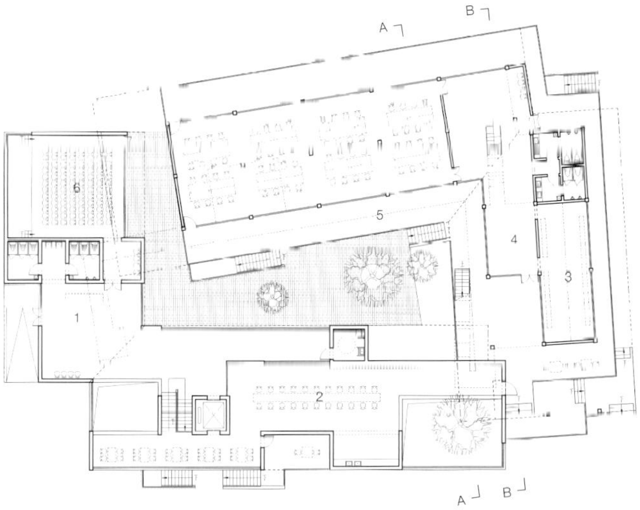

Ground-floor plan

1. Entrance hall of gallery
2. Book bar
3. Shop
4. Entrance hall of culture creation area
5. Workshop
6. Lecture hall
7. Gallery
8. Office
9. Artist workshops
10. Platform under wooden frame
11. Pavilion

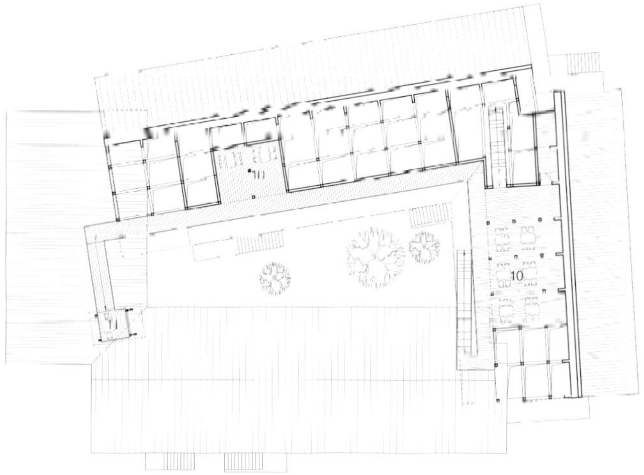

Second-floor plan

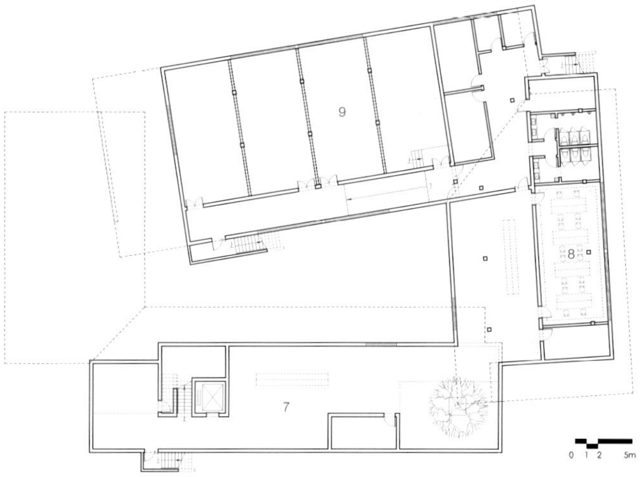

Basement-floor plan

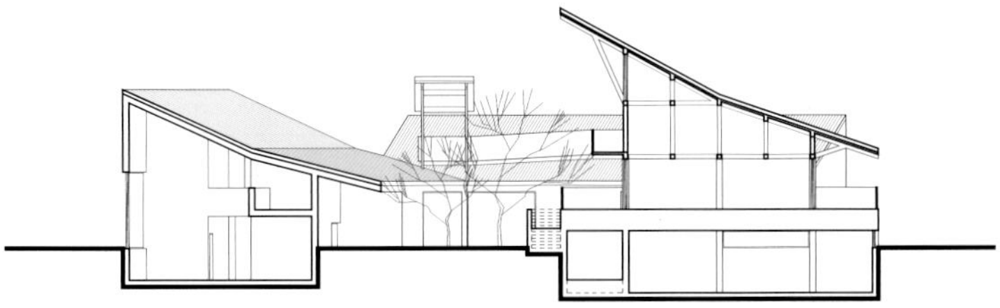

Section A-A

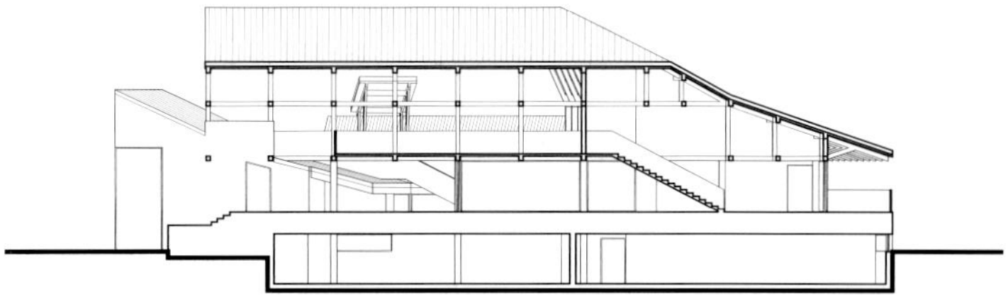

Section B-B

Axonometric drawing of the wooden frame

EXPLORATION AWARD IN TECHNOLOGY

Exploration Award in Technology focuses on projects with a humanistic spirit and which display continuous innovation with architectural technologies through two or more high-quality works created in recent years. This award also encourages cross-professional and cross-disciplinary exploration.

Li Xinggang
Atelier Li Xinggang

Laureate

Zhang Zhun
AND Office

Shortlisted

Li Xinggang

Atelier Li Xinggang
Founder and Principal Architect, Atelier Li Xinggang

Li Xinggang is a distinguished architect renowned for his exceptional achievements in the field. He holds the titles "Winner of the National Engineering Survey and Design Master," "Winner of the 10th Liang Sicheng Architecture Prize," and is a member of the Jiusan Society. Presently, he serves as the chief architect of the renowned China Architecture Design & Research Group. He also holds the following positions: professor-level senior architect, director (China Construction Technology Group Large-scale Complex Architecture Research Center), doctoral tutor (Tianjin University), design tutor (Tsinghua University's School of Architecture), and part-time professor (Shanghai Jiaotong University), as well as positions in other esteemed institutions.

Throughout his career, Li Xinggang has dedicated himself to the study and practice of large-scale complex architectural designs. He has developed his own contemporary complex architectural design theory, methodology, and technical system, which is centered around the principles of "integrated geometry and poetic scenery" and "engineering-integrated architecture." Under his guidance, numerous significant national engineering and design projects have been successfully completed. He has also presided over the creation of iconic venues for the 2022 Beijing Winter Olympics and 2022 Beijing Paralympic Games, like the "Bird's Nest" National Stadium, the Yanqing Competition Area of the Beijing Winter Olympics, the National Sliding Center, and the National Alpine Ski Center. His portfolio also includes outstanding works like Museum for Site of Xanadu, Jixi Museum, Gymnasium of New Campus of Tianjin University, The THIRD SPACE in Tangshan, and the innovative "Silo Pavilion" at the Holiday Inn Express Beijing Shougang. These projects collectively exemplify Li's unique and groundbreaking approach to contemporary architecture, which embraces Chinese characteristics while fostering innovation.

Li Xinggang's exceptional contributions to the field and fraternity have garnered him numerous accolades and awards. He has been honored with the China Youth Science and Technology Award, Architecture Gold Award from Asian Association of Architects, the National Excellent Engineering and Design Gold and Silver Awards, National Most Beautiful Scientific and Technological Work Award, National Candidate for Millions of Talents Award, and the National May 1st Labor Medal. He also received commendation from the CPC Central Committee and the State Council for outstanding contributions made to the 2022 Beijing Winter Olympics and 2022 Beijing Paralympics, as well as a special merit with the Beijing Olympics' Engineering Award. He has also had the privilege of serving as a torchbearer for both the 2008 Beijing Olympics and 2022 Beijing Winter Olympic Games.

Selected Works

2022 2022 Beijing Winter Olympic Games, Yanqing Zone, Beijing, China
2021 "Chongtai"—Winter Olympics Taizicheng Exhibition Hall, Hebei Province, China
2021 Yuhuan Museum and Library, Taizhou, Zhejiang Province, China
2021 Anren Great Craftsman Culture Center, Sichuan Province, China
2019 Mountain Garden Cultural Center for the Horticulture Village in Yanqing, Beijing, China
2018 "Silo Pavilion," Holiday Inn Express Beijing Shougang, Beijing, China
2017 "Miniature Beijing"—Renovation of No. 28 Dayuan Hutong, Beijing, China
2015 The THIRD SPACE in Tangshan, Tangshan, Hebei Province, China
2015 Gymnasium of New Campus of Tianjin University, Tianjin, China
2013 Jixi Museum, Anhui Province, China
2011 Museum for Site of Xanadu, Inner Mongolia, China
2008 National Stadium—Main Stadium for 2008 Olympic Games, Beijing, China

Yanqing Winter Olympic Village (2022 Beijing Winter Olympics) © Xiao Jie

Interviewer: *Architecture China*
Interviewee: Li Xinggang (LI)
Editor: Wang Ying

How do you interpret nature within the context of architectural practice?

LI: The most general sense of the term "nature"—the sky, vegetation, earth, mountains, and waterways, as well as wind, rain and snow—is what I call "primordial nature." It's the environment that humans depend on for survival. But we can expand upon that definition to include what architects often deal with in their work—"artificial" or "civilized" nature. These terms refer to a special state of nature resulting from human intervention.

Artificial nature is central to our work as architects, because we very rarely deal with nature in a primordial state. Most of the time, we deal with nature in the context of highly dense urban environments. New buildings should form mutual connections not only with primordial, but also artificial, natural surroundings. That's how I interpret "nature."

In current architectural practices in China, how can we strike a balance between construction and poetic expression?

LI: There's a recent trend of certain types of materials, structures, and techniques being used in the construction of a building to emphasize the notion of craftsmanship. I, personally, view that as a type of poetic construction.

However, there's also an interdependence and interconnectedness between buildings and the natural environment that, in my opinion, constitute a more powerful form of poetry. Poetic construction can inspire a spiritual dialog between the people of today and those of the past, as it harks back to the building practices of our ancestors, but while incorporating recent innovations. By doing so, the past and the present are able to communicate with each other. That's another form of poetry using the wisdom of construction to convey human sentiments.

"Miniature Beijing"—Renovation of No. 28 Dayuan Hutong © Su Shengliang

What opportunities and challenges do you believe China's unique construction practices present to today's architects?

LI: Truthfully, there exists a certain contradiction between technology and poetry: the former is quantifiable, while the latter isn't. Technology looks toward the future, while poetry finds its origins in tradition; technology revolves around humans, while poetry emphasizes an equal union between people and nature. However, we need to make efforts to reconcile their differences—to use measurable technology as a means of creating immeasurable poetry.

Jixi Museum © Qiu Jianbing

How do we create a fusion between forward-facing, human-oriented technologies on the one hand, and past traditions that emphasize harmony with nature on the other? This is the main challenge that we as architects face today; but it also offers many opportunities for experimentation as we attempt to attain this ideal in our practice.

National Stadium—Main Stadium for 2008 Olympic Games © Zhang Jin

Gymnasium of New Campus of Tianjin University © Sun Haiting

2022 BEIJING WINTER OLYMPIC GAMES: NATIONAL SLIDING CENTER

Site plan

Location: Yanqing District, Beijing, China
Lead architects: Li Xinggang, Qiu Jianbing, Zhang Yuting
Architecture: Liu Ziqim, Zhu Lingli, Liu Yang, Yuan Zhimin, Li Bizhou, Yang Ru, Wang Xiang, Jiang Wenlin, Lu Jingyao, Chen Yimin
Structure: Ren Qingying, Liu Wenting, Li Zheng, Zhang Xiaomeng
Master plan: Gao Zhi, Zhu Gengxin
Landscaping: Shi Lixiu, Guan Wujun, Zhu Yanhui
Interior design: Cao Yang, Zhang Chao
Bridge engineering: Zhao Hongwei, Chi Xiaoqi
Gross floor area: 59,363 square meters
Design period: December 2018
Construction period: June 2021
Photography: Sun Haiting, Zhang Jin, Liu Ziqi, Zhu He, Zhang Muzi

The National Sliding Center is situated in the valley at the southern foot of Xiaohaituo Mountain in Yanqing District near Beijing, China. It encompasses a land area of 18.3 hectares, with the venue itself covering 9.5 hectares, and a gross floor area of approximately 59,000 square meters. The center was designed to host the bobsleigh, skeleton, and luge events during the 2022 Beijing Winter Olympics. These sports are known for their thrill factor, with speeds reaching up to 135 kilometers per hour and gravitational pull peaking at 5 g. Because of this, bobsleigh has been nicknamed "Formula 1 on ice." The track stretches a total length of 1,975 meters and features sixteen curves. The venue spans 800 meters from north to south and has a maximum east–west width of 300 meters. With a vertical drop of 141 meters, the site presents an average slope , with a 16 percent incline.

The National Sliding Center is China's first sliding venue. Given the rigorous requirements of the sport (and its arena), as well as the high level of professionalism associated with of the sport (and its arena), as well as the high, only sixteen Olympic-level sliding centers exist worldwide, and with only just two located in Asia. Embracing the core design concepts of the Yanqing Competition Area, which emphasize the location of a "mountain forest venue" and an "ecological Winter Olympics," the design of the National Sliding Center takes into account the challenges posed by the mountain forest environment in terms of venue planning and construction. Through a synergistic and innovative approach to track design, architectural design, and landscape design, the architectural landscape seamlessly integrates with the natural surroundings. This approach ensures that the venue not only meets the requirements to host an exceptional competition, but also fosters a symbiotic relationship between sports and the ecological forest environment, embodying the spirit of the 2022 Beijing Winter Olympics.

Overview of the National Sliding Center from a mountain top

Bird's-eye view of the Yanqing Zone of the 2022 Winter Olympic Games from southwest to northeast

Model of the sliding track's roof

Aerial view of the National Sliding Center from southeast

Roof walkway of the National Sliding Center

Pavilion on the sliding track's roof

As a newly constructed venue for the Yanqing Zone of the 2022 Beijing Winter Olympics, the National Sliding Center makes use of innovative technologies and methods. The entire design and construction process of the track and venue underwent comprehensive reviews by the International Olympic Committee, different international sport federations, and the Beijing Organizing Committee for the Winter Olympic Games. Adding to that, the venue also successfully passed all the required tests and obtained the necessary international certifications, positioning it at the forefront of similar venues worldwide in terms of quality and standards.

Spectator seats inside, at the finish area

Start of the sliding track

Sliding track beneath the roof

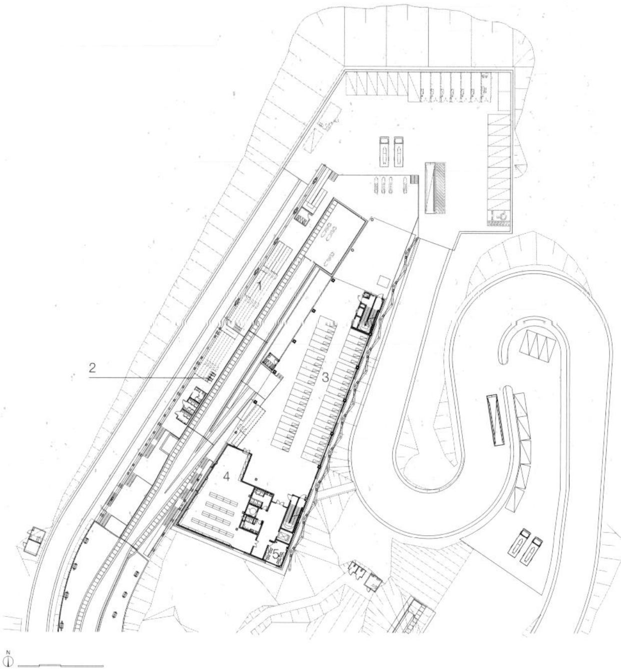

Floor plan of the start area

1. Standing area for departure zone 1
2. Barrier-free viewing platform (two seats)
3. Sled preparation zone
4. Athletes' changing room
5. Referees' room

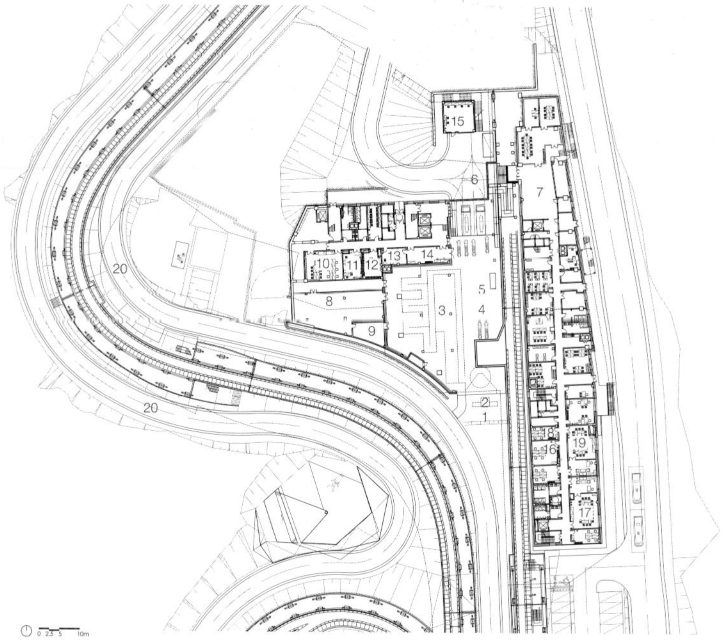

Cross section of the finish area

1. Award ceremony area
2. Podium
3. Interview area
4. Sled reception area
5. Sled weighing
6. Docking area
7. Ceremony preparation area
8. Electrical substation
9. Duty office
10. Sled racing office
11. Medical station
12. Athletes' changing room
13. Sled measuring room
14. Measure control room
15. Sled storage and repair
16. IBSF staff office
17. IBSF meeting room
18. FIL staff office
19. FIL meeting room
20. Sidewalk

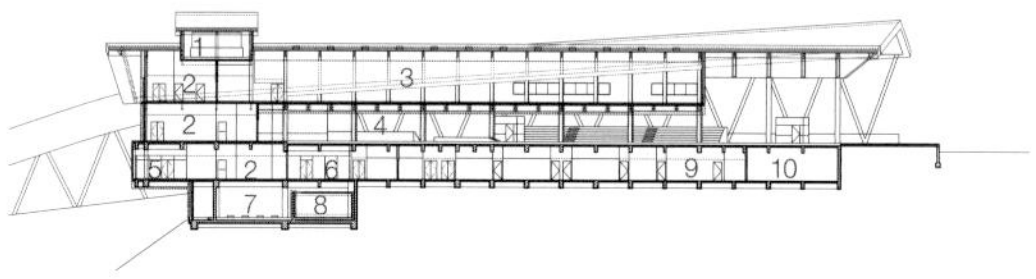

Cross section of the start area

1. Water tanks
2. Hallway
3. Athletes' warm-up area
4. Athletes' changing room
5. Athletes' rest area
6. Officials' rest area
7. Fire-water pump room
8. Fire-water reservoir
9. Walkway
10. Electrical substation

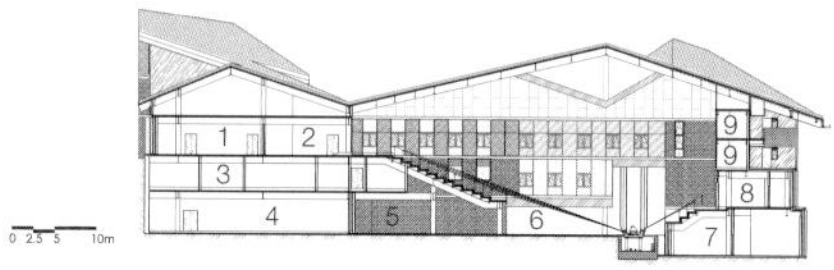

Cross section of the finish area

1. Heated area for spectators
2. Sports exhibition room
3. Merchandise store
4. Electrical substation
5. Interview area
6. Sled reception area
7. Award office
8. Olympic family
9. Commentary area

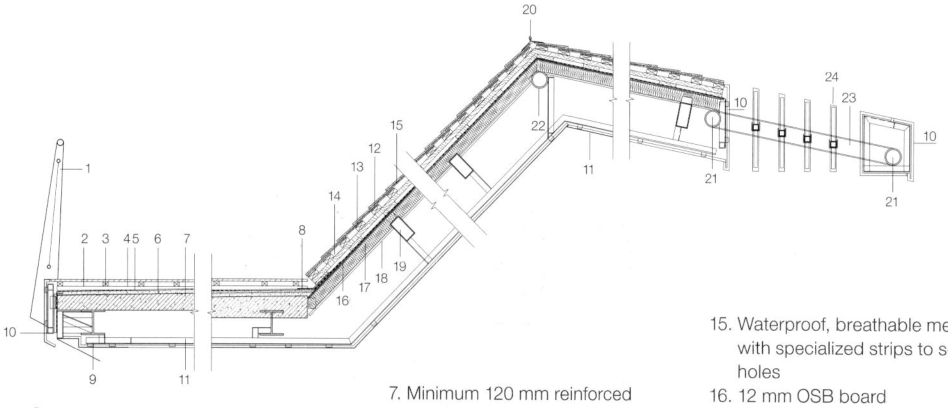

Cross section of the roof structure

1. Stainless-steel handrail
2. 38 mm x 89 mm treated timber walkway
3. 38 mm x 45 mm treated timber keel
4. 38 mm x 89 mm treated timber counter battens
5. 3+3 self-adhesive waterproof membrane with added 20 mm cement protective layer
6. Minimum 30 mm fine cement leveling layer
7. Minimum 120 mm reinforced concrete slab with 2% outward inclination
8. Additional water-proofing layer
9. Curved H-beam for the walkway
10. 3 mm aluminum finish for the cornice
11. 3 mm aluminum ceiling boards
12. 6-16 mm wedged wooden shingles
13. 38 mm x 90 mm treated timber hanging bar @ 190 mm
14. 38 - 100 mm x 140 mm treated timber counter battens @ 400 mm
15. Waterproof, breathable membrane with specialized strips to seal nail holes
16. 12 mm OSB board
17. 38 mm x 89 mm SPF timber lattice @ 406 mm (the inside is filled with insulation material of the same thickness)
18. 12 mm calcium silicate board
19. Steel purlin between timber beams
20. Curved, tubular steel tubes for the roof ridge
21. Curved, tubular steel tubes for the gable ends
22. Aluminum alloy coping
23. Square steel contact beams
24. Aluminum grating on the eaves

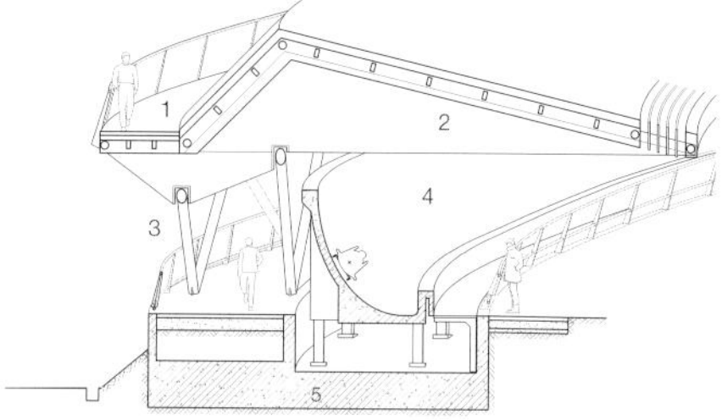

Roof and race track structure

1. Rooftop walkway
2. Roof support frame
3. V-shaped steel beams
4. Ice track
5. U-shaped slits

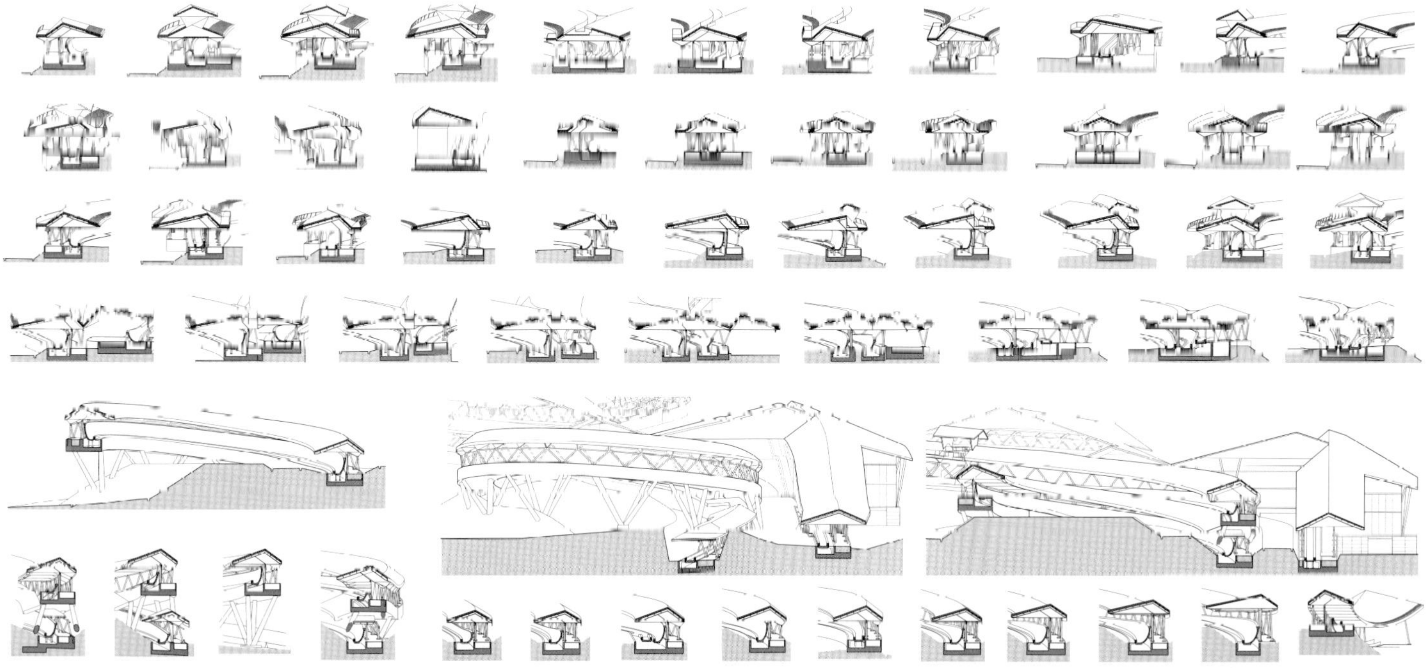

Collection of different cross sections

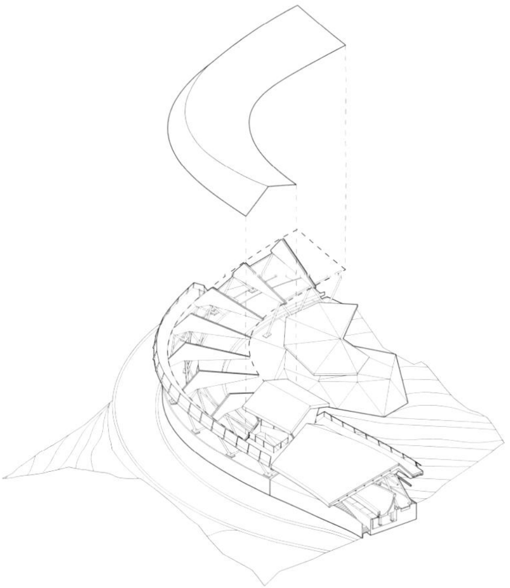

Axonometric section of the National Sliding Center

Axonometric overview of the National Sliding Center

"CHONGTAI"—WINTER OLYMPICS TAIZICHENG EXHIBITION HALL

Location: Chongli, Hebei Province, China
Lead architects: Li Xinggang, Yuan Zhimin
Architecture: Yuan Zhimin
Structure: Sun Hailin, Sun Qingtang
Master plan: Qi Haijuan, Jin Shang
Landscaping: Li Li, Kong Weiyi, Cao Lei, Zhang Li, Li Jia, Zhang Yubin
Exhibit and interior design: Wang Guobin, Yu Shenhong
Gross floor area: 6,371 square meters
Design period: August 2018
Completion: December 2021
Photography: Li Ji, Yuan Zhimin

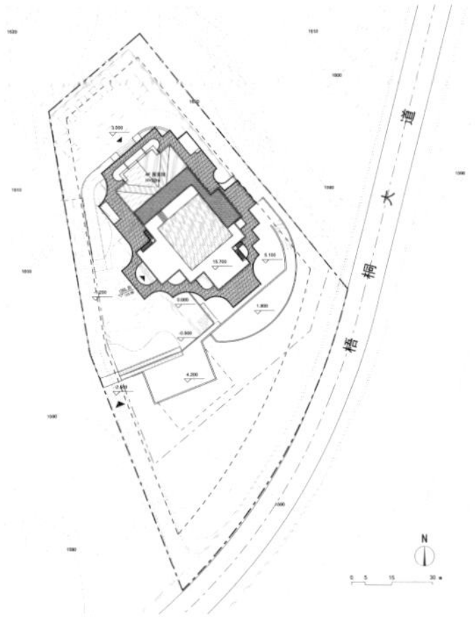
Site plan

View from the Olympic Village

Aerial view

"Chongtai"—the 2022 Beijing Winter Olympics Taizicheng Exhibition Hall was first designed in August 2018 and successfully completed in December 2021. It is situated in the Chongli Taizicheng area in Hebei Province, China, surrounded by magnificent mountains. This was a renovation project of an existing unfinished building that featured an original structure that had a distinct sense of solidity and verticality, contrasting sharply with the surrounding mountains and natural environment.

The design concept of the exhibition hall is shaped around the idea of "*chongtai*," which translates to "a platform near Chongli." In Chinese, *chong* represents the reverence for nature and the preservation of traditional customs—a notion that suited the Olympic Games' mountain venue. The remarkable central axis formed by Chongli's mountains reveals the historical significance of Taizicheng, also known as Prince's City.

The building project transformed the existing vertical volume into a horizontal landscape platform. The previous building platform was extended horizontally, blending harmoniously with the natural mountain landscape to create a rooftop viewing platform by opening up a section of the existing roof. The remodeling of the main structure evenly removed beams based on the mountain's environmental conditions. Curved and rectangular structural plates were arranged between the beams, forming a continuous building boundary along with the walls and roof. Roof and wall openings with varying properties were strategically placed, guided by walkways, visual perspectives, and lighting conditions, thereby offering "framed views" of the ruins, Xuehua Town, and scenic mountain peaks, allowing visitors to appreciate both distant and nearby landscapes.

The building consists of a dark gray base and a white horizontal cantilever section. The base is firmly anchored in the mountain environment, while the "suspended" landscape platform extends horizontally, adapting to the unique site characteristics, reducing the building's impact on the surrounding environment. This design approach not only gives the building the image of a "platform" embedded in the mountains, but also offers a continuous public viewing space amid natural surroundings. Visitors can explore the exhibition hall and access the roof landscape platform through an external walking system. The integrated walkway system seamlessly connects the indoor and outdoor spaces, both at ground level and on the roof, effectively incorporating the building into the mountain ice-and-snow sports park.

Semi-aerial view from northwest

Sketch

Courtyard at the western entrance

1 | 2
3 | 4

1. Staircase on the side of the building
2. Foundation and cantilevered viewing space
3. Northern side of the cantilevered viewing space
4. Eastern side of the cantilevered viewing space

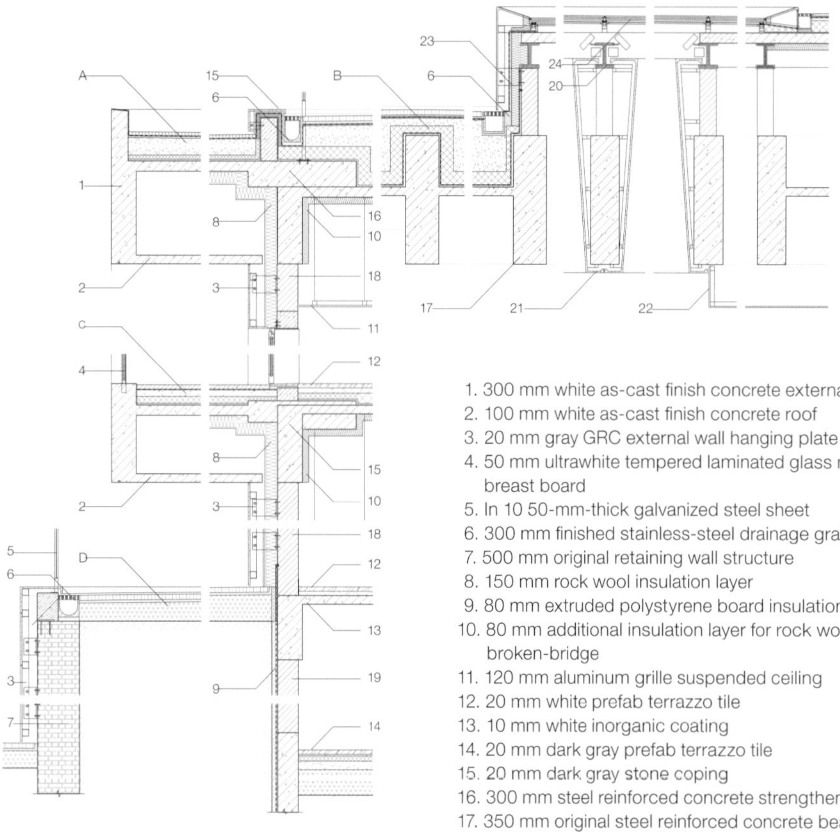

1. 300 mm white as-cast finish concrete external wall
2. 100 mm white as-cast finish concrete roof
3. 20 mm gray GRC external wall hanging plate
4. 50 mm ultrawhite tempered laminated glass metal breast board
5. In 10 50-mm-thick galvanized steel sheet
6. 300 mm finished stainless-steel drainage grate
7. 500 mm original retaining wall structure
8. 150 mm rock wool insulation layer
9. 80 mm extruded polystyrene board insulation layer
10. 80 mm additional insulation layer for rock wool broken-bridge
11. 120 mm aluminum grille suspended ceiling
12. 20 mm white prefab terrazzo tile
13. 10 mm white inorganic coating
14. 20 mm dark gray prefab terrazzo tile
15. 20 mm dark gray stone coping
16. 300 mm steel reinforced concrete strengthened beam
17. 350 mm original steel reinforced concrete beam
18. 300 mm aerated concrete block wall
19. 300 mm concrete block wall
20. 250x150 mm roof steel structure
21. 20 mm 2.5x0.8-m dark-gray GRC hanging plate
22. 12 mm white gypsum board suspended ceiling
23. 8 mm dark-gray stainless-steel hanging plate
24. 20 mm tempered laminated insulating glass roof

A. Construction method of inaccessible pebble roof:
- 40-mm-thick white pebble
- Non-woven polyester fiber cloth isolating layer
- 3+3-mm-thick SBS modified asphalt waterproof coil
- 20-mm-thick DS mortar leveling course
- Minimum thickness 30 mm type A composite lightweight aggregate cushion, sloping 2%
- 50-mm-thick extruded polystyrene board insulation layer
- 20-mm-thick DS mortar leveling layer
- 120-mm-thick steel-reinforced-concrete roof panel

B. Construction method of accessible water permeable brick accessible roof:
- 60-mm-thick dark-gray water permeable brick
- 30-mm-thick 1:6 dry cement mortar
- 4-mm-thick SBS modified asphalt waterproof coil
- 10-mm-thick DS mortar leveling course
- Minimum thickness 50 mm type B composite lightweight aggregate cushion, sloping 1%
- 150-mm-thick extruded polystyrene Board insulation layer (80 thickness of top of the beam)
- 4-mm-thick SBS modified asphalt waterproof coil
- 20-mm-thick DS mortar leveling course
- Original steel-reinforced-concrete roof panel

C. Construction method of cantilevered viewing volume floor:
- 80-mm-thick C25 abrasion resistant concrete surface
- 4-mm-thick SBS modified asphalt waterproof coil
- Minimum thickness 35 mm C15 fine aggregate concrete surface, sloping 1%
- 50–80-mm-thick class B1 extruded polystyrene board
- 20-mm-thick DS mortar leveling layer
- Steel-reinforced-concrete structural slab

D. Construction method of water permeable brick floor:
- 60-mm-thick dark-gray water permeable brick
- 30-mm-thick 1:6 dry cement mortar
- 200-mm-thick stepless crushed stone, sloping 2%
- Plain soil compaction

1. Café
2. Cafe Logistics
3. Main entrance
4. Entrance hall
5. Temporary exhibition hall
6. Office
7. [illegible]
8. Power distribution room
9. Kitchen
10. Restroom
11. Exhibition hall
12. Secondary exhibition hall
13. Cantilevered viewing volume
14. Auditorium
15. Motor room
16. Roof platform

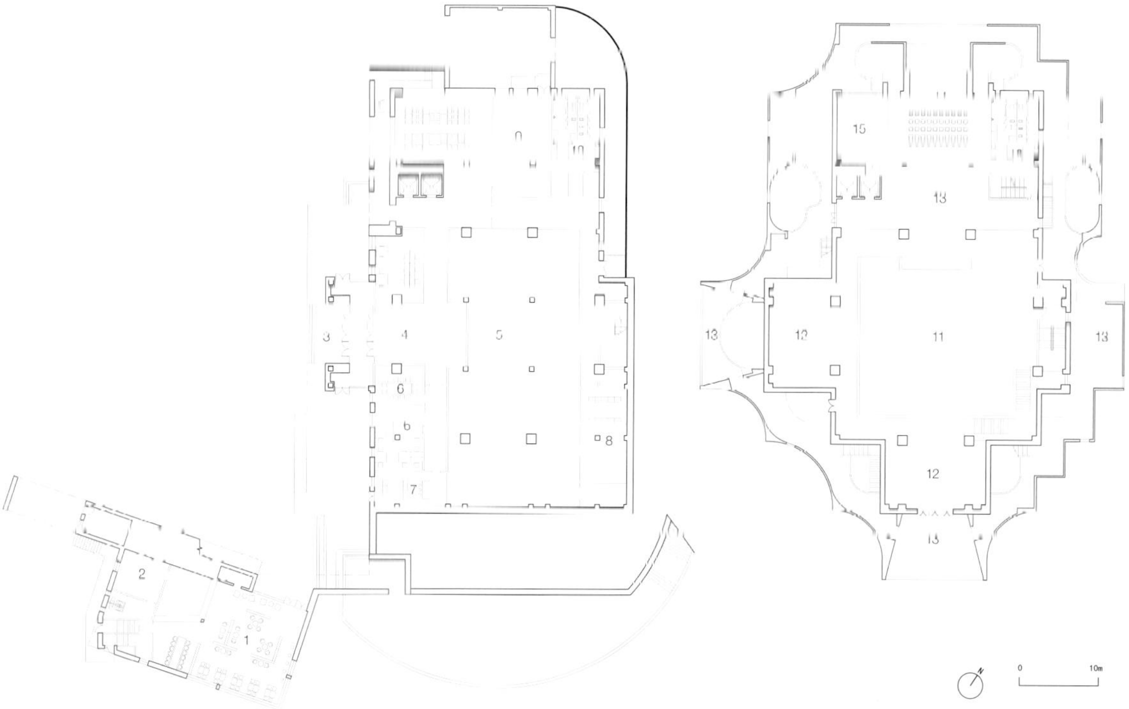

First-floor "foundation" plan

Third-floor plan of the cantilevered viewing space

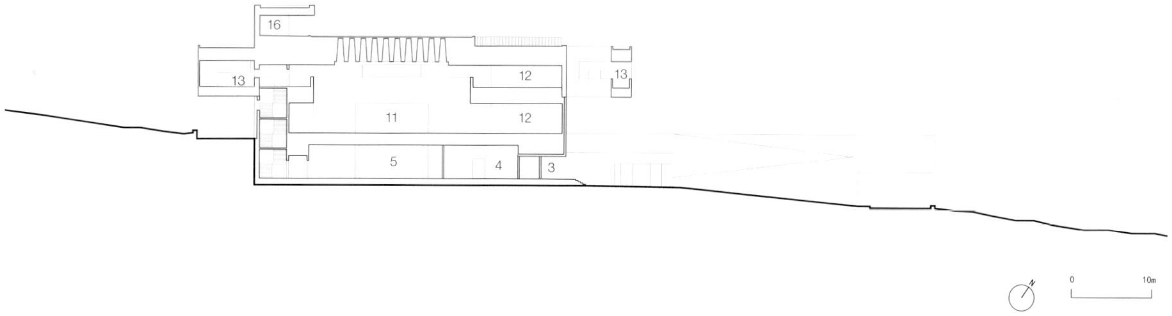

Section

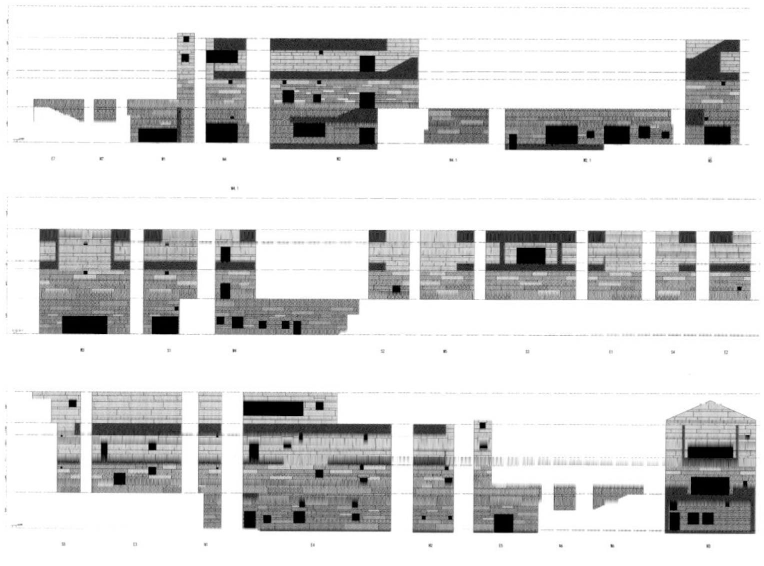

Developed pattern of GRC external wall hanging plate

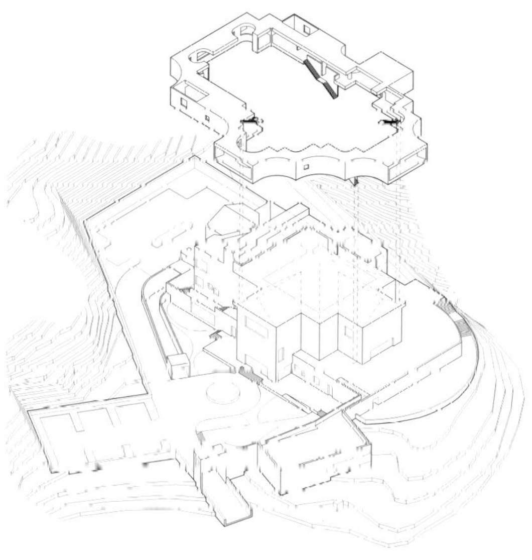

Axonometric diagram

YUHUAN MUSEUM AND LIBRARY

Location: Taizhou, Zhejiang Province, China
Lead architect: Li Xinggang
Architecture: Zhang Yinxuan, Yan Yu, Zhang Siteng
Structure: Ren Qingying, Liu Wenting, Li Sen, You Tianzhi
MEP: Fan Gaina, Wei Hang, Jiang Hong, Wang Li, Li Jia
Landscaping: Yang Chen
Interior design: Cao Yang, Ma Mengxue
Lighting consultant: Zhangxin Lighting Studio
Gross floor area:
Museum: 7,682 square meters
Library: 12,000 square meters
Design period: October 2014
Construction period: October 2021
Photography: Li Ji, Zhang Siteng

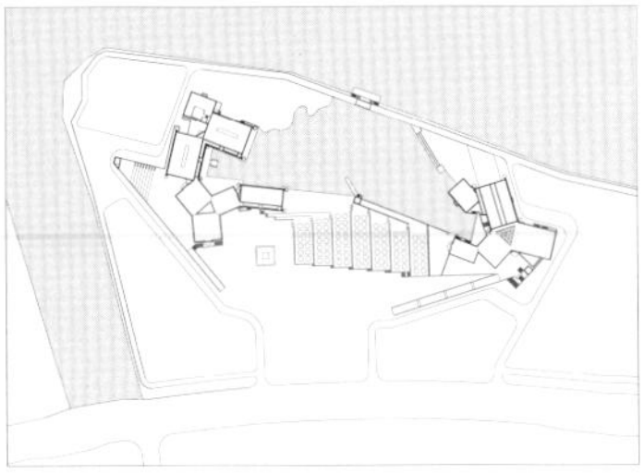

Site plan

View of the Yuhuan Museum and Library from across Yuhuan Lake

The Yuhuan Museum and Library, along with the public landscape space between the two building groups, were first designed in October 2014. The complex is situated on a reclaimed plot of land in the New Town Development Zone of Yuhuan, an island county in Taizhou City, Zhejiang Province, China. The design draws inspiration from the unique characteristics of the Kanmen neighborhood in the old city of Yuhuan, which is known for its fishing port, tunnels, mountains, bays, channels, and islands. The architect incorporated these spatial forms into the design of the two building groups, as well as the landscape square and water area in between them, creating a multilevel overall spatial environment that resembles a "mountain-sea" landscape.

Both the museum and library can be seen as modern interpretations of a fishing village, featuring a combination of horizontally and vertically overlapping and enclosing curved-roof building units. The two building groups are situated on a large stone foundation and are accessed along long ramps or steps. Visitors enter the halls or semi-enclosed atriums at the rear through hidden entrances, which resembles the experience of "crossing the mountains and entering the harbor." The building units interact with each other, and are connected in a series or stacked, to form various spaces. The inner courtyards of the two building clusters are relatively distant, yet orientated toward each other and connected by a large water feature. Combined with landscaping elements, such as a fishing pavilion, wharves, dikes, steps, and trees, they create an impression of a "fishing port" within the New Town Development Zone of Yuhuan. By incorporating the distant mountains and a nearby river, the design aims to create a "poetic scenery."

The project further explores the study of basic architectural units and their combinations to generate buildings and group spaces. The two building clusters are constructed with a concrete suspension structure featuring anti-curved surfaces and large-span fish belly beam structures. The basic structures and spatial units are repeatedly combined, adjusted, connected, and enclosed, in both horizontal and vertical directions, resulting in unique column-free indoor and outdoor spaces that respond to various functional requirements, different human behaviors, the terrain, views, and contexts.

The use of fair-faced concrete in both internal and external spaces highlights and expresses the significance of columns, beams, and plates in the anti-curved suspension and fish belly beam structures. The roof drainage system and its extensions also contribute to the buildings' visual appearance. Locally processed rubble walls are used for the foundation of the buildings, as well as the spaces between the buildings' structural supports, establishing a link between the museum, the library, and the traditional construction methods and terrain treatment found in local fishing villages and stone houses. In addition to concrete and stone, glass and wood curtain walls create a transparent appearance that softens the overall cold and hard expression of the buildings.

View of the museum

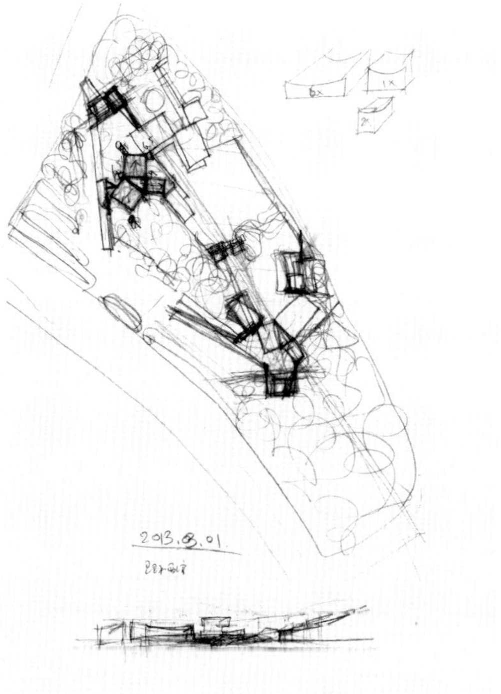

Sketch

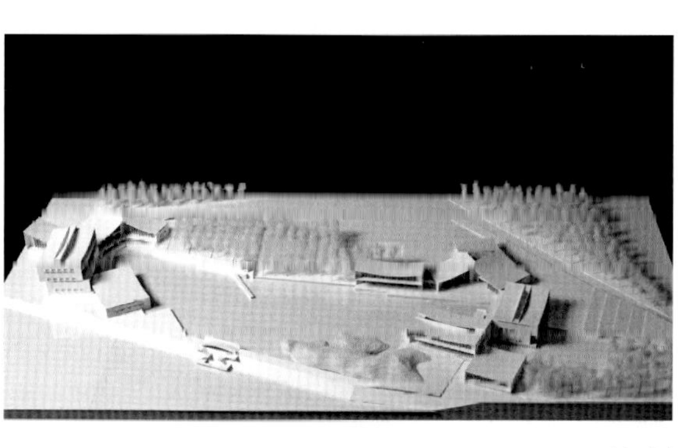

Model

View of the steps and the eave

A waterside library

View from under the eaves of the library

Interior space of the reading room

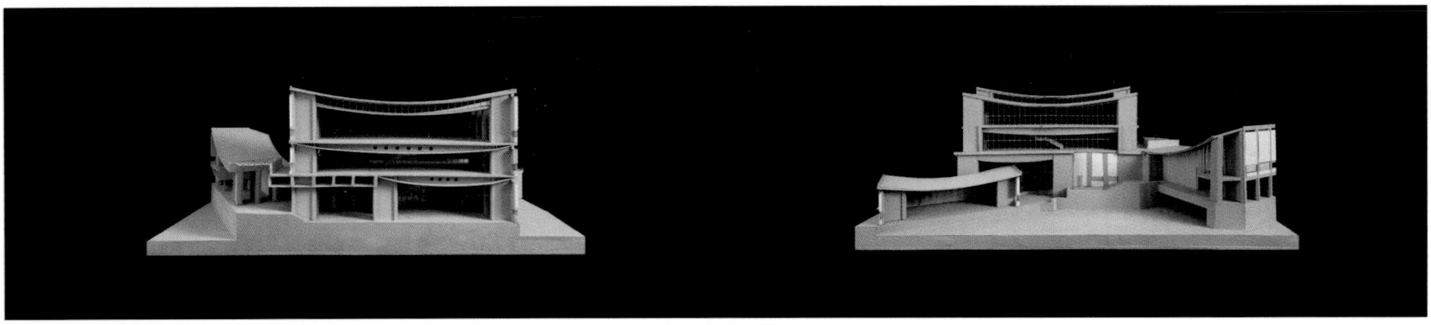

Section model

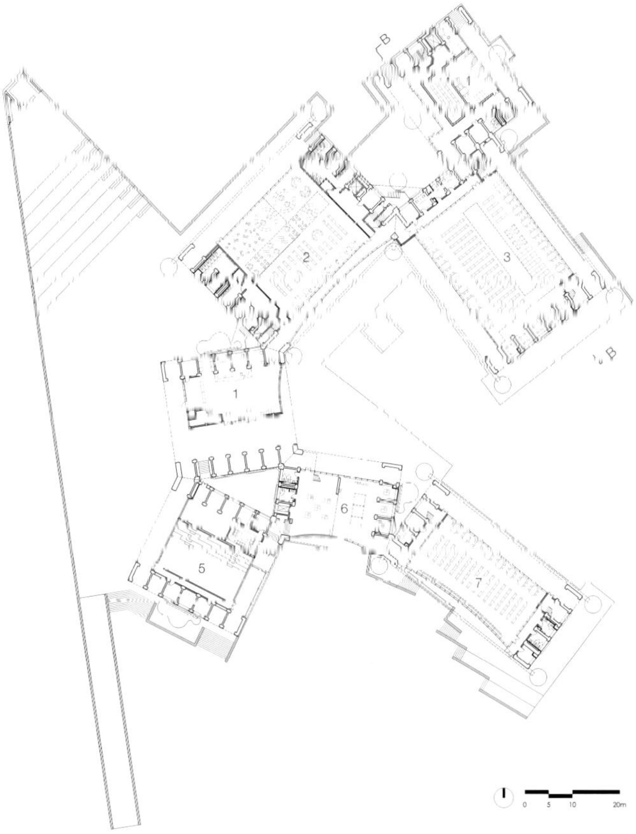

Entrance floor plan of the library

1. Entrance hall of the library
2. Children's reading room
3. Open-stack reading room
4. Special collection reading room
5. Lecture hall
6. Exhibition hall
7. 24-hour reading room

Entrance floor plan of the museum

1. Entrance hall of the museum
2. Comprehensive hall
3. Temporary exhibition hall
4. Pavilion
5. Preface hall
6. Exhibition hall
7. Multifunction hall

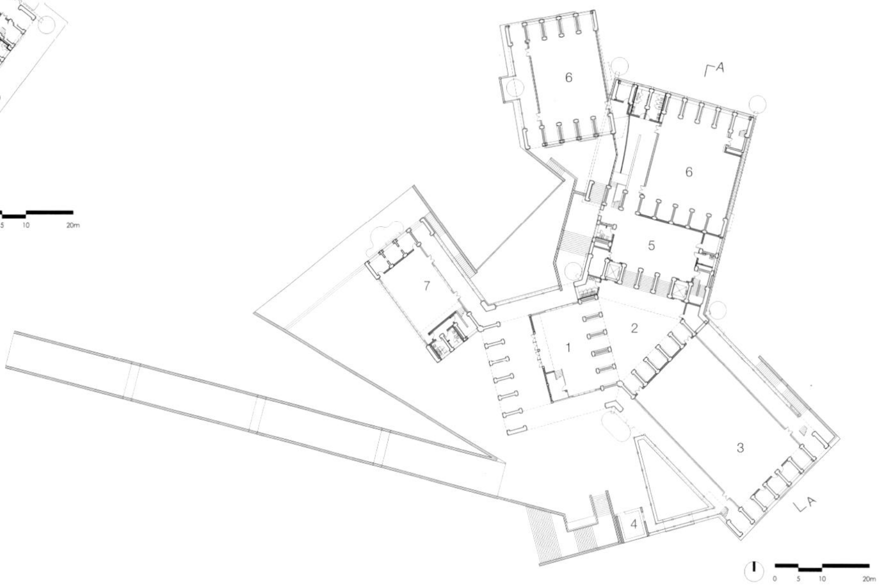

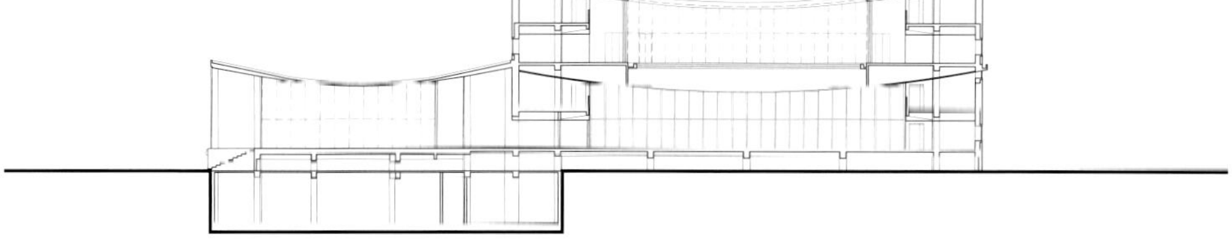

Section A-A

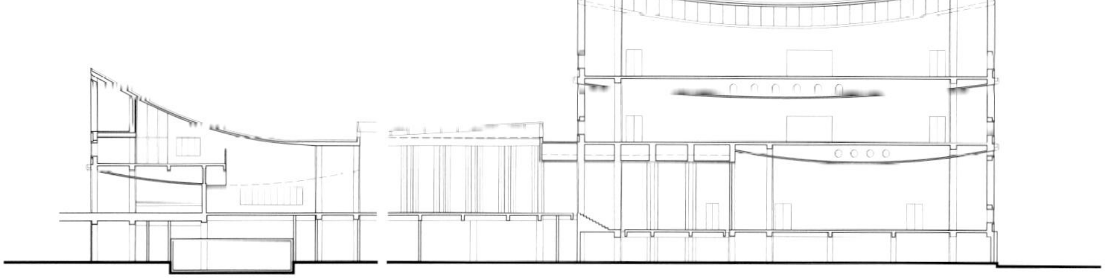

Section B-B

Zhang Zhun

AND Office
Co-founder and Lead Engineer, AND Office

Born in 1982, Zhang Zhun graduated in 2007 from Tongji University's College of Civil Engineering, China, with a Master of Structural Engineering. Shortly after, he began working for Tongji Architectural Design Group, where his early work revolved around the specialized fields of design and construction, such as unconventional steel structures, curtain walls, prestressed structures, renovation and reinforcement, and geotechnics.

In 2016, he co-founded AND Office with Liu Yichun and Guo Yimin. Since then, he has focused primarily on structural design, practice, and teaching, from an architectural perspective. Although his background in engineering means that objectivity and scientific rigor form the core of his practice, on a broader level, he skillfully integrates structure with spatial, cultural, and societal factors in order to find sustainable uses for new materials, technologies, and systems. In all the projects that he's partaken in, structural ingenuity is incorporated in subtle ways, silently ensuring the building's integrity with sound mechanical logic, while contributing to its abstract significance.

Selected Works

The following works were completed in collaboration with architects:
2022 Upper Cloister in Aranya, Golden Mountain (Jinshanling), Chengde, Hebei Province, China
2021 Dingshu Vocational School of Pottery, Yixing, Jiangsu Province, China
2021 Swallow's Wing, Shenzhen, China
2020 Bridge of Nine Terraces, Nanjing, Jiangsu Province, China
2020 Radisson Collection Resort, Nanjing, Jiangsu Province, China
2019 Baozhu Chamber, Ningbo, Zhejiang Province, China
2019 "Light of Internet" Expo Main Exhibition Hall, Wuzhen, Zhejiang Province, China
2018 Nanjing Qinhuai Bay Bridge, Nanjing, Jiangsu Province, China
2018 House ATO, Beijing, China
2018 Edge Garden, Shanghai, China
2018 Artificial Intelligence B Hall, Shanghai, China
2018 B Hall, Shanghai Westbund World Artificial Intelligence Conference, Shenzhen, China
2018 Pingshan High School Pedestrian Bridge, Shenzhen, Guangdong Province, China
2017 Soft Matter, Shanghai, China
2017 Swan Science Museum, Rongcheng, Shandong Province, China
2017 XY Yun House Yoga Pavilion and Pool, Guilin, China
2016 Dongyuan Qianxun Community Centre, Suzhou, Jiangsu Province, China
2016 Li Garden Teahouse, Shanghai, China
2016 Yicang Modern Art Museum, Shanghai, China
2015 Blossom Pavilion, Shanghai, China
2014 Long Museum (West Bund), Shanghai, China

Baozhu Chamber © Chen Bin

B Hall, Shanghai Westbund World Artificial Intelligence Conference © Archi-Union

Interviewer: *Architecture China*
Interviewee: Zhang Zhun (ZHANG)
Editor: Wang Ying

What is your understanding of the term "Building with Nature"?

ZHANG: When I think of the term "nature" (*ziran*), I'm reminded of the Daoist classic *Daodejing*, in which the term *ziran* can be interpreted as "occurring in and of itself." In my understanding, "building with nature" should incorporate elements of Chinese culture and philosophy. It's not just a matter of isolated building practices, it should be present throughout the entire field of architecture. By taking part in the judging process for the Architecture China Award as a structural engineer, I hope to contribute certain structural principles to architectural culture.

Swallow's Wing © Zhangyu Jianzhu

Swan Science Museum © Yao Li

XY Yun House Yoga Pavilion and Pool © Tian Fangfang

What direction are you currently exploring in your practice?

ZHANG: I think structure is a reflection of how we view the world. Although it's about rigorous mathematical calculations, it's also capable of expressing a variety of creative design elements. That expressivity is something that we focus on in our practice. Based on this idea, we've sought ways of using structure as a means of mediating the relationship between our projects and their natural surroundings. There's so much that needs to be taken into account when it comes to the incorporation of natural elements in architecture. If we isolate structure from that process, viewing it purely as a means of ensuring a building's physical viability, then we risk diminishing the building's overall significance, as well as its degree of harmony with the surrounding environment.

What is the relationship between structure and nature?

ZHANG: When it comes to the role of nature in a building's surroundings, architects often come up with all kinds of ideas that serve as inspiration to structural engineers such as myself. Though structural engineering may appear to be a purely logical undertaking, at its essence, it's really about arriving at solutions based on observations of natural phenomena—or you could say, it's about using mechanics as a means of interpreting nature. Conversely, we can identify mechanical laws in nature to help architects realize their environmental principles. When these elements overlap, it can inspire unique forms of structural innovation. Obviously, taking inspiration from architecture doesn't mean straying from mechanical laws—it's more a question of using these laws as the foundation for subjective creativity in design. Ultimately, the result is that both architects and structural engineers sufficiently reflect on the environment in order to arrive at an idea that wholly conforms to the notion of "building with nature".

Bridge of Nine Terraces © Scenic Architecture Office

Pingshan High School Pedestrian Bridge © Chen Yongyu

As a structural designer, how do you collaborate with architects?

ZHANG: Generally, we get involved fairly early on in the project and rely on architects to explain its central principles and key ideas to us. Structural engineers tend to interpret these ideas primarily in terms of their physical and material significance. But if architects can convey the underlying logic behind these ideas to us, we can contribute not only our mechanical expertise, but also our imagination. This gives rise to a kind of cross-pollination between our fields. In this way, in the initial stages of the project, we can launch a dialogue regarding the form that the structure should take, making our subsequent work more efficient.

What opportunities and challenges do you believe China's unique construction practices present to today's structural designers?

ZHANG: I believe there are two aspects to this. The first is purely technical, and largely pertains to how we take advantage of technological advancements. That includes improved computational power, more sophisticated analyses, the ability to carry out a greater number of experiments, as well as seeking second opinions from experts.

The second is about how to coordinate the relationship between structural and architectural design. I think this is largely a matter of accumulating experience and engaging in discussions with architects, so that collaborations are more harmonious and smoother. Together, the two aspects—one technical and the other communicative—can help us face and overcome challenges.

"LIGHT OF INTERNET" EXPO MAIN EXHIBITION HALL

Location: No. 1, Yunxiang Road, Tongxiang City, Jiaxing City, Wuzhen, Zhejiang Province, China
Designer: Archi-Union Architects
Lead architect: Yuan Feng
Project architect: Han Li
Digital construction director: Zhang Wen
Architect: Kong Xiangping, Huang Jinyu, Gu Huajian, Chen Hao, Zhang Haobo, Li Yuying, Lou Yu, Tao Xi, Jin Jinxi.
Interior: He Fuzi, Wang Ju, Wang Yifei, Wang Tuomeng, Liu Luwen, Tang Jingyan, Cui Mengmeng, Jiang Haiyan
Structure: Zhang Zhun, Huang Tao, Wang Rui
Landscaping: Dong Nannan, Wei Weixuan, Ye Jun
Gross floor area: 19,466 square meters
Surface area: 18,152 square meters
Construction period: 2019
Photography: Schran Images, Tian Fangfang, AND Office

Bird's eye view © Tian Fangfang

Situated in the northwest of central Wuzhen, Zhejiang Province, China, the project is surrounded on all sides by rural residences and tourist attractions, except for the pavilion area, where the first phase of construction has already been completed. The site is immediately adjacent to the ancient architectural complex, Xizha, embodying how historical and modern districts are increasingly getting intertwined as the region undergoes a process of urbanization, in the process creating complex and diverse landscapes. Following its construction, the project served as one of the venues for the 2019 World Internet Conference.

The venue needed to be ready for the conference in October, however, the design process only began in February. The initial requirement for the venue's design was that it needed to be a continuous, column-free space of approximately 90 by 200 square meters. By implementing a tiered façade, the architect aimed to reduce the perceived scale of the space and at the same time form a visual parallel with the rooftop, which features an undulating shape that recalls Jiangnan's characteristic waterways. Initially, the roof's design featured oblique ridges to diversify the interior space, but it was revised to parallel ridges when the team realized that oblique ridges would require more non-standard components and would, therefore, be more difficult to implement given the time constraint.

In keeping with the client's requirement to preserve the appearance of the ancient town, real tiles were used as the material for the roof, deviating from the usual standard of using light materials for the rooftops of long-span exhibition halls. The biggest challenge in the initial structural design of the project was to develop a viable solution for a heavy, long-span rooftop within a tight timeframe.

Northeastern corner of the exhibition hall © Schran Images

Bird's-eye view of the Red Pavilion © Schran Images

To address this, a beam-string structure that would also serve as a skylight was proposed. The structural engineer ensured that the concave shapes formed by the beams and strings between ridges would provide optimal load-bearing support where it would be most needed. This suspended load-bearing system came to pass as the best solution to effectively support the heavy tile rooftop.

The project utilizes a semi-rigid suspended roof system with a continuous span of five sections. Although each beam-string structure used in the roof ridge exhibits good vertical stiffness, their out-of-plane stiffness and overall torsional resistance were relatively weak. The horizontal dragging forces exerted on both ends of the beam-string structure by the suspended roof needed to be carefully mitigated to ensure the integrity of the building under various conditions.

To this end, structural engineers continually fine-tuned the span and inclination of the roof in each area. Although form-finding algorithms could have been used to determine the "catenary line" of each beam to obtain the optimal degree of inclination for each span, strictly adhering to these algorithms in structural design would require numerous components with miniscule dimensional differences, and would, therefore, hinder construction. Instead, a more approximative approach was employed, whereby all the beams would have a nearly identical curvature. This meant that, in order to reduce horizontal dragging, the span and inclination of the roof sections were optimized by considering the spatial requirements of each exhibition area and the acceptable beam height.

Once the plan for the suspended beams had been finalized, the team took into account the overall layout of the space in order to determine

Red Pavilion © Schran Images

Interior of the exhibition hall © Schran Images

Construction process © AND Office

Ground-floor hall of the Control Center © Schran Images

the best way of integrating them with strings and columns. V-shaped supports and vertical ground anchors were utilized to reduce span and increase the structure's lateral resistance, at the same time delimiting a semi-outdoor porch area.

Further, H-section steel suspended beams were installed along the roof at 2-meter intervals, which is a structurally efficient distance as it aligns with the economical span of the roof structure. They played the additional role of purlins, simplifying the architectural composition of the roof while reinforcing its stability. To increase efficiency in construction, the roof tiles were embedded into standing seam panels with the use of prefabricated components.

After careful selection and analysis, it was determined that the suspended beam system would utilize H-shaped steel beams with a spacing of 2 meters and a height of 200 millimeters (with a few exceptions using square sections). This configuration allowed for a continuous roof that spanned five sections with lengths measuring 35.5, 18, 18, 44, and 35.5 meters respectively. Toward the center of the roof, the beam-string structure has a height of 6 meters. Its upper "strings" consist of circular pipes with a diameter of 475 millimeters. It is additionally supported by two tension rods with a diameter of 150 millimeters and diagonal braces with a diameter of 194 millimeters. Hinges were used to connect the suspended beams and the beam-string structure, the beam-string structure and the V-shaped supports, and the straight columns and the ground.

Just when the team thought that the structural design of the building was finally complete, the requirements for the project changed dramatically: instead of a continuous space, the venue now needed to be divided into four independent exhibition zones. Although the design was compatible with this change, the division of the space opened up other possibilities for ensuring the building's structural integrity that were less complicated than the one the team had originally settled upon.

For instance, now, more standing columns could be introduced into the space, which could be paired with a four-span continuous truss structure. However, after weighing out the cost, construction period, rooftop structure, as well as the nature and long-term flexibility of the interior space, the original "suspended beams and string-beam structure" solution was adopted. At the space division, an auxiliary wind-resistant cable has been added; it also serves as the keel of the inner curtain wall.

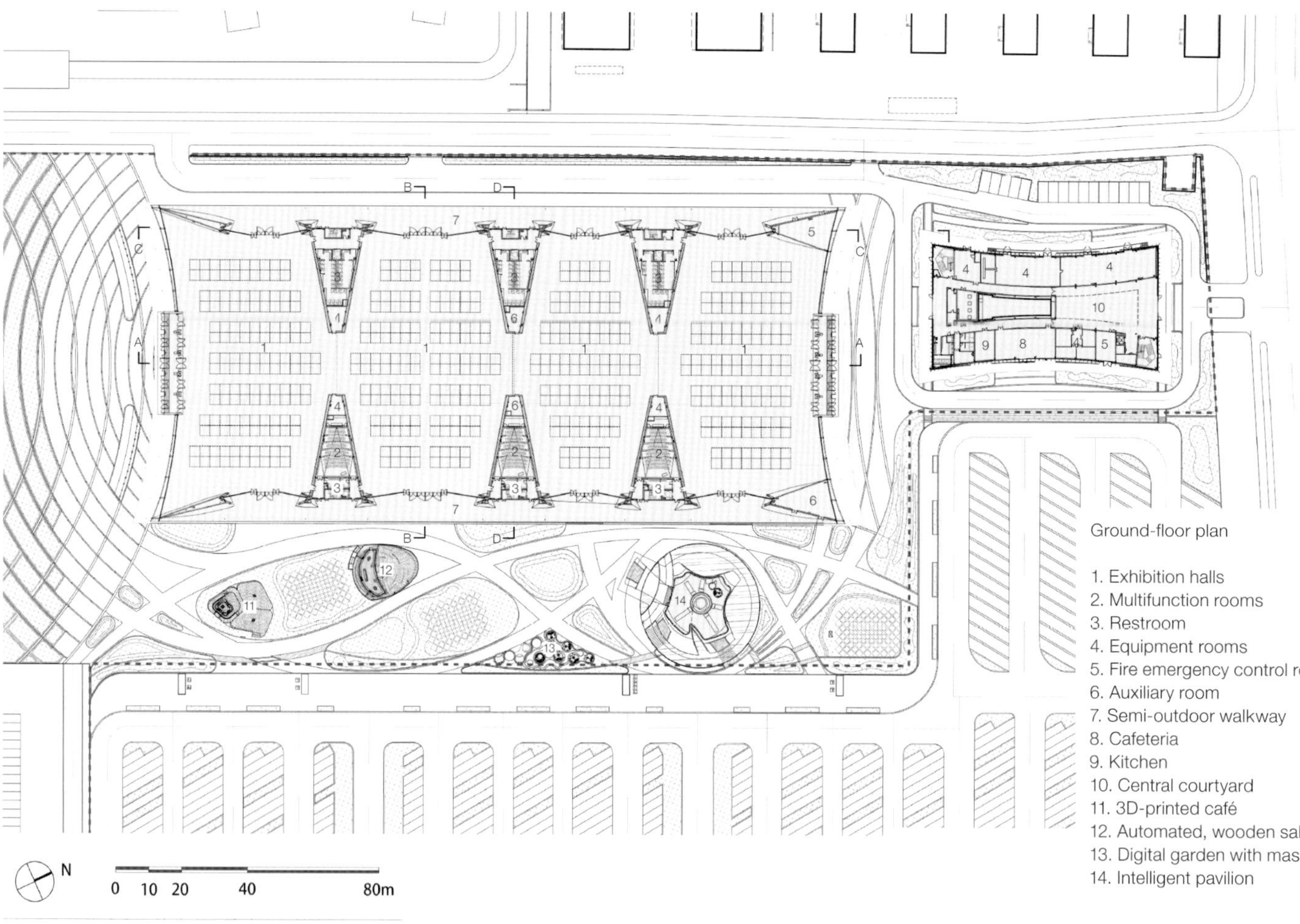

Ground-floor plan

1. Exhibition halls
2. Multifunction rooms
3. Restroom
4. Equipment rooms
5. Fire emergency control rooms
6. Auxiliary room
7. Semi-outdoor walkway
8. Cafeteria
9. Kitchen
10. Central courtyard
11. 3D-printed café
12. Automated, wooden sales booth
13. Digital garden with masonry robot
14. Intelligent pavilion

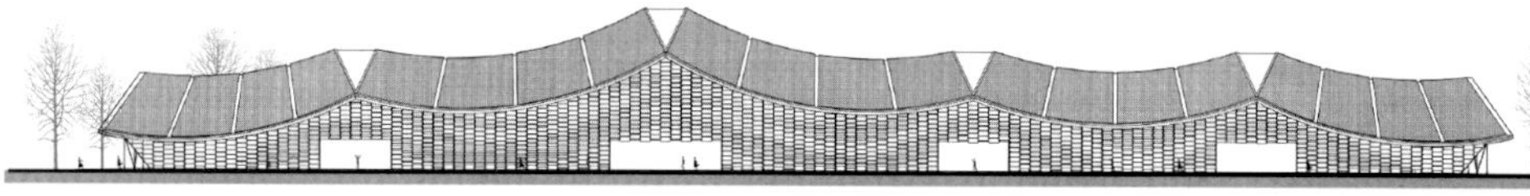

East elevation

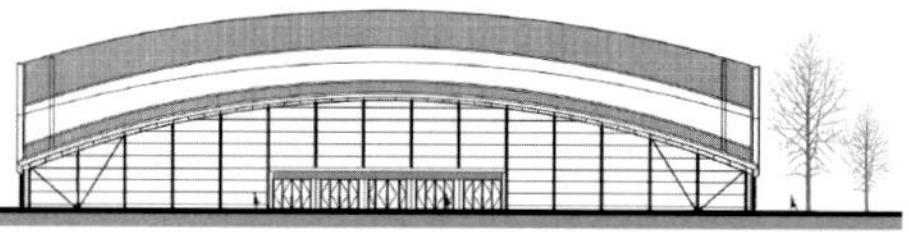

South elevation

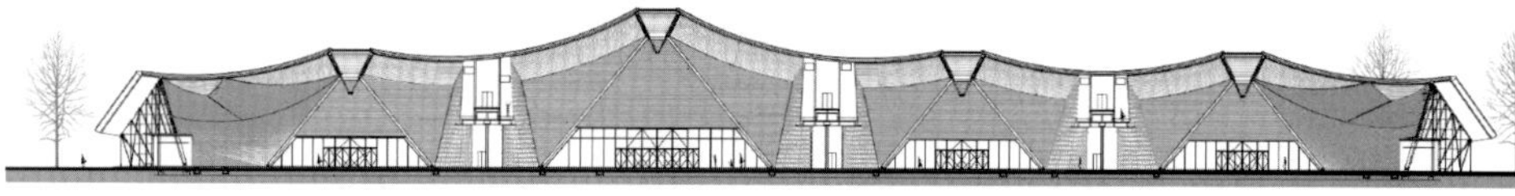

Section A-A

Section B-B

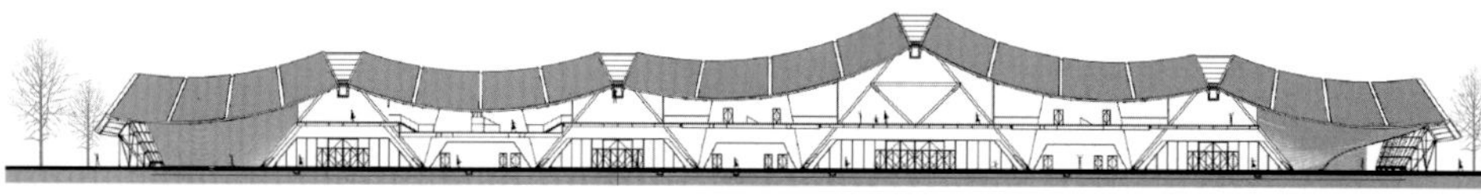

Section C-C

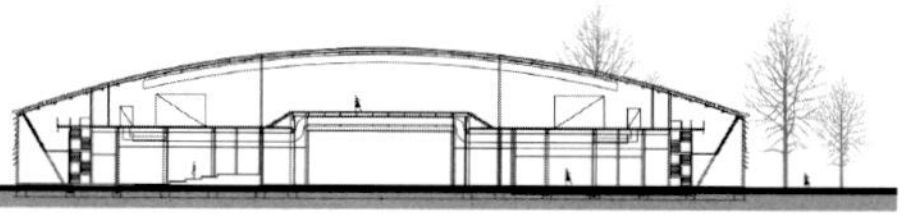

Section D-D

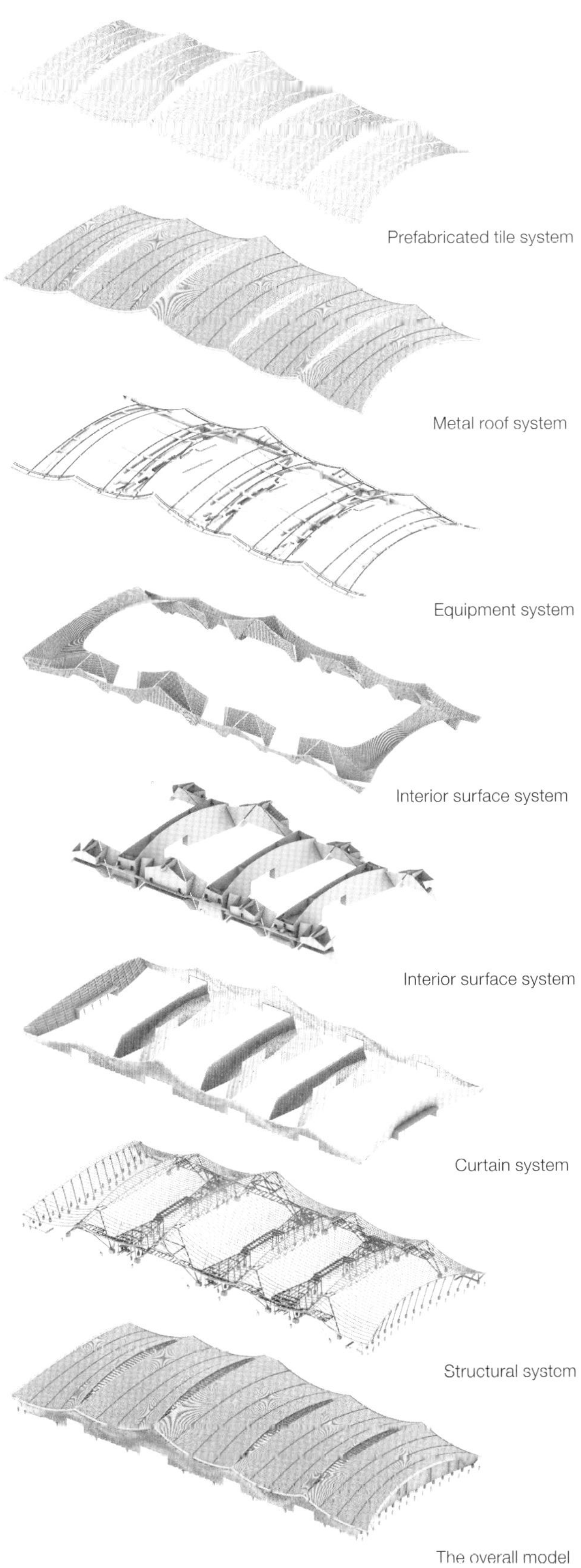

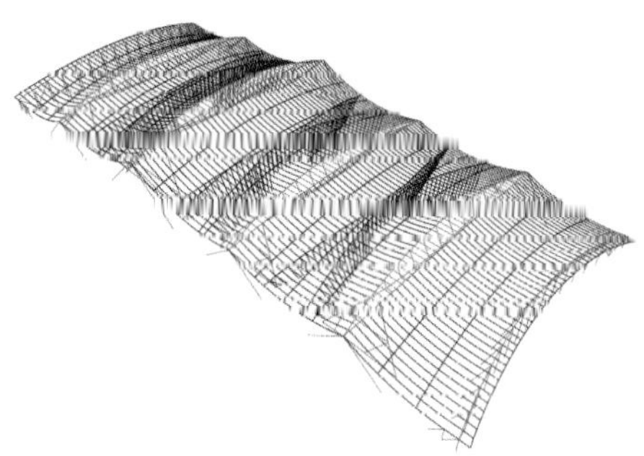

Catenary beam as roof structure system

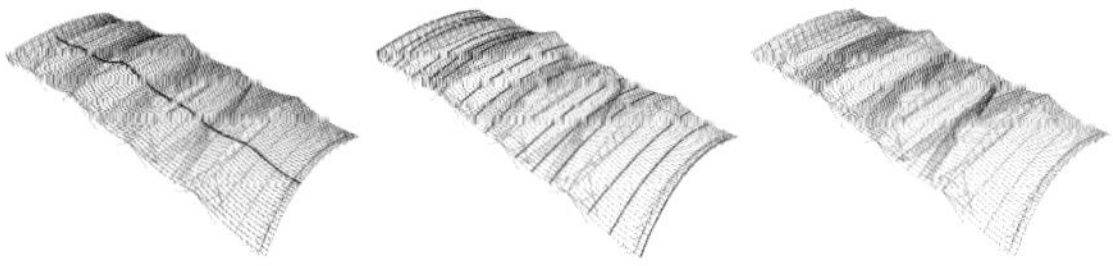

Semi-rigid suspended beam

Reverse curvature stable cable

Auxiliary wind cable

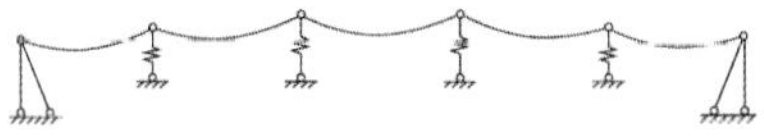

Continous span sem-rigid suspended beam in long direction; 40-meter-span, 200-millimeter high suspension beam

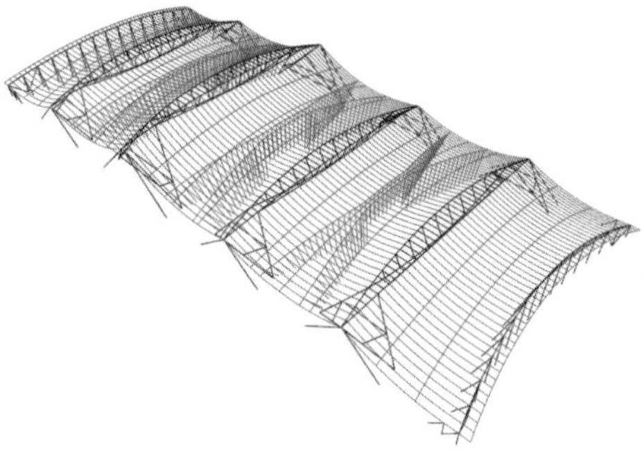

The string beam and the end arch beam are used as the main beam structure system

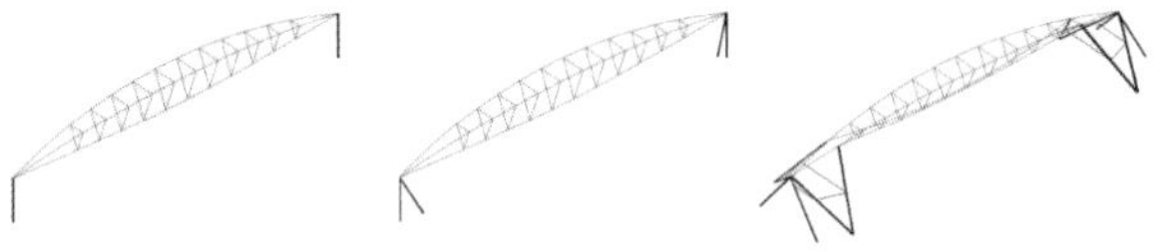

Increase lateral resistance and reduce structural span by combining functional space

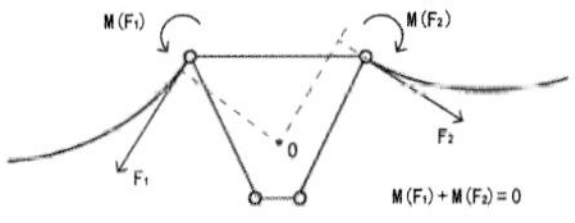

Optimize roof shape to avoid tortion of beam string

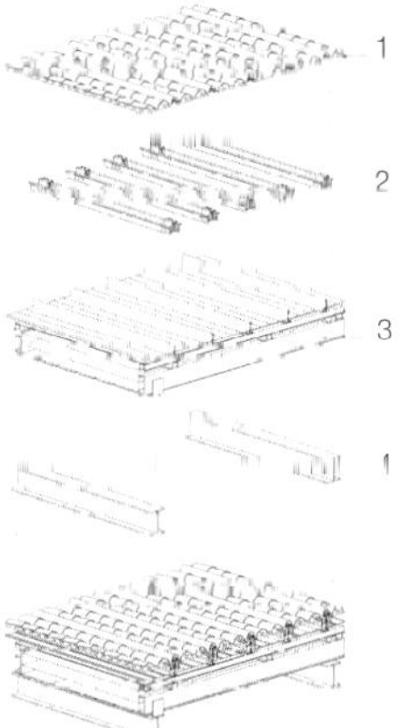

Roof system

1. Prefabricated tiles
2. Support beams
3. Metal roof
4. Steel structure

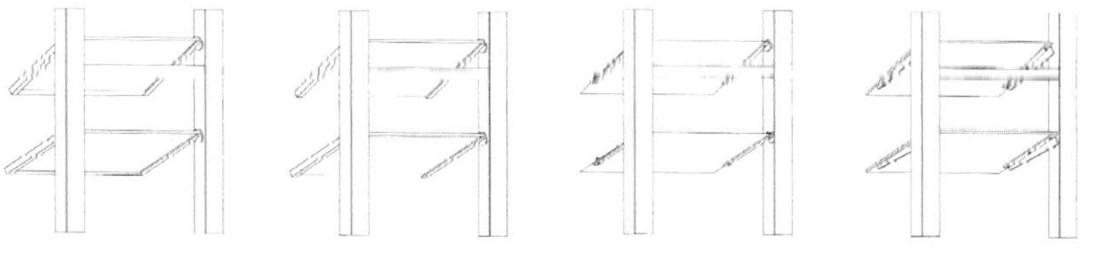

U-shaped slit scheme

Double-sided slit scheme

Threaded fastener scheme

Dotted connection scheme

Detailed view of the eastern and western curtain walls

HOUSE ATO

Location: South Square, Beijing ("Bird's Nest") National Stadium, Beijing, China
Lead architects: Liu Yichun/Atelier Deshaus
Design team: Liu Yichun, Shen Wen, Deng Rui, Gong Yu; (structure) Zhang Zhun, Zhang Chongchong
Gross floor area: 160 square meters
Design period: March 2008–April 2018
Construction period: April 2018
Photography: Wu Qingshan, Tian Fangfang

Clear and open veranda © Wu Qingshan

Open space under the eaves © Atelier Deshaus

This project is part of the architect's ATO ("亼屮囗") series and was initially conceived as a zen Buddhist meditation hall to be built on Golden Mountain in Chengde Province, China. Although the meditation hall is still to be constructed,, the proposed design was already put to the test in the form of a temporary venue for the 2018 China House Vision exhibition.

In this project, the architects put a contemporary, multicultural spin on their "亼屮囗" concept, in which the essence of an architectural structure is distilled into three elements, represented visually using Chinese ideograms: 亼 (roofs), 屮 (support columns/beams), and 囗 (foundation/surrounding walls). Meanwhile, the structural components of the building were represented using the minimalist design language of points, lines, and surfaces.

The model of the construction created little doubt for the structural engineer as to the building's overall viability. The approach of integrating slender supporting columns with other architectural elements to provide greater stability almost extended like a continuation of two of the engineer's previous projects: Blossom Pavilion and Li Garden Teahouse. However, with its unconventional shape and extreme thinness, House ATO's roof posed a significant challenge.

In terms of its layout, the building took inspiration from the *Building Standards*, a Song dynasty text, to divide the space into two concentric sections using columns. The unique curvature of the roof—such that it rose gradually toward the center into a kind of spout—allowed for two types of load-bearing modes, that together ensured its resilience. In keeping with the principle of axial load bearing, the intense curvature toward the center of the roof made it better suited to the load-bearing needs of rooftops covering long-span shell structures. By contrast, the surrounding, flatter surface makes use of bending load bearing and was, therefore, better suited to functional layouts with shorter spans. This coherence between space, form, and load bearing provided the foundation for achieving a structurally feasible building with a shell-like exterior of uniform thickness. The extremely thin and unusually shaped rooftop also helped convey the metaphorical significance of the project.

Even after the roof's dual load-bearing concept had been elaborated, further mechanical analysis was necessary to achieve the desired thinness. Although the building's initial model conformed to mechanical principles, slight undulations in certain parts of the roof's surface impacted the structure's load-bearing capacity. Therefore, the idea of minimal surface was used to enhance the roof's performance.

Rooftop view © Wu Qingshan

In the shape-finding process, the target surface was initially expanded based on the architect's opinions. Then the team continually displaced and exerted varying degrees of external force on the surface until a minimal surface shape that closely matched the envisioned architectural form was obtained. Finally, the shape was cropped to the necessary size. Although the end result didn't appear all that different from the original, its load-bearing capacity and constructability had been significantly improved.

As the roof was a freeform surface, its accurate construction was crucial to the project's success. While steel hyperbolic molding, 3D printed concrete templates, and other digital technologies would have realized the desired shell structure, budget and time constraints made these solutions unviable in the specific context of the temporary exhibition hall.

After comparing different options, the relatively old-fashioned, yet nonetheless effective, method was adopted: a ferro-cement vessel. The process of this approach bears some resemblance to another earlier project, Soft Matter. However, in this case, there were even stricter standards for accurately replicating the desired form.

A combination of steel supports and sheets were used to create a skeleton onto which steel mesh was applied to achieve the desired surface area. The team discovered that the minimal surface could be created using an arrangement of geodesics, so that the steel sheets—which consist of interwoven geodesics—were a crucial reference that allowed the process to maintain accuracy.

Once an appropriate construction method had been determined, through a mechanical analysis, the minimum thickness of the steel mesh and polymer mortar of 50 millimeters was established. To extend safety precautions, it was decided that all columns used in the structure should have a width and depth of 50 millimeters by 50 millimeters. These slender columns allowed for an interactive relationship between the building's structural components and its architectural functions.

In the completed exhibition hall, the artisanal texture of the roof formed a vivid contrast with the building's overall minimalist, industrial aesthetic. This coexistence of high and low technology is a prominent characteristic of contemporary architectural practices. The building will be adapted to a new setting when the initially planned mediation hall project on Golden Mountain commences and will help further architectural and structural experimentation, in particular exploring the use of carbon fiber-reinforced polymers.

Evening view © Tian Fangfang

Interior space © Tian Fangfang

Detailed view © Wu Qingshan

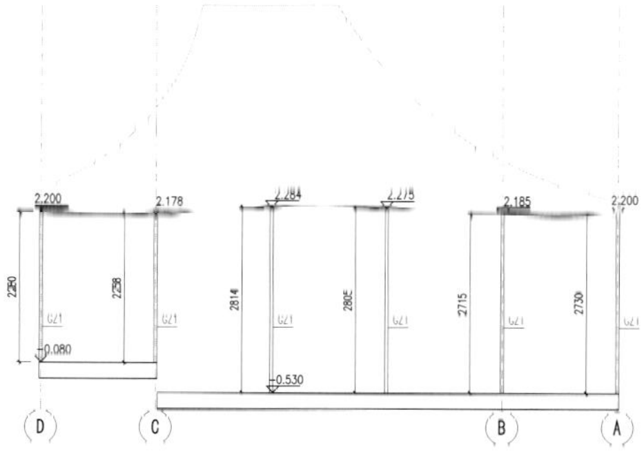

3-1 Structural arrangement

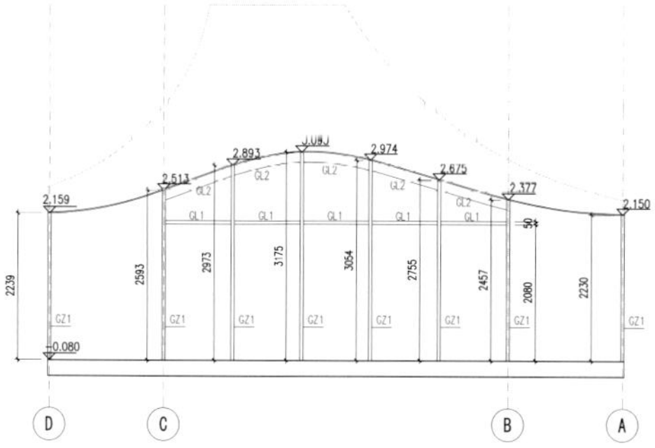

3-2 Structural arrangement

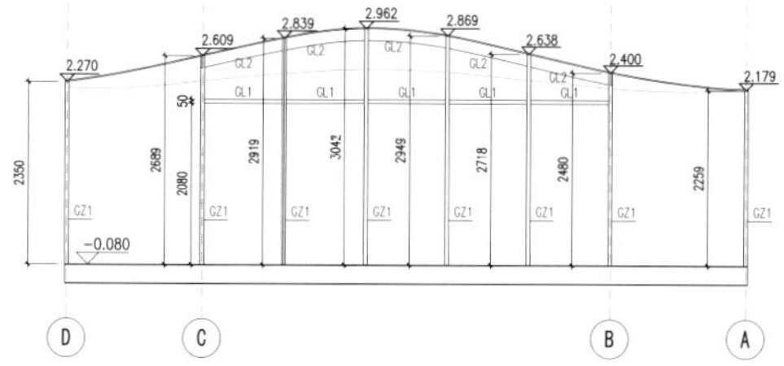

3-3 Structural arrangement

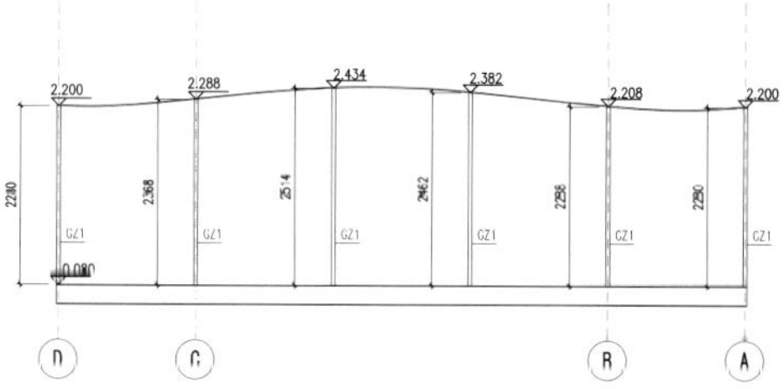

3-4 Structural arrangement

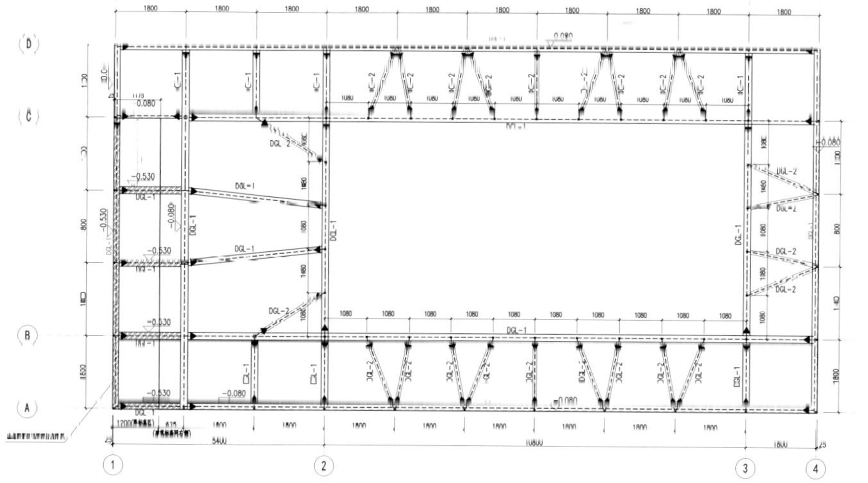

Basic structural floor plan (on stilts)

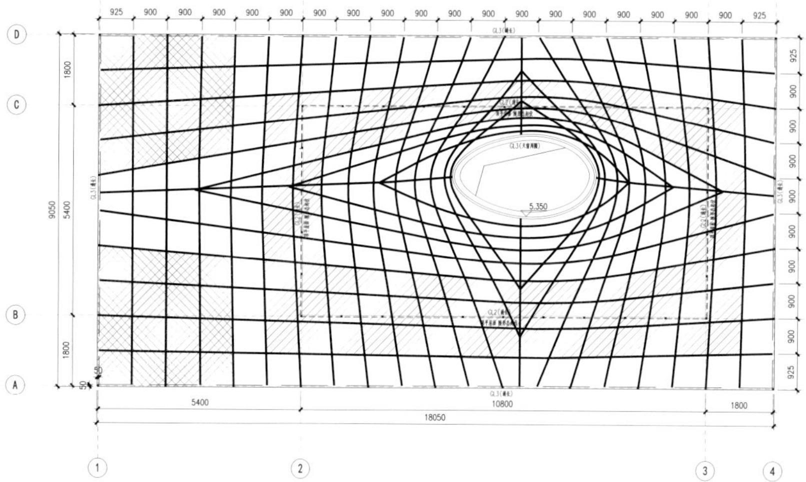

Structural arrangement of the roof

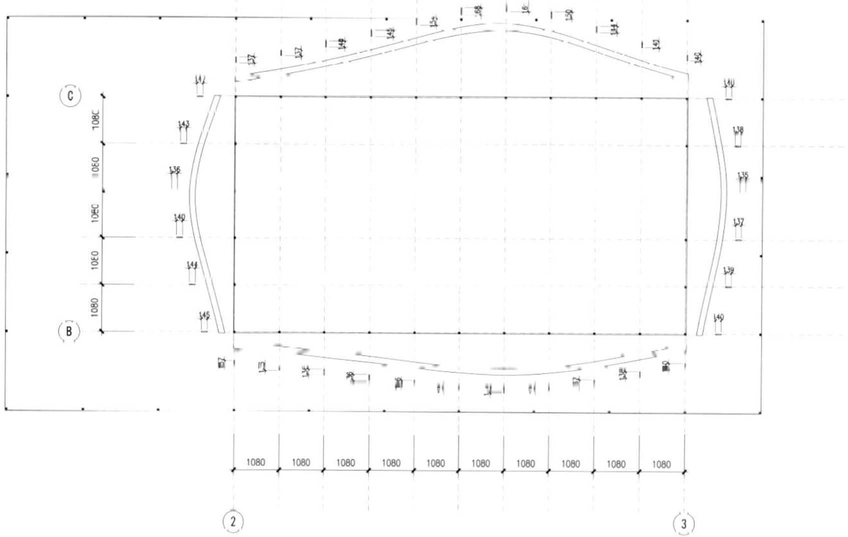

GL2 expansion plan

自然建造
ARCHITECTURE
CHINA
AWARD

EXPLORATION AWARD FOR YOUNG ARCHITECTS

Exploration Award for Young Architects is granted to young architects under the age of forty-five who have completed two or more high-quality works in recent years. It aims to show professional recognition while encouraging the experimental spirit of young architects.

Wang Baozhen
Yinyuan Studio

Laureate

Shui Yanfei
Yanfei Architects

Laureate

Xu Lang
CLAB Architects

Shortlisted

Wang Bin
Gebie Architects

Laureate

Fan Beilei, Kong Rui, Xue Zhe
gcnarchitects

Shortlisted

Wang Baozhen

Yinyuan Studio
Founder and Principal Architect, Yinyuan Studio
Lecturer, School of Architecture, Zhengzhou University

After graduating from Peking University, China, in 2008, Wang Baozhen began teaching at Zhengzhou University, China. In 2015, he founded Yinyuan Studio. Two years later, he published a book titled *Craft of Three Gardens*, which recounts three of his projects as an architect in Guangxi Province, China. In 2020, he was nominated for the Exploration Award for Young Architects in that year's Building with Nature: Architecture China Award; his Rong Garden (Rong Yuan) project won a Special Project Award. In the 2023 Architecture China Award, he won an Exploration Award for Young Architects.

Yinyuan Studio explores the following directions in their practice:

1. Courtyard language

In contrast to the West, Chinese architecture has always been a holistic notion encompassing houses, courtyards, and gardens. In their pursuit of creating successful architecture, the studio asks questions like: How can we make use of Chinese architectural wisdom to create structures that are adapted to today's complex and diverse lifestyles? How can we find ingenious ways of facilitating a complementary relationship between artificial structures and natural surroundings?

2. Seeking inspiration from the earth

Modern architecture tends to overlook the relationship between buildings and the land. The word *di* in traditional Chinese culture encompasses virtually all the connotations of modern words such as land, earth, setting, base, location, environment, and venue. *Di* is not only the foundation of natural growth, it is also the basis for human activity and the continuation of human culture. Exploring the multiple connotations of *di* is an important source of inspiration when it comes to landscaping and architectural design.

3. Stroll, or the curation of promenades

In the northern Song dynasty text *The Lofty Message of Forest and Streams*, famous eleventh-century painter/gardener Guo Xi suggests four criteria for appraising landscapes: walkability, viewability, inhabitability, and stroll. The studio believes these criteria constitute the definition of an ideal place according to traditional Chinese culture. The modern world, from West to East, has embraced the first three criteria while ignoring the last to produce an architectural paradigm similar to Martin Heidegger's idea of the "poetic dwelling." Though Le Corbusier and Frank Lloyd. Wright both touched upon the idea of stroll in their work—with the former also evoking it under the term *promenade architecturale*— they didn't elaborate on or emphasize it to the same degree as Guo Xi. So then, what is "stroll" and how can it be implemented in spaces?

Selected Works

2022 Dong Lu Yuan, Henan Province, China
2016 Zhe Yuan, Henan Province, China
2015 Rong Yuan, Guangxi Province, China
2014 Pitaya Yuan, Guangxi Province, China
2010 Tuo Yuan, Guangxi Province, China

1 | 2
  | 3

1. Zhe Yuan © Wang Baozhen
2. Rong Yuan © Wang Baozhen
3. Tuo Yuan © Weng Zitian

Interviewer: *Architecture China*
Interviewee: Wang Baozhen (WANG)
Editor: Wang Ying

What new insights have you developed on the idea "Building with Nature"?

WANG: Obviously, "building" needs no explanation, but "nature" is more complex: it has both a narrow definition and broader connotations. The narrow definition is what we commonly refer to as the natural world—mountains and rivers, wind and rain, thunder and lightning, forests, insects and fish, and flowers and birds. Its extended meaning, which corresponds to its use in Chinese philosophy, is "unrestricted," "unaffected," "flexible," letting things follow their natural course. I personally feel a little uneasy with concepts that aren't clearly defined, so I limit my definition of "Building with Nature" to the coexistence between artificial and natural environments.

What direction are you currently exploring in your practice?

WANG: The main direction I am currently exploring is courtyard architecture. As our discipline evolves, architecture has become divided into various sub-disciplines, such as building design, landscape architecture, and interior design. This division has led to a growing disjuncture between architecture and nature. My focus is now on approaching courtyards as a cohesive whole, designing them in a systematic manner. This approach, which I refer to as "courtyard architecture," aligns well with the principles of "Building with Nature."

How can we interpret nature in landscaping?

WANG: When we talk about nature, we usually define it in opposition to things that are "created by humans." Truthfully, Chinese people's definition of "nature" doesn't completely overlap with how it's used in the West. Our understanding of nature has more to do with a balance of mutually opposed elements: *yin* and *yang*. So, even though Chinese gardens are based in and inspired by nature, there's a greater degree of human intervention. For instance, the nature in the Gardens of Suzhou, as they exist today, has actually been artificially created by humans. That's not to say that the trees aren't really trees, or that the ponds aren't ponds. I just mean that it's an idealized representation of nature, where the underlying concept is broader than the natural world.

What's the connection between contemporary architectural practices and traditional Chinese gardens?

WANG: Traditional Chinese gardens are a treasure trove of inspiration when designing modern buildings. When we reference them in our work, we're not merely carrying on their symbolism or methods, but rather their creators' wisdom in dealing with certain problems from the era in which they were built. This wisdom is timeless and can be found in a lot of our traditional gardens and artificial structures. There's a quote from *The Treatise of Gardens* by Ji Cheng that I think sums it up well: "Its ingenuity lies in its adaptation [of nature]; its beauty, in its sense of moderation."

DONG LU YUAN

Location: Linzhou, Henan Province, China
Lead architect: Wang Baozhen
Design team: (structure, interior, and landscaping) Wang Baozhen, Wang Honggen, Duan Jingna, Shang Liguo; (interns) Dong Bo, Zhao Zihan, Wu Yue, Zhao Zhenning
Site area: 4,000 square meters
Gross floor area: 3,000 square meters
Design period: 2019
Construction period: 2022
Photography: Ke Yunfeng, Wang Baozhen, Wang Dan, Yinyuan Studio

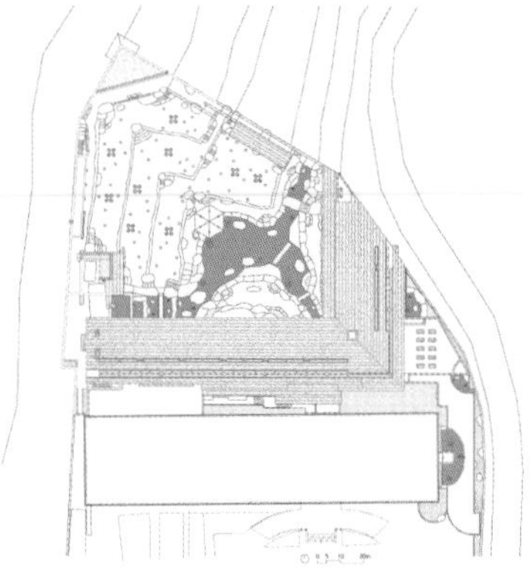

Site plan

Main courtyard and Taihang Mountains in the background © Wang Dan

Pre-exisiting workshop on the site

Structure and Topography

Though the project is located in the mountains, it's built on a very gentle incline. The design aims to curate a kind of promenade or "implied itinerary" that, beyond a mere difference in altitude, would truly give occupants the feeling of being in a mountain grove. Taking into consideration functionality, as well as budgetary concerns, the integrity of the structure is ensured using a standard column grid. Now, using such a simple medium, how can the design vision of an immersive mountainside experience be brought to life?

Interior and Exterior

The team though about how the design could "borrow the landscape" in as creative a way as possible to evoke not only its aesthetic, but also sentimental significance, rather than merely exposing it with the use of glass curtains? In traditional Chinese architecture, the implementation of this notion was often very simple: the boundaries between the building and its surrounding landscape were clearly delimited, with the former paying homage to the latter by "framing" it or guiding visitors' line of sight toward it—thus "borrowing" it for one's own private courtyard. The architects, therefore, sought to create—using the language of modern architecture—a more reciprocal and symbiotic relationship between buildings and landscapes as a means of fulfilling people's longing for nature in an increasingly denatured world.

Materials and Construction

The materials that have been used are an organic fusion of local and contemporary construction materials and techniques. The former includes rubble, slab stone, fieldstones, and plaster, while the latter includes steel structures, aerated concrete bricks, white paint, and concrete.

1 | 2
3

1. Narrow walkway and a stony shed © Ke Yunfeng
2. Courtyard, building, and the distant mountains © Ke Yunfeng
3. Rock hut and corner pavilion © Ke Yunfeng

Typical materials and construction styles of local houses © Yinyuan Studio

Entrance hall, overhang, panoramic window front, and the mezzanine exhibition hall © Ke Yunfeng

1 | 2 | 3

1. Hidden turn courtyard with small pond © Ke Yunfeng
2. Chensi (Resting area) © Ke Yunfeng
3. Entrance hall, stone stairs, mezzanine walkway, and entrance © Ke Yunfeng

Meditation room, elevated viewing point, overhang, and panoramic window front © Ke Yunfeng

1	2
3	4

1. Panoramic window front and main courtyard © Wang Baozhen
2. Second-floor hallway with natural lighting © Ke Yunfeng
3. Room F © Ke Yunfeng
4. Corner hall filled with natural lighting © Ke Yunfeng

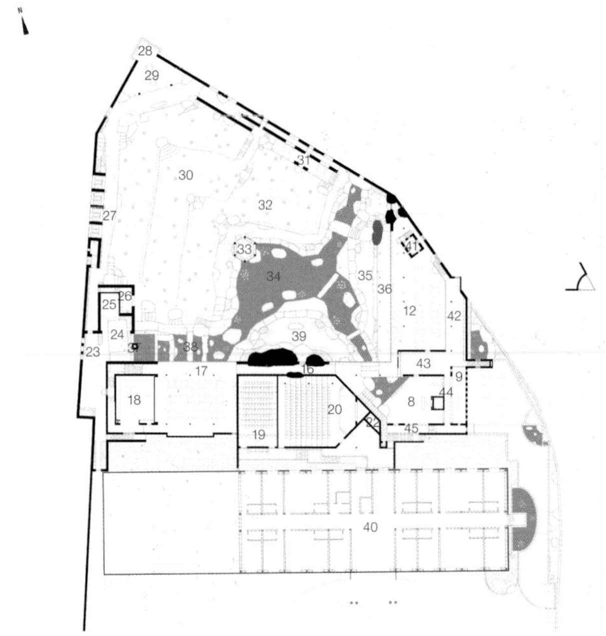

Mezzanine floor plan

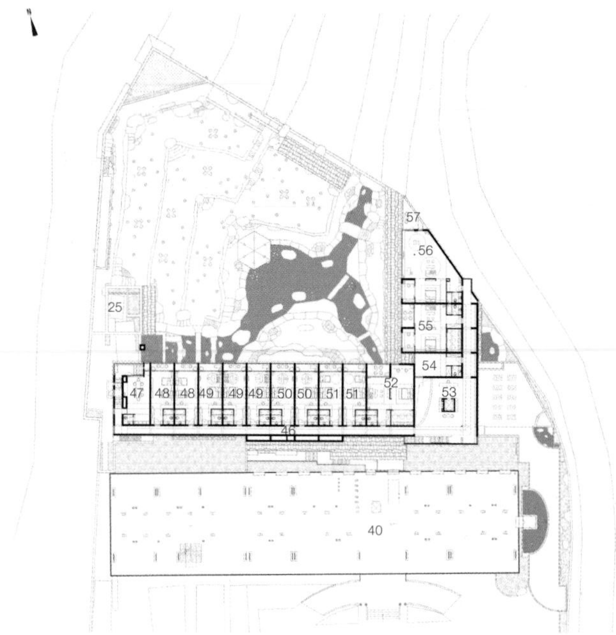

Second-floor plan

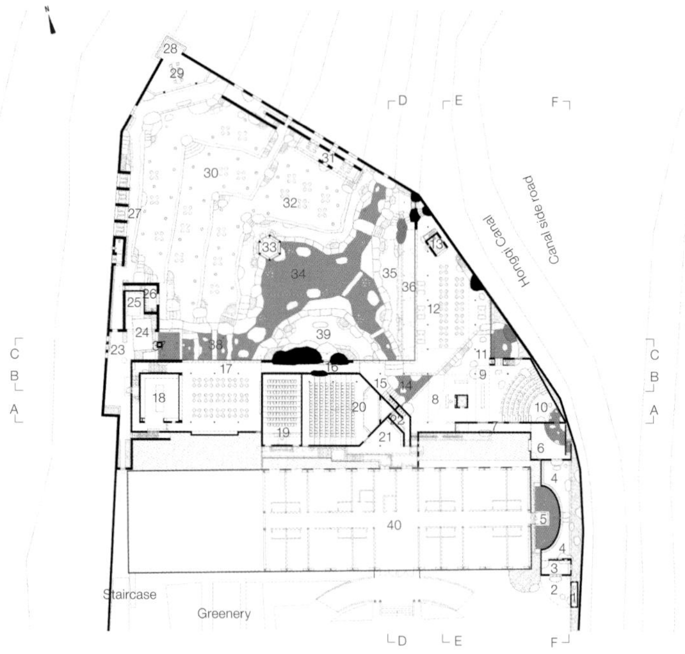

Ground-floor plan

1. Staff room
2. Buzheng (Entrance)
3. Xiaoyin (Small foyer)
4. Banjiu (Corridor hall)
5. Bantui (Lotus Hall)
6. Wanzhuan (Transitional hall)
7. Shiqi (Sloped corridor)
8. Youpeng (Main hall)
9. Gaogu (Main hall)
10. Chensi (Resting area)
11. Linyuan (Main hall)
12. Hanshan (Café)
13. Bar (Remodeled from a well)
14. Small stone pond
15. Shijingxie (Stone stairs)
16. Xiaxiang (Sloped corridor)
17. Linhao (Restaurant)
18. Kitchen
19. Mingjian (Small lecture hall)
20. Dongcha (Large lecture hall)
21. Yanqi (Semi-outdoor resting area)
22. Equipment room
23. Suyuan (Small courtyard)
24. Pre-existing underground firewater reservoir
25. Pre-existing water tank
26. Bar
27. Sijuan Shanlin (Coffee house)
28. Yiting (Small pavilion)
29. Qiyan (Big pavilion)
30. Liangmu Taoli (Orchard)
31. Wuyue (Semi-outdoor café)
32. Yaoyue (Resting platform)
33. Huangu (Pavilion)
34. Qingxi (Water pond)
35. Taihang (Leisure platform)
36. Yanxu (Space beneath the canopy)
37. Bafengta (Stone tower)
38. Haoliang (Stone bridge)
39. Liubu (Resting platform)
40. Former guesthouse building
41. Guao (Small coffee room)
42. Dazuo (Exhibition hall)
43. Xiaoyin (Exhibition hall)
44. Huandu (Sky bridge)
45. Xianbu (Corridor)
46. Yixiantian (Corridor)
47. Zhiwei (Private room for the restaurant)
48. Room A
49. Room B
50. Room C
51. Room D
52. Room E
53. Zhoudao (Second-floor service space)
54. Office
55. Room F
56. Room G
57. Yilan (Roof terrace)

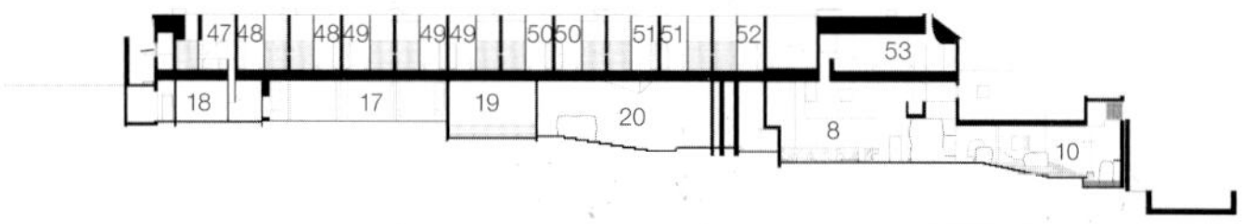

Section A-A

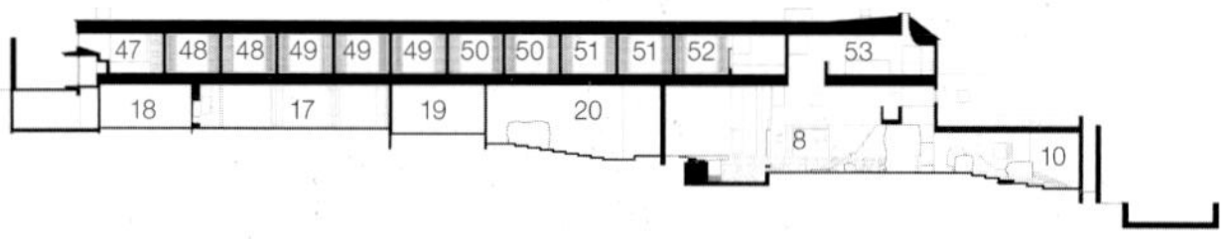

Section B-B

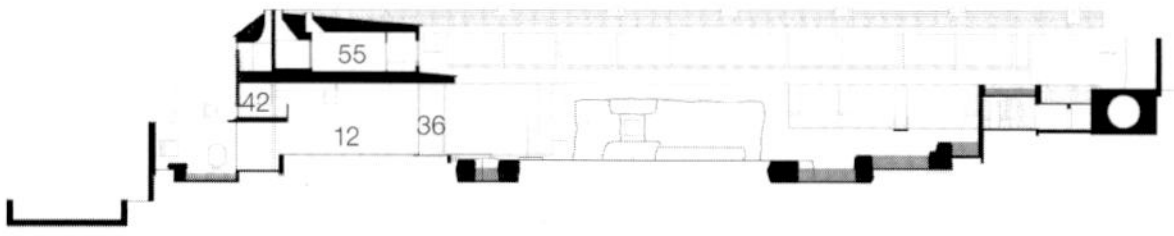

Section C-C

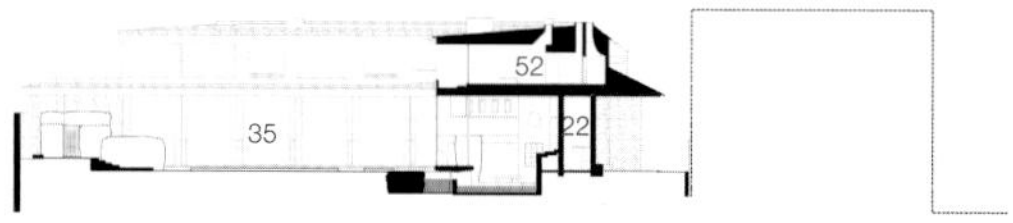

Section D-D

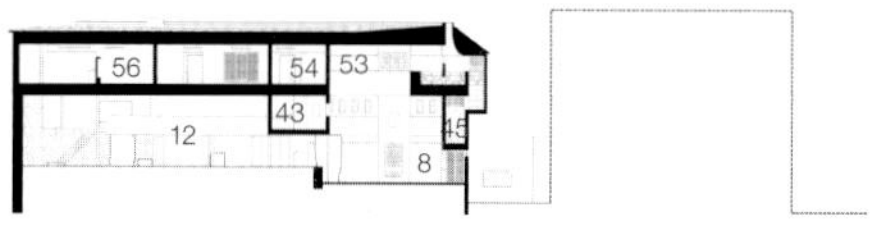

Section E-E

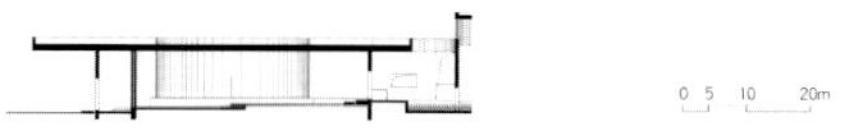

Section F-F

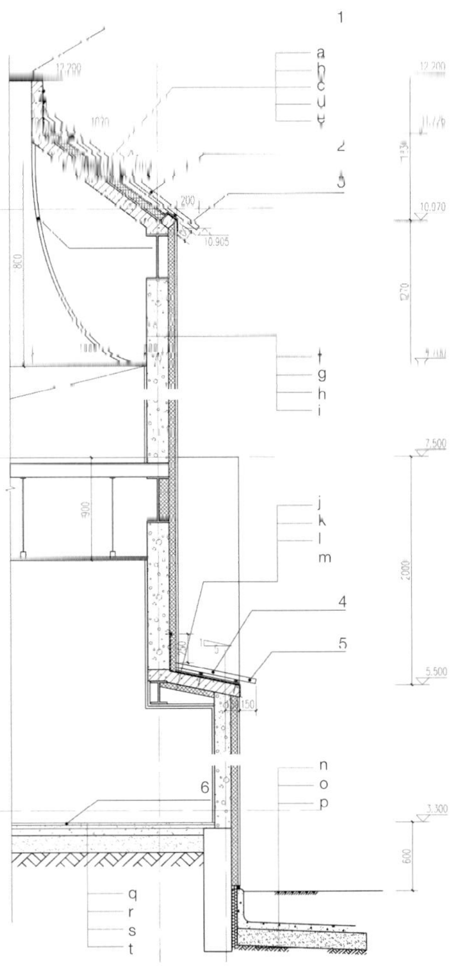

Wall details

1. Glass roof (tempered laminated glass; thickness of the lamination should not be less than 0.76 mm)
2. Local stone slab roofing
3. Overhang with a width of 200 mm
4. Local stone slab roofing
5. Overhang with a width of 200 mm
6. Local stone slab flooring with cracked ice texture

a. Stone slabs
b. Plaster
c. Insulation
d. Plaster
e. Reinforced concrete
f. Plaster
g. Aerated concrete
h. Insulation layer
i. Plaster
j. Stone slabs
k. Plaster
l. Reinforced concrete
m. Insulation
n. Concrete
o. Sand and limestone
p. Rammed earth
q. Sand and limestone
r. Concrete
s. Sand and limestone
t. Rammed earth

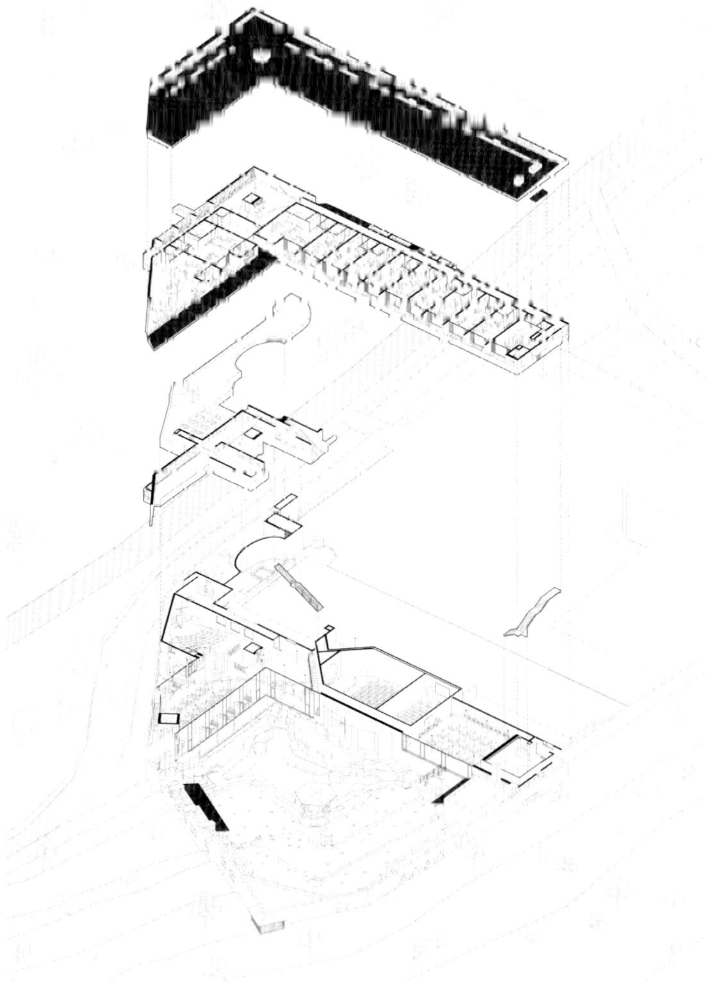

Axonometric projection

Detailed view of the building nodes

1. Polymer cement mortar, pressed into a layer of alkali-resistant fiberglass mesh cloth
2. Glass roof (tempered laminated glass; thickness of the lamination should not be less than 0.76 mm)
3. Local stone slab roofing
4. Overhang with a width of 200 mm
5. Local stone slab roofing
6. Overhang with a width of 300 mm

a. Stone slabs
b. Plaster
c. Insulation
d. Plaster
e. Reinforced concrete
f. Building plaster
g. Aerated concrete
h. Building plaster

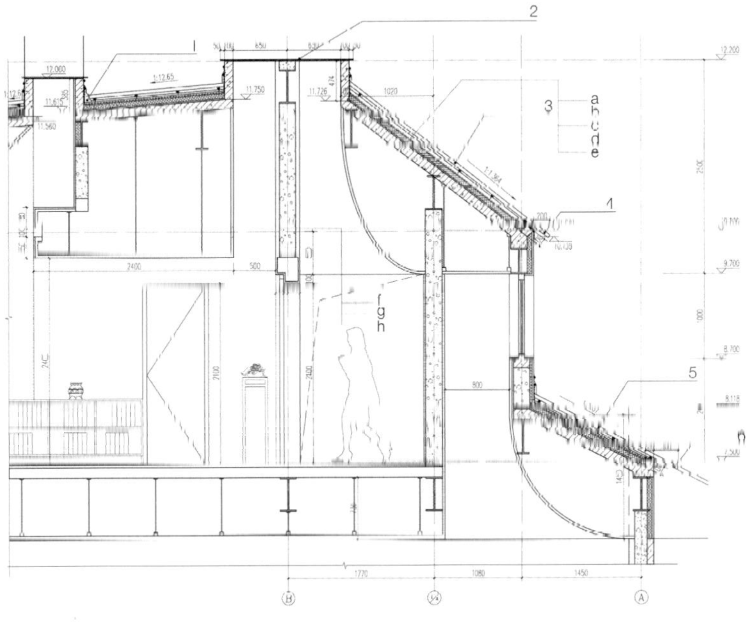

PITAYA YUAN

Location: Guangxi Province, China
Design team: Wang Baozhen, Duan Jingna, Chen Haiyi (foreman)
Functions:
Bamboo Pavilion—a place for local farmers to eat, rest, and receive guests
Hu Chamber—a space for receiving guests, working, and cooking food, with a bathroom included
Gross floor area:
Bamboo Pavilion—160 square meters
Hu Chamber—290 square meters
Design period: 2013
Construction period: 2014
Photography: Wang Baozhen, Weng Zitian

Site plan

Evening view of the Bamboo Pavilion © Weng Zitian

Hu Chamber © Wang Baozhen

The goal in this project was to craft a poetic garden dwelling amid an idyllic natural setting of mountains and rivers.

Bamboo Pavilion

Construction: The foundation was built using ordinary red bricks, with stainless-steel pipes (with a diameter of 55 millimeters and protruding 200 millimeters above the ground) serving as column bases. The columns and roof truss have been made from locally sourced Moso bamboo rods, which have a diameter of approximately 50 millimeters; they cost around five yuan per piece and were treated with several coats of diesel oil. The lookout platforms were constructed using local cedar planks, while the roof surface was made from cedar tree bark. First, the stainless-steel pipes were inserted into the concrete layer of the foundation. Then, the bamboo columns were inserted into the pipes and sealed with waterproof adhesive. Finally, the bamboo columns were connected to each other using threaded rods. Since the time it has been constructed, the Bamboo Pavilion has withstood two typhoons without suffering any damage.

Artistic inspiration: Bold "borrowing" of the landscape inspired by a poem by Du Fu:
"My window contains the perennial snowcaps of the Western ranges.
In my doorway, a thousand boats are moored on the Eastern Wu."

A sense of effortlessness is conveyed in terms of structural support, similar to the pavilion depicted in the Five Dynasties painting by Dong Yuan, *Summer Mountains*. (Underneath, a reclusive scholar leisurely admires the scenery; the columns are long and slender, with little space between them—like a bamboo grove. The ease with which they appear to prop up the huge roof of the pavilion adds to the languor of the scene.) Homage to traditional craftsmanship is conveyed by the elevated tie-beam (*tailiang*) structure and interlocking framework (*chuandou*), where the triangular shapes form a striking visual parallel with the space at the bottom of the slope; dense but flexible partitions between spaces. Finally, is the building's ability to channel refreshing breezes and filter out strong winds.

Hu Chamber

Construction: The walls are made using the folk construction method of "tiger-skin" bricks [illegible] with orange mud; the roof is made from reinforced concrete and the main openings are supported and decorated with 10-millimeter-thick steel panels. Concrete is used for drainage outlets and wall copings.

Artistic Intentions: The sturdy "tiger-skin" walls are covered in climbing ivy and reinforce the landslide-prone slopes. They also create a sense of privacy for the logistic space inside. They serve as a protective backdrop against the cliffside for the Bamboo Pavilion, creating a harmonious interplay of openness and seclusion, lightness and density, and height and depth. Stones present at the site have been preserved and embedded into walls or used for pathways. Irregular staircases lead to the top of the mountain, as well as the roof, to enjoy reviving fresh air and compelling views.

	1	
2	3	4
	5	6

1. View from the Hu Chamber through one of the circular gates © Wang Baozhen
2. View from within the Hu Chamber © Wang Baozhen
3. Bamboo Pavilion and Hu Chamber © Weng Zitian
4. Roof structure of the Bamboo Pavilion © Wang Baozhen
5. Detailed view of the Hu Chamber's stairs © Weng Zitian
6. Rooftop platform of the Hu Chamber © Wang Baozhen

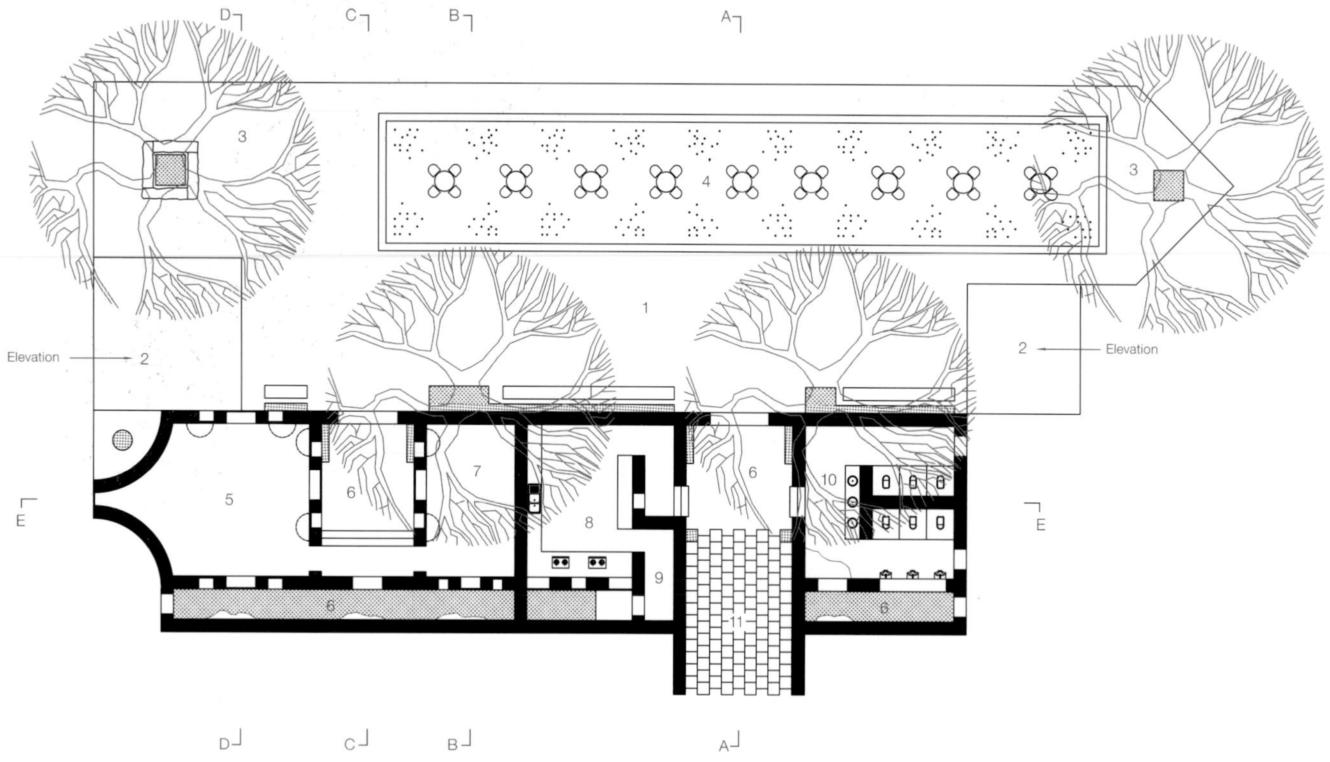

Ground-floor plan

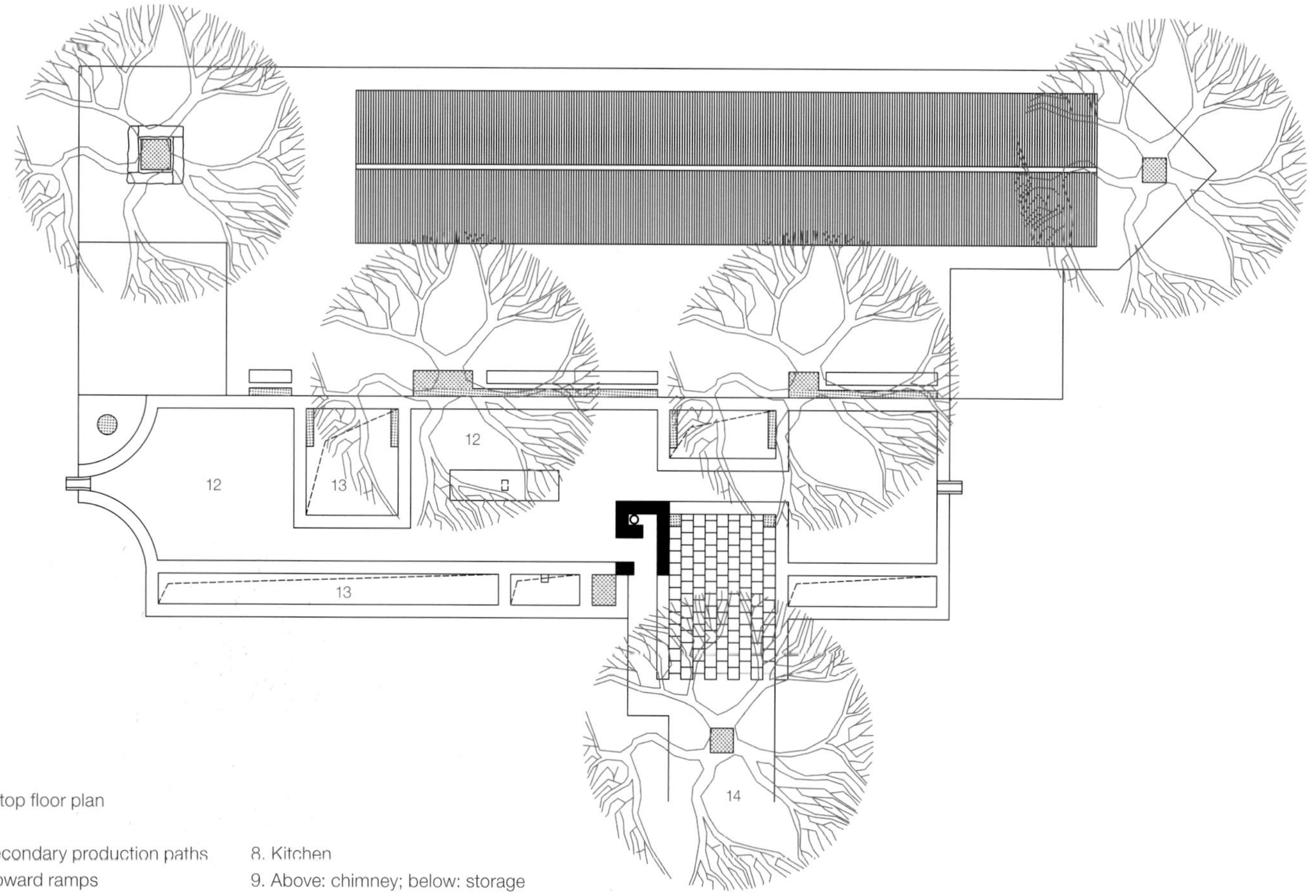

Rooftop floor plan

1. Secondary production paths
2. Upward ramps
3. Platforms
4. Bamboo Pavilion
5. Reception
6. Courtyard
7. Office
8. Kitchen
9. Above: chimney; below: storage
10. Restrooms
11. Large steps
12. Hu Chamber rooftop platform
13. Courtyard opening
14. Access to Section II

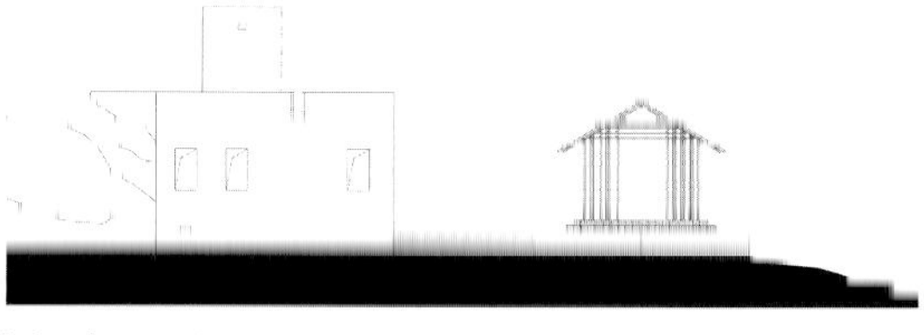

East elevation

North elevation

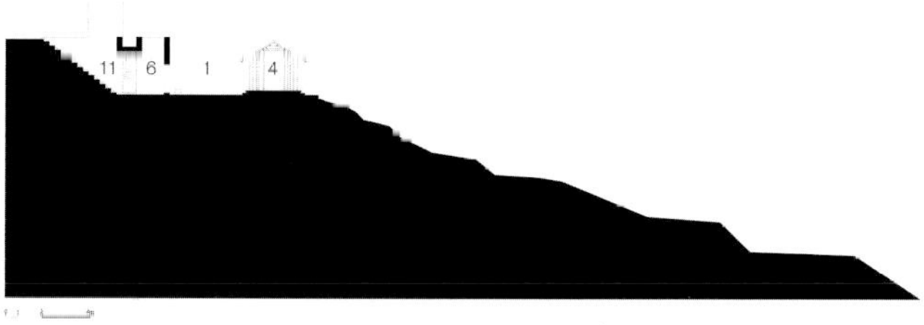

Section A-A

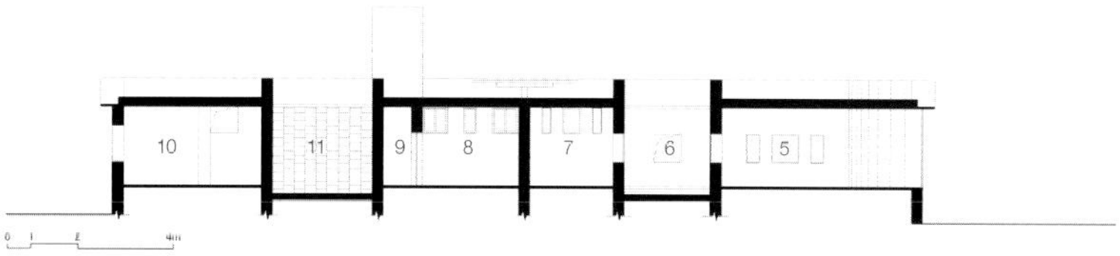

Section E-E

Design inspiration for the Bamboo Pavilion: *Summer Mountains* by Southern Tang dynasty painter Dong Yuan

Pictures of the original site © Yinyuan Studio

Wang Bin

Gebie Architects
Founder and Principal Architect, Gebie Architects

Wang Bin earned a bachelor's degree from Southeast University, China, in 2006, a master's degree from the University of California, Berkeley, United States, in 2008, and a PhD from Tongji University, China, in 2020. He previously worked at KPF Architects in New York City. During his studies at Berkeley, Wang won the Eisner Prize, the school' s most distinguished award for the creative arts. He founded Gebie Architects in 2012.

The field of architecture currently faces major challenges in China. On the one hand, it seems like one can only arrive at the vanguard of the industry and have their designs validated with the aid of external forces; on the other hand, free access to information in the digital age also means that almost anyone can be an architect today. Uniform value systems have eroded and the cultural ties which architecture depends on have been severed. In their work, Gebie Architects attempt to play the role of a "rearguard," seeking out solutions between upholding academic standards and defending individual expression in architecture. At the same time, the studio also hopes to represent local identities and cultures.

The vast majority of their flagship projects are located in the villages of China's Jiangnan region. The practice's most recent project, a private residence in Shaoxing's Yuecheng District, is their only work in an ancient city with well-preserved cultural ties. Although the studio has only produced a small number of works to date, they already reveal two major objectives: The first, is to abandon the obsession with past idyllic beauty in Jiangnan villages and instead create contemporary rural landscapes that are in keeping with today's eclectic, fragmented reality. Second, is to identify models and construction methods for contemporary living spaces that pay homage to and take into consideration rich reserves of cultural heritage. Underlying these two objectives is a desire to conserve the essence of modern architecture.

Selected Works

2021 Qiu Residence in Xuanhuafang, Shaoxing, Zhejiang Province, China
2020 Avalokitesvara Asrama, Xiaogan, Hubei Province, China
2020 Rice Field Restaurant in Changyangli, Suzhou, Jiangsu Province, China
2019 Chenxi Community Center, Shangyu District, Shaoxing, Zhejiang Province, China
2019 Changyangli Community Center, Suzhou, Jiangsu Province, China
2016 Cunshang Lake House, Suzhou, Jiangsu Province, China

Avalokitesvara Asrama © Zhao Yilong

Changyangli Community Center © Hao Ping

Interviewer: *Architecture China*
Interviewee: Wang Bin (WANG)
Editor: Wang Ying

What is your understanding of the term "Building with Nature"?

WANG: The Building with Nature: Architecture China Award is, to an extent, a manifesto against commercialism. "Building with nature" is about respecting the essence and inherent properties of things, rather than acting out of a desire to flatter. In commercialized society, architects have often been guided by the need to appeal to the market, but the Architecture China Award is critical of this trend.

In this regard, I think that many of our memories of traditional urban and rural images don't result from a desire to please someone. For example, little bridges over streams, white walls with gray roof tiles, or smoke spiraling upward from kitchen chimneys—these images are the product of the functional needs of ordinary people, and yet, we now to romanticize them. So, I think that "building with nature" is about real functions, building new and authentic images using readily available materials and contemporary techniques, rather than emulating grandiose scenes from elsewhere or from the past.

What direction are you currently exploring in terms of your practice?

WANG: Two directions are of interest to me at the moment. One is rural construction, because China's countryside (particularly in the region of Jiangsu and Zhejiang Provinces) has undergone a remarkable transformation and couldn't be more different from the outdated images we tend to imagine. How, then, should we go about creating contemporary rural landscapes in this rapidly changing environment? Another direction I'm interested in is using modern perspectives and techniques to carry on past traditions in relatively well-preserved fabrics of villages and cities.

How do young architects take part in rural initiatives?

WANG: To be frank, in rural construction, we usually start off serving the interests of capital as part of the bigger picture of architects going to the countryside. Around two or three years ago, I started to become aware of this as a problem. Now, we've been exploring a new approach, that is, attempting to get close to local inhabitants and see things from their perspective when designing new buildings.

For example, we once worked on a project in Wujiang, Jiangsu Province, about 5 kilometers from where Fei Xiaotong—regarded as the founding father of Chinese sociology—carried out research for his work *Peasant Life in China*. However, we didn't realize that at the time and so didn't use his work as a reference. We approached the design purely from our own subjective standpoint as architects, as well as that of the project's investors. When we later found out, I was full of regret. I keep thinking that, had we taken inspiration from sociology or anthropology and considered problems from a more grassroots perspective, the results would have been completely different; that's something that I'm keen to try in our future projects.

What are the greatest challenges and opportunities faced by young architects today?

WANG: The greatest challenge is that the context is broken apart in China. Different places have different speeds of development, which destroyed the original urban and rural system. We might see all kinds of styles in one single village. Collage cities and villages are everywhere. In those places, it's hard to know what kind of new architecture would be the best to carry on local traditions. That's the most frustrating and painful part of my work: trying to design a building that at once displays a contemporary quality and connects the cultural traditions of a specific place.

Our work as architects isn't to create nature itself—we are definitely not able to. Instead, we might be able to reconcile and stitch up the context and create a unique culture that has a dialectical relationship with nature.

RICE FIELD RESTAURANT IN CHANGYANGLI

Location: Wujiang District, Suzhou, Jiangsu Province, China
Lead architect: Wang Bin
Design team: (Architecture) Liu Kaiqiang, Xie Xuanji, He Zhenglin, Jing Qi; (structure) Li Fengqing; (heating) Yu Jiuyi; (water supply and sewer system) Zhang Chengfu; (electricity) Zhang Daoguang
Gross floor area: 1,000 square meters
Design period: 2019
Construction period: 2020
Photography: Xia Zhi, Xue Liang, Wang Bin, Zhang Honggui

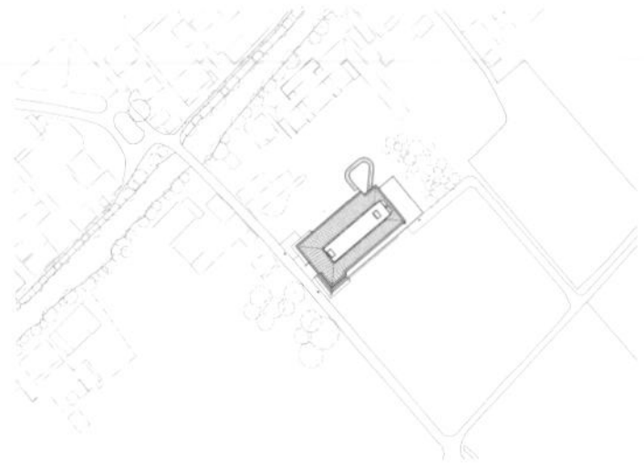

Site plan

Bird's-eye view © Zhang Honggui

View from a distance, looking across a rice paddy field © Xue Liang

The defining qualities of China's traditional villages weren't conferred directly by aesthetics, but instead grew spontaneously, as the result of agricultural production. In other words, they're the fruit of so-called natural architecture. The classic rural landscapes that were produced by farmers working the land have come to form an aesthetic ideal, even if they didn't result from a conscious design process. It was only when we traveled to villages in the Jiangnan region, as part of our involvement in rural construction initiatives, that we realized that these landscapes have, to some degree, been altered or broken as the farming systems upon which local populations depend on to make a living have become rapidly industrialized. This has left some villages abound with carelessly constructed factory buildings. Low-grade factories producing screws, clothing, and flour are roofed with cheap, blue, steel tiles or polycarbonate boards that have been allowed to fall into disrepair. By pushing practicality to an extreme, villages have become overrun by a hodgepodge of colored glass tiles, dated mosaic walls, gaudy terrazzos, windows with blue or green panes, and bland boxes made of concrete and brick interspersed with steel panel huts. On top of that, village dwellings also increasingly compete with one another in terms of scale and often adopt faux-European styles that seem out of place in the Chinese countryside. This eclecticism has become the predominant shared trait of China's villages today.

The location of the Rice Field Restaurant in Changyangli was no exception. High-voltage cables crisscrossed in the sky, slicing into pieces romantic visions of little bridges over bubbling brooks and whitewashed walls with black tiles. It was impossible to take a photo in the area without being photobombed by a variety of such eyesores.

Ramp in the northeastern corner © Xia Zhi

Northern façade © Xia Zhi

Eastern façade © Xia Zhi

Upward view of the stairs © Xia Zhi

Concrete along the stairwell © Xue Liang

Therefore, with its decidedly industrial aesthetic, Rice Field Restaurant attempts to reflect this reality—rather than denying it—while also asserting order over the chaotic rural skyline. The building's structural elements are on full display, free of all unnecessary embellishments. The main body of the building is composed of a combination of steel and concrete structures, with the former being more apparent along its north–south axis and the latter along the east–west axis. For the rooftop, prefabricated lightweight concrete slabs were used to create an interplay between lightness and heaviness. The four corners of the building are marked by entrances with overhangings in different shapes, which add variation to its otherwise minimalistic geometry.

Economical construction materials have been adopted and presented authentically. For example, concrete paired with cheap red quarry tiles and green terrazzo serve to adapt the building to its context. The roof is covered with white steel tiles, as these were virtually the only material that the budget would allow. The roof's sturdy cornices are used to hide the cheap, lightweight textile of these tiles, as well as create a more angular and precise visual effect.

Curation of spaces is another important aspect in contemporary rural construction. In today's villages, public edifices no longer serve to educate or enlighten the community, like the churches and temples of yesteryear. These spaces once played an important role in the self-

Interior of the stairwell © Xue Liang

1. The big staircase in the southwest corner © Xia Zhi
2. Western view of the main hall © Xia Zhi
3. Passage from the first to the second floor © Xia Zhi
4. Eastern view of the main hall © Xia Zhi
5. View from the staircase toward the exterior © Wang Bin

governance of rural communities, but rural autonomy—though once necessary due to the limited reach of centralized power—has since significantly diminished. At the same time, an influx of capital and increased interaction with urban populations have created a need for collective spaces in today's rural areas. Rather than being limited to one function, these spaces need to be highly adaptable, serving as venues for team-building activities, weddings, funerals, press conferences, and everyday workplaces. This multiuse approach reflects the openness and flexibility of contemporary society. It's precisely through the work of interior design and curation that long-span, continuous, or ceremonial spaces acquire contemporary significance. The architects consistently sought to emphasize this multifunctionality throughout the design of Rice Field Restaurant. The first floor is occupied by private rooms, the second by a large space, and the third by a multifunction hall. On either side are different staircases that allow visitors to experience each floor as part of a distinct, continuous itinerary. As people travel up and down the stairs, they can appreciate the independent space of the stairwell without being entirely divorced from the neighboring large rooms. At the same time, the stairwell beckons them to step outside onto the expansive balconies and admire the rice fields.

While Wang Bin refers to this method of creating spaces through bold structural expression and modest cheap materials as "rural brutalism," the core value of this method isn't brutality, but courage—the courage to face reality head-on. Contemporary rural construction is often plagued by conflicts between aesthetic and ethical concerns. The Rice Field Restaurant in Changyangli expresses a clear statement in this regard. Above all else, architects must honor the constraints of their discipline and find more intelligent ways of resolving practical problems within the parameters of a project.

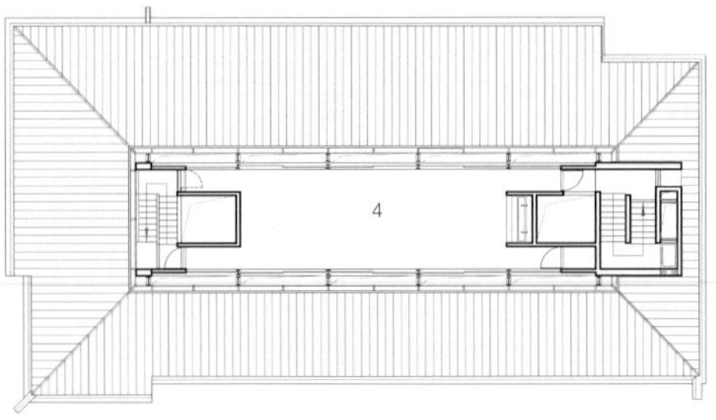

Roof floor plan

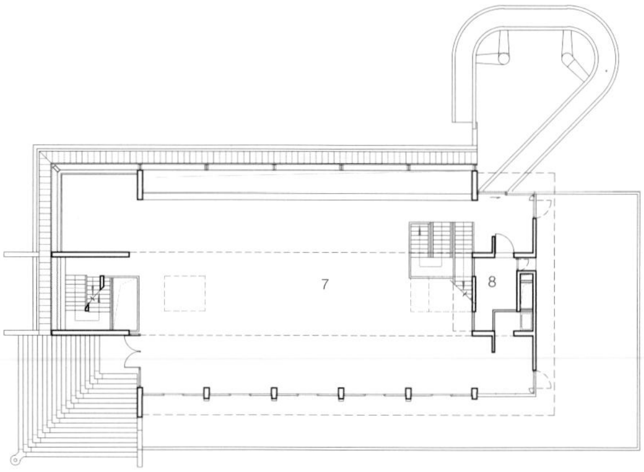

Second-floor plan

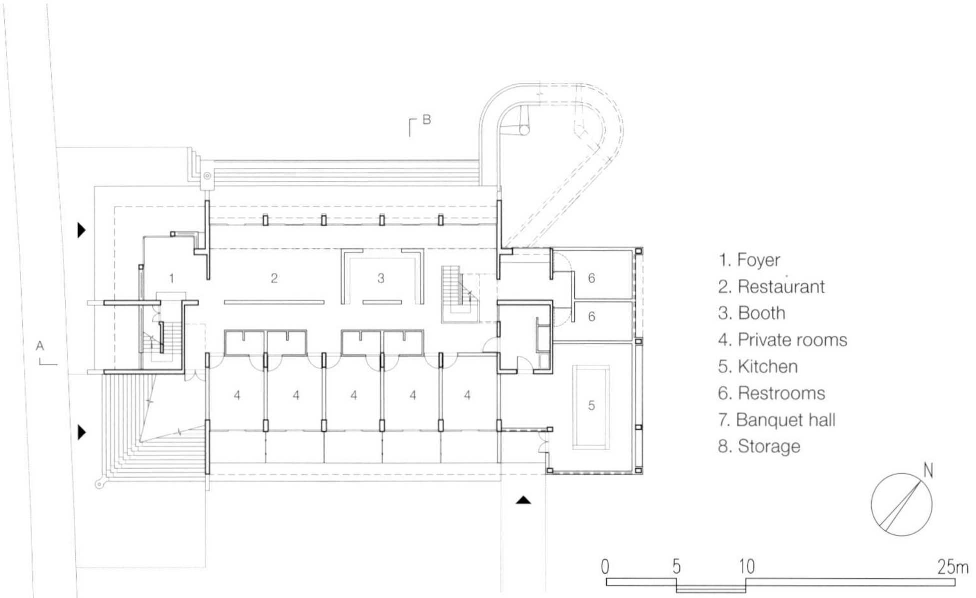

Ground-floor plan

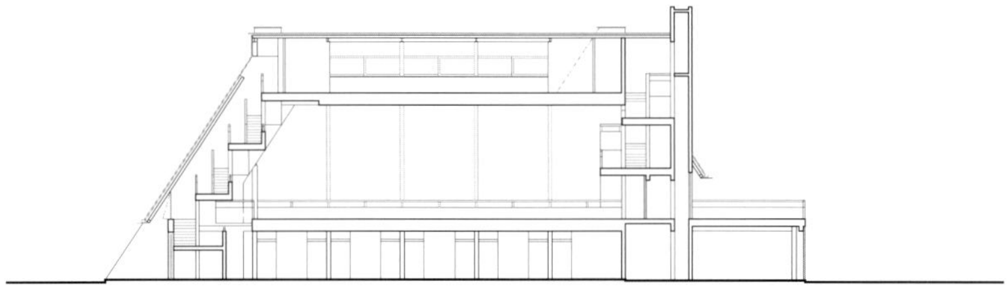

Section A-A

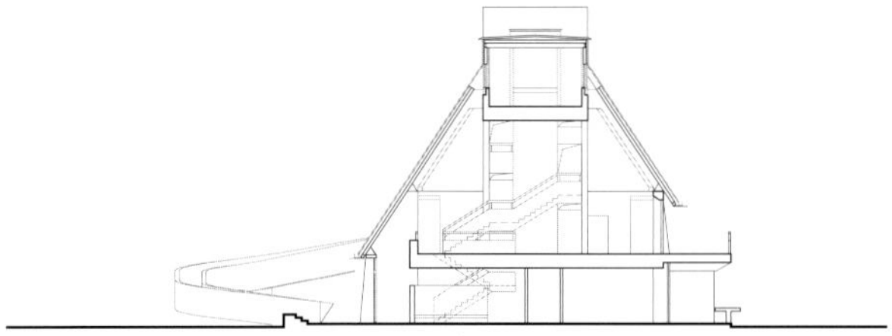

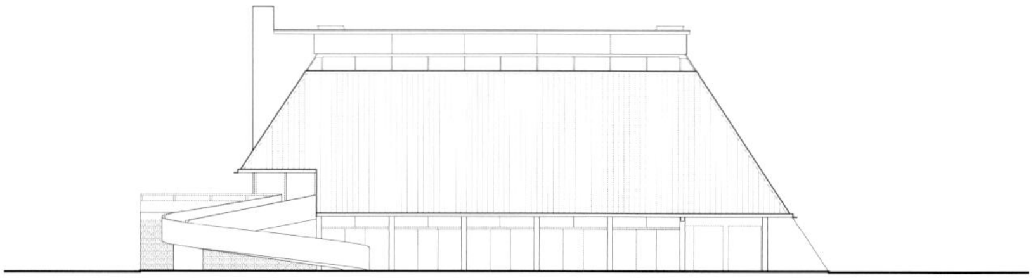

Section B-B

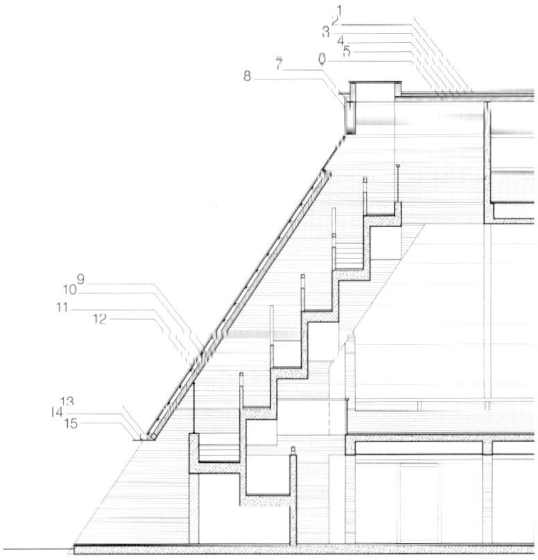

Detailed cross section of the short side

1. Aluminum alloy support for 0.8 mm-thick wave-shaped color steel tile H75
2. 40x40x3-mm square pipe keel @ 600 mm, vertical main steel beams
3. 20 mm-thick 1:2.5 cement mortar protective layer, sloping to both sides
4. 3 mm-thick SBS waterproofing membrane with 10 mm overlap at the end
5. 20 mm-thick 1:2.5 cement mortar for leveling and slope formation
6. 150 mm ALC boards, pre-sprayed with a waterproof sealing paint
7. 0.8 mm-thick stainless-steel drainage boards
8. 0.8 mm-thick white wave-shaped board with a 50 series special keel
   Installation of angle code purlin on the back @ 1,050 mm
9. Aluminum alloy support for 0.8 mm-thick wave-shaped color steel tile H75
10. 40x40x3-mm square pipe keel @ 600 mm
    100x100x100x3-mm square pipe sections are installed underneath to raise the support
11. 150 mm ALC boards, pre-sprayed with a waterproof sealing paint
12. 200x300-mm I-beam main steel beams
13. 150x200x3-mm stainless-steel guttering
14. 40x40x3-mm galvanized square tubes with two coats of anti-corrosive paint
15. 3 mm-thick steel plate with two coats of anti-corrosive paint

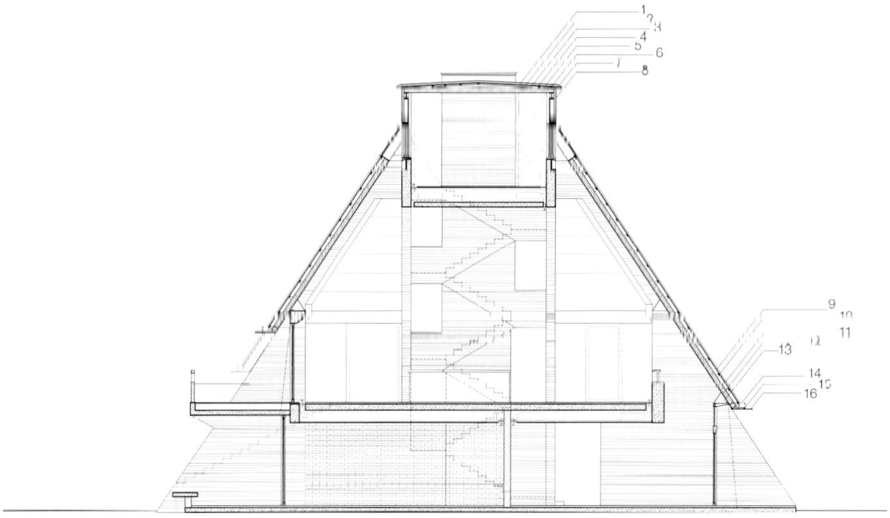

Detailed cross section of the western staircase

1. Aluminum alloy support for 0.8 mm thick wave shaped color steel tile H75
2. 40x40x30-mm square pipe keel @ 600 mm
   100x100x100x3-mm square pipe sections are installed underneath to raise the support
3. 150 mm ALC boards, pre-sprayed with a waterproof sealing paint
4. 200x300-mm I-beam main steel beams
5. Steel support
6. 150x200x3-mm stainless-steel guttering
7. 40x3-mm galvanized square tubes with two coats of anti-corrosive paint
8. 3 mm-thick steel plate with two coats of anti-corrosive paint
9. Aluminum alloy support for 0.8 mm-thick wave-shaped color steel tile H75
10. 40x40x3-mm square pipe keel @ 600 mm
    100x100x100x3-mm square pipe sections are installed underneath to raise the support
11. 150mm ALC boards, pre-sprayed with a waterproof sealing paint
12. 200x300-mm I-beam main steel beams
13. Steel support
14. 150x200x3-mm stainless-steel guttering
15. 40x3-mm galvanized square tubes with two coats of anti-corrosive paint
16. 3 mm-thick steel plate with two coats of anti-corrosive paint

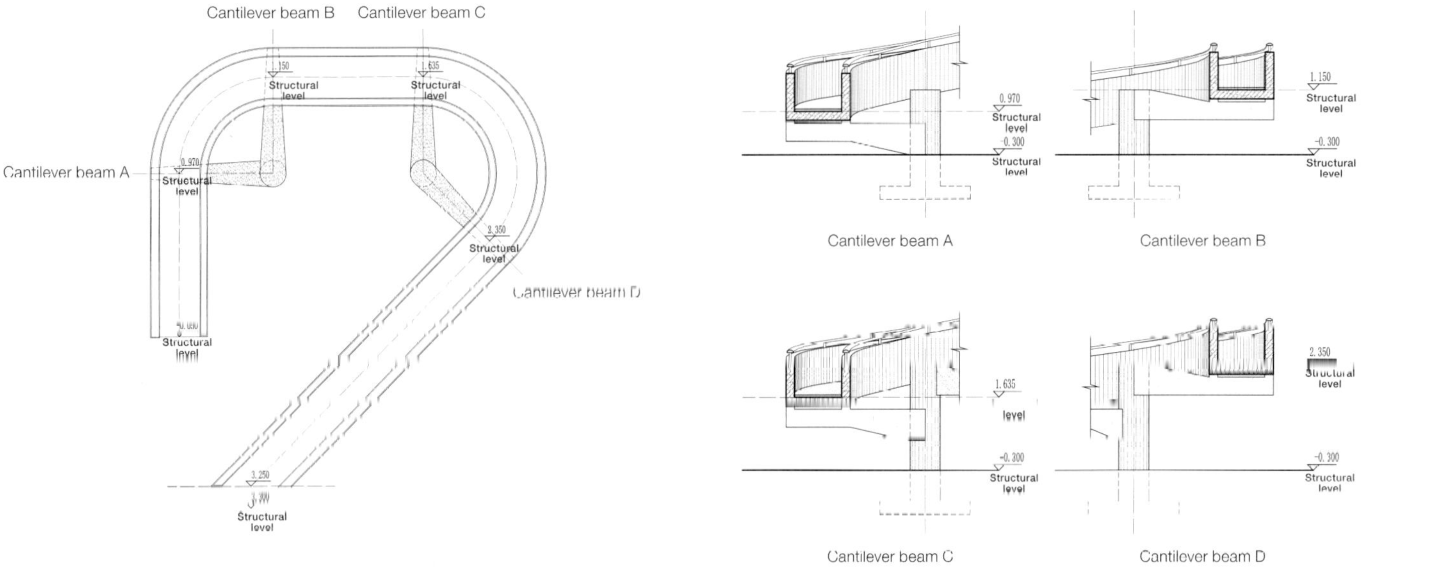

Detailed view of the ramp

QIU RESIDENCE IN XUANHUAFANG, SHAOXING

Location: Yuecheng District, Shaoxing, Zhejiang Province, China
Lead architect: Wang Bin
Design team: (Architecture) He Zhenglin, Xie Xuanji, Liu Kaiqiang; (structure) Zhang Zhun, Li Fengqing; (heating) Yu Jiuyi; (electricity) Zhang Daoguang; (water supply and sewage) Zhang Chengfu
Gross floor area: 230 square meters
Design period: 2019
Construction period: 2021
Photography: Xue Liang

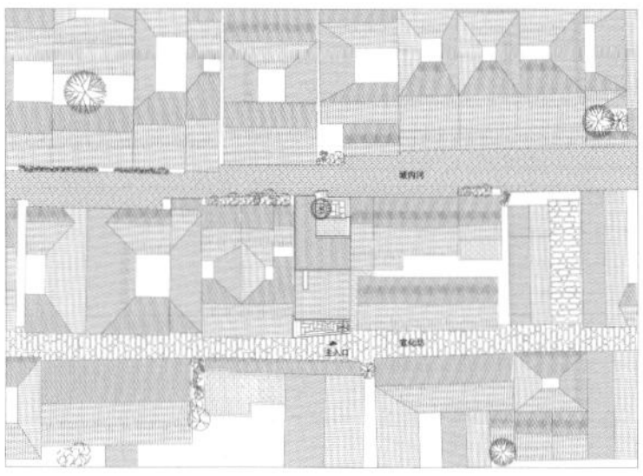

Site plan

Bird's-eye view © Xue Liang

View of the south elevation from the alley © Xue Liang

Fushan Hill, in the west of Shaoxing, Zhejiang Province, China, is one of the main landmarks remaining of the ancient kingdom of Yue. Two thousand and five hundred years ago, Fan Li, advisor to the kingdom's famous King Goujian, had actually planned for Shaoxing to be a unique east-facing "juxtaposed city."[1]

Then, a water source from the Huiji mountain range in the south flowed north into Shanhui Plain. One river ran through Shaoxing via what was then the eastern reaches of the small city of Goujian (which is the west city of the juxtaposed city). A community settled and grew parallel to this river section no further than 100 meters from the southeast foot of Fushan Hill. In this settlement, was an alley about 200 meters long and 2 meters wide, known as Xuanhuafang.

Qiu Residence is located between Xuanhuafang and that river. The site is occupied by buildings from the 1970s that were built by the homeowners themselves; most of them have fallen into disrepair. The site spans approximately 16 meters from east to west, and 6.6 meters from north to south, hinting at the ancient city's eastward-facing layout. On the southern side of the site is a road that intersects with Xuanhuafang, known as Siyushiqian (meaning the front yard of prison administration), which was formed by filling in a river. These ancient names that have been preserved to this day evoke the zone's former prestige and convey its once importance in local governmental affairs. However, all other traces of that history have since been replaced by the smog and clamor of modern urban life.

As a result of the ancient city's dense layout, the original building's gables, which follow the north–south axis, stand inches from neighboring properties. The stream to the east, and the only entrance from Xuanhuafang, to the west, define the plot's remaining boundaries. To preserve the old street's appearance and render the building more discreet, a traditional plaster composed of lime mortar and paper strips was applied to the surrounding walls. On the side adjacent to the river, the building's contours were recessed to reduce its sense of scale and ensure that it fits in with the neighborhood. The riverside courtyard was also preserved. Although the perimeters of the property were severely constricted, the original building had the advantage of being the tallest in the neighborhood, giving the design the opportunity to incorporate a visual extension along the north–south axis. Therefore, at the beginning of the design process, four interconnected, overlapping spaces of different heights were conceived; when experienced from the inside, they would draw people's gaze upward. These spaces are positioned to allow natural light and fresh air to filter through the building from top to

Entrance on Xuanhuafang Alley © Xue Liang

Foyer © Xue Liang

Living room © Xue Liang

bottom, almost as if the cross-sectional layout of a traditional courtyard had been vertically transposed.

The neighborhood is so dense that on the northern and southern sides of the property there are two bungalows that have wooden beams that have been directly secured into the original building. This meant that demolishing some of the original structure would also result in large parts of neighboring houses being pulled down. This tricky situation motivated the architect to consider other possibilities regarding the building's structure and construction. The expression *"jin chan tuo qiao,"* translating to "a golden cicada breaks free of its shell"—which means to escape a predicament through a cunning [illegible] to mind and was applied literally. The original building's external walls and most of its structure were preserved, as a kind of "shell" in which a new structure was built. At the same time, the foundations were dug up and replaced with a concrete slab foundation. First, as few as possible of the prefabricated floor slabs were removed; then, newly constructed columns were passed through the gaps before sealing them with concrete. When the structure of the new building was sturdy enough to support the gables, the rest of the original building's floor slabs were removed. In this way, the gables were preserved without disrupting the neighbors' buildings.

The final product is almost like a new skeleton within the shell of an old building, creating an interesting temporal juxtaposition. When the window on the south side of the building—placed higher than neighboring roof pitches—is opened, a column of intense natural light floods in, giving the space new life. To provide additional reinforcement and pre-emptively resolve potential issues with mold and humidity, wall-length bookshelves and cabinetry have been built along the old wall on the property's north–south axis, with a moisture-control layer sandwiched in between.

The design for Qiu Residence in Xuanhuafang demonstrates how buildings can be updated and modernized in extremely dense traditional Chinese neighborhoods. The challenges encountered on this project were about more than the preservation of historical and cultural ties—they also included more practical construction related concerns. The objective wasn't to rigidly preserve or emulate the so-called traditional appearance of the original structure; rather, the intention was to impart the ancient city's millennium-old essence and adapt one of its dwellings to a current, modern-day lifestyle using contemporary materials and technologies.

1. *Pilingcheng* or "juxtaposed city" is a historical notion that describes cities juxtaposed next to each other with connected city walls—for example, the ruler's palace in the west small city, with the rest of the people living in the east bigger city. This layout can, therefore, also be called "Big-small City."

Living room © Xue Liang

Second-floor study © Xue Liang

Kitchen © Xue Liang

Stairwell © Xue Liang

Second-floor study © Xue Liang

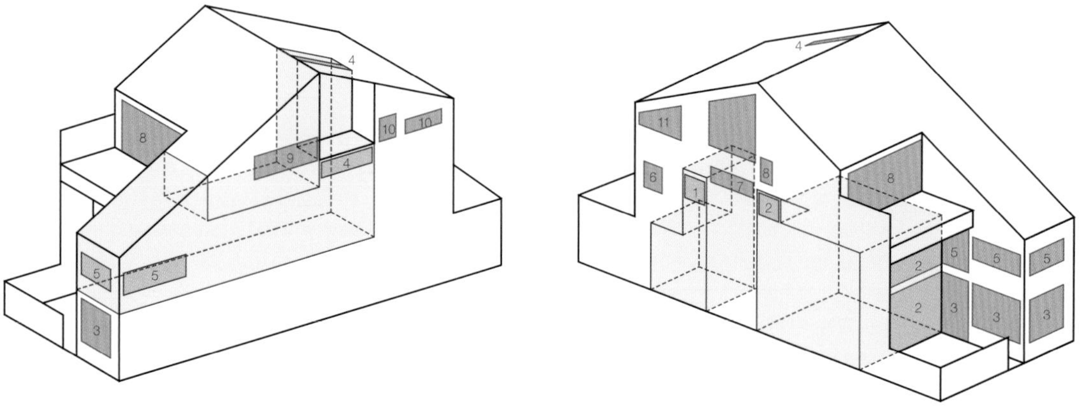

Axonometric analysis

1. Foyer
2. Living room
3. Tea room
4. North side of staircase
5. Reading pavilion
6. Bathroom of the second bedroom
7. South side of staircase
8. Main bedroom
9. Small study
10. Bathroom of the main bedroom
11. Laundry room

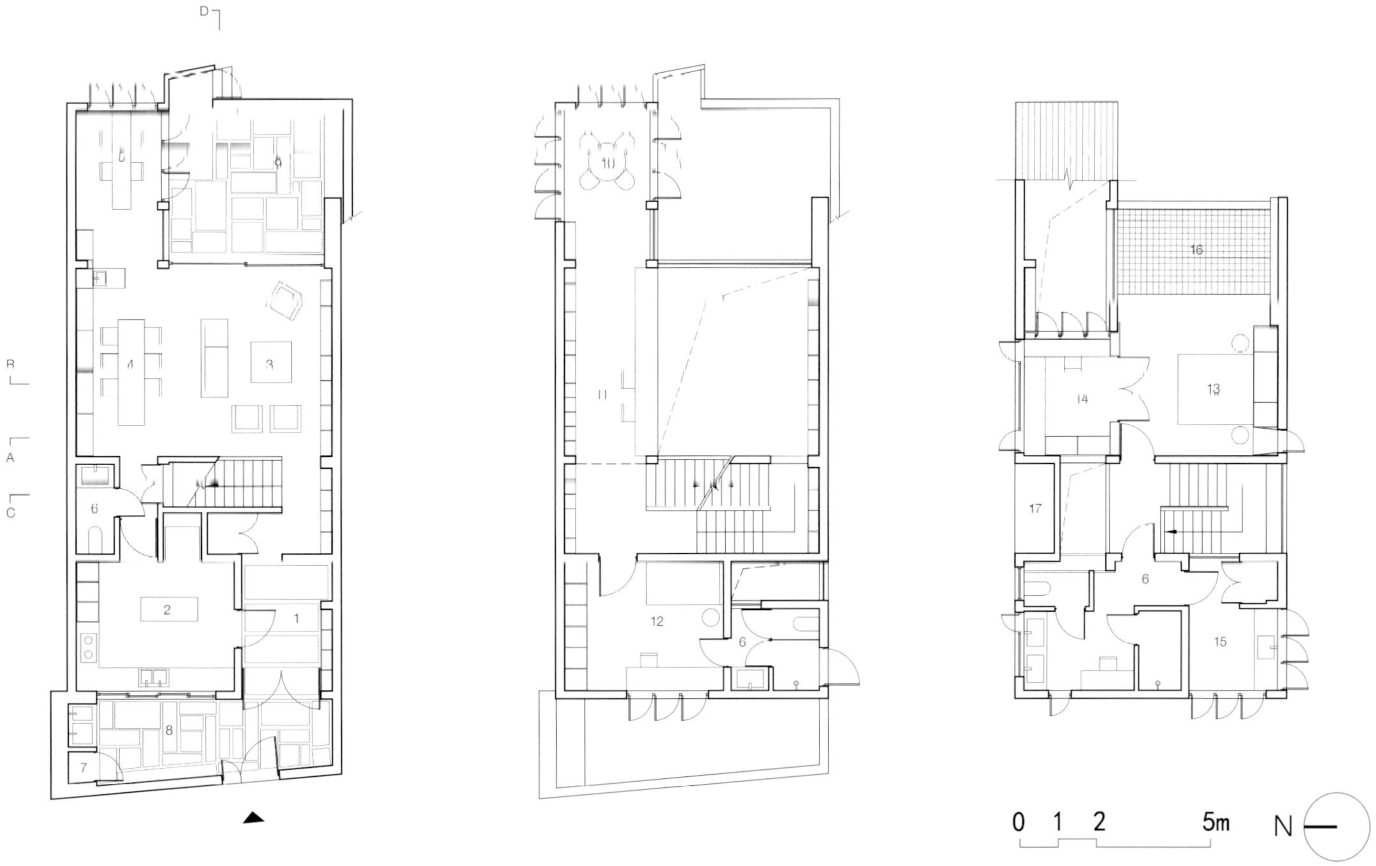

Ground-floor plan

1. Foyer
2. Kitchen
3. Living room
4. Dining room
5. Tea room
6. Bathroom
7. Utility room
8. Western courtyard
9. Eastern courtyard
10. Reading pavilion
11. Study
12. Second bedroom
13. Main bedroom
14. Small study
15. Laundry room
16. Terrace
17. Utility deck

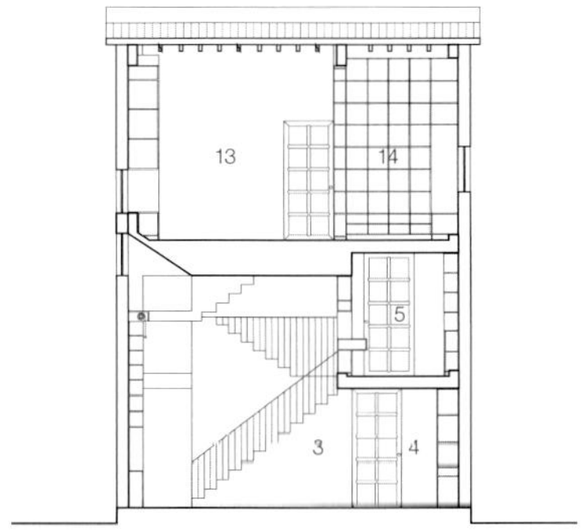

Section A-A

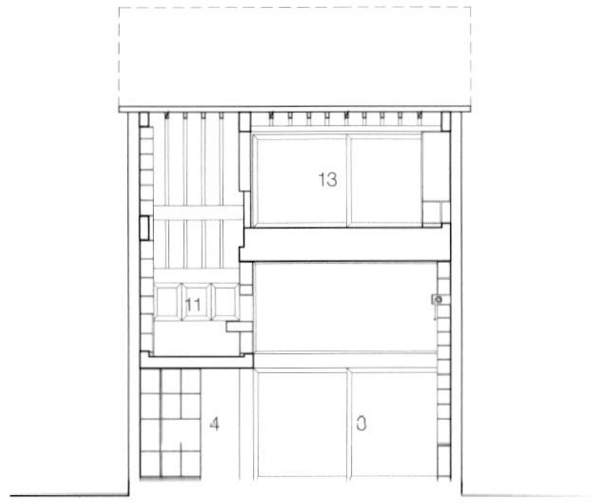

Section B-B

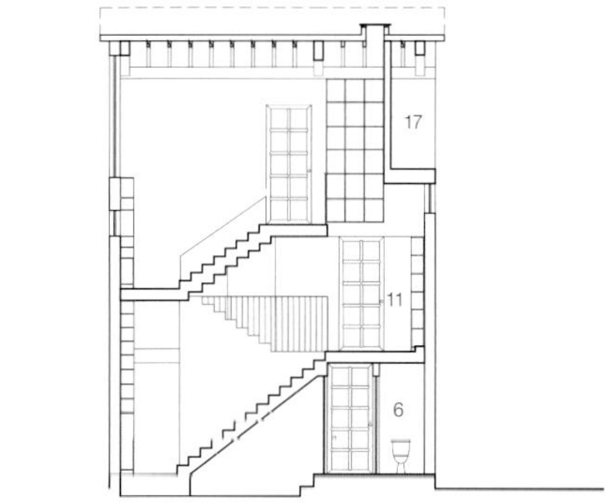

Section C C

Section C-C

Shui Yanfei

Yanfei Architects
Lead Architect, Yanfei Architects
Visiting Professor, Syracuse University
Chartered member, Royal Institute of British Architects (RIBA)

Shui Yanfei holds a Master's in Architecture from Princeton University. Thereafter, he worked at the Office for Metropolitan Architecture in Rotterdam, The Netherlands, and in 2012 co-founded Yanfei Architects with Su Yiqi.

His design creations and research have been published by academic reviews and media platforms such as *A+U, The Plan, PASAJES arquitectura, Architecture Journal, Wallpaper*, dezeen,* and *designboom*. He has also given lectures at academic institutions such as Harvard and Syracuse Universities, United States, the Chinese University of Hong Kong, Hong Kong, China, and Tongji University, China. His work has been displayed at multiple exhibitions in both China and abroad, such as an exhibition of contemporary independent Chinese architects organized by Harvard University, as well as the Shanghai Urban Space Art Season. In 2018, he won the American Institute of Architects' Award for Excellence in Design and was also invited to take part in the Venice Biennale that year. The following year, he contributed to the traveling exhibition at Aedes Architecture Forum in Berlin titled Building A Future Countryside in China. In 2023, he won an Exploration Award for Young Architects in the 2023 Building with Nature: Architecture China Award.

In 2020, he was appointed as a visiting professor at Syracuse University's School of Architecture. In 2021, he became a chartered member of the Royal Institute of British Architects (RIBA) in the UK.

Selected Works

2023 Wind Bunker (under construction), Qinhuangdao, Hebei Province, China
2023 Equilix Winery (under construction), Penglai, Shandong Province, China
2023 Papago Land (under construction), Lishui City, Zhejiang Province, China
2023 Climate Muesum (under construction), Chengdu, Sichuan Province, China
2022 Xianlin School, Nanjing, Jiangsu Province, China
2021 Jebum-Gang Art Center, Tibet, China
2021 Xinfan Market, Lishui City, Zhejiang Province, China
2021 M House, Lishui City, Zhejiang Province, China
2019 Future Garden Station, Nanjing, Jiangsu Province, China
2019 Shibantai Hotel, Beijing, China
2019 Yushan Summer House, Suzhou, Jiangsu Province, China
2018 J House, Shanghai, China
2018 RV Campground Club, Shanghai, China
2017 Soft Matter, Shanghai, China
2017 Lostvilla Boutique Hotel in Yucun, Zhejiang Province, China

Equilix Winery © Yanfei Architects

Jebum-Gang Art Center © Chen Hao

Interviewer: *Architecture China*
Interviewee: Shui Yanfei (SHUI)
Editor: Wang Ying

What new insights have you developed on the idea of "Building with Nature"?

SHUI: In Chinese, the term "nature" refers to the concept of "Daofa ziran," which represents a resonance between the macro cosmo and micro cosmo. This idea is deeply rooted in Eastern cosmology, which is not aimed at making the transcendent understanding of the world, but rather consciously maintaining the immanent continuity between the subject and the object; between the human and the universe. Therefore, instead of establishing a set of rules or creating the doctrine of the means, "nature" or *ziran*, from my perspective, is more about focusing on the familiarity of our everyday life to find its new meaning and poetic engagement in the quotidian banality.

What direction are you currently exploring in your practice?

SHUI: In recent years, we have been re-evaluating China's economic construction history from the 1950s to the 1970s, and observed how modern construction technology was integrated into the Chinese context on a large scale. After that extremely challenging period, the standardized design principles imported from the Soviet Union gradually evolved into a cooperative interplay between "codes and recipes," which to some extent facilitated the unprecedented rapid urbanization of the past three decades, resulting in a built landscape across China characterized by extreme banality

This overwhelming phenomenon has become the fundamental condition for every Chinese architect; we need more than Haus-Rucker's famous claim of "amnesty for built reality." Similarly, when we use *ziran* (nature) within the Chinese context, it is not merely a critique of the extreme banality, but rather an attitude; an opportunity to discover novelty in our everyday lives, and a possibility for poetic transformation rooted in Eastern cultural tradition.

Therefore, in our practice, on the one hand, we aim to navigate the boundaries between standardization and uniqueness, conducting a series of attunement operations through a precise understanding of limitations. On the other, we have broadened the definition of economic factors in a comprehensive sense, developing a range of adaptable frameworks to address emerging issues such as programmatic and content instability, political envelope systems, and the suppressed construction rights of individuals and organizations. This ongoing series of research and practices is not intended to become a manifesto, but rather to achieve a contemporaneity that integrates Western and Eastern influences.

What are the greatest challenges and opportunities faced by young architects today?

SHUI: I believe that the greatest challenge for Chinese architects lies in navigating the cultural differences between the East and the West. In my opinion, the most effective approach is not fusion, but rather finding resonance between the two, encompassing geographical, cultural, and temporal dimensions. For instance, exploring the connections between postmodernism and ancient Chinese civilization. If we aim to overcome the sense of "othering" between ourselves and others, the approach should involve establishing parallel references rather than assigning one as superior to the other. In our practice, we strive to preserve and reconcile these conflicts, contrasts, and resonances in a subtle and implicit manner, rather than by being overtly explicit.

XINFAN MARKET

Location: Huzhen Town, Jinyun County, Lishui City, Zhejiang Province, China
Lead architect: Shui Yanfei
Design team: Ding Xiang, Zou Yongjun, Deng Junwen, Liu Heng, Zuo Zhuangzhuang, Tan Jiaqi, Zhang Yijia
Gross floor area: 3,120 square meters
Design period: May 2019–November 2020
Construction period: February 2021
Photography: Chen Hao

Site plan

Aerial image © Chen Hao

Xinfan Market is an architectural reconstruction project located in Huzhen Town, Jinyun County, Zhejiang Province, China. After more than twenty years of intensive use, the old farmer's market was demolished due to structural safety hazards and poor sanitary conditions. This project aimed to enhance the market's architectural design and create an open, hygienic, and friendly environment for its users. In doing so, we wanted to hark back to a collective lifestyle unique to China's countryside.

The new building follows the original layout of the old market, comprising eastern and western sections, allowing it to retain its connection with the local context. The east building is covered by a triple-arched roof and provides local retailers with a small business space that can be flexibly divided. Meanwhile, the western building is a long and narrow single-story structure covered by a large-span arched roof that serves as the market's main venue. Its simple structure allows the space to be organized and used in a multitude of ways. The arched corridor between the two buildings connects the streets on the north and south sides of the lot, while the interior promenade extends east to west, from the riverbank to a village street. Stalls are organized around the promenade, thereby improving the market's accessibility.

Aerial image © Chen Hao

Five types of stall structures, all formed by a cantilevered system made of welded steel components, feature in the interior layout of the west building; they can be used and adapted by sellers in a multitude of ways. They also allow the installation of signs, electric cables, lighting devices, and other features. In the interest of convenience, industrially produced materials were selected, and the market is covered with a 0.9 millimeter thick arched corrugated steel roof—a common feature of large-span factories. Since the roof didn't need to be insulated, it can support its own weight without the need for additional columns or beams. This made the project much more cost-effective, not to mention easier to construct and more water-resistant. The exterior walls of the market are made from Jinyun tuff, a local accessible raw material, which echoes the architectural and historical context of Jinyun, the Stone City. The exterior walls feature modern industrial materials and traditional Jinyun tuff juxtaposed to create a striking visual contrast.

As a new form of rural infrastructure, Xinfan Market has the potential to help foster closer social ties and address future challenges in rural communities.

Western façade, as seen from across the river © Chen Hao

Western façade © Chen Hao

Interior view of the market © Yanfei Architects

Interior view of the market © Chen Hao

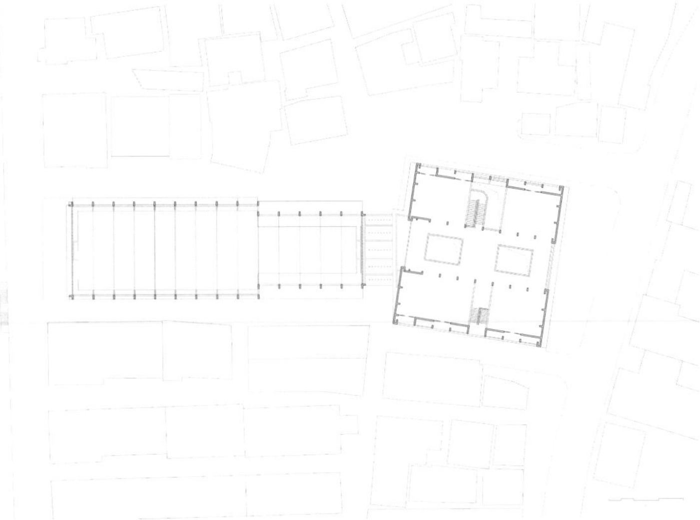

Second-floor plan

Ground-floor plan

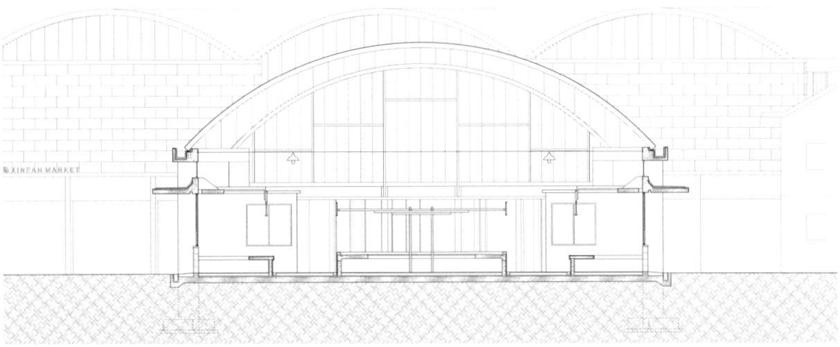

Section A-A

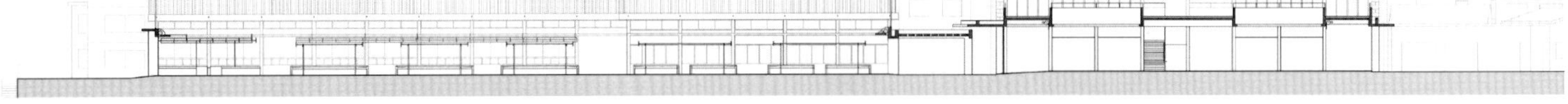

Section B-B

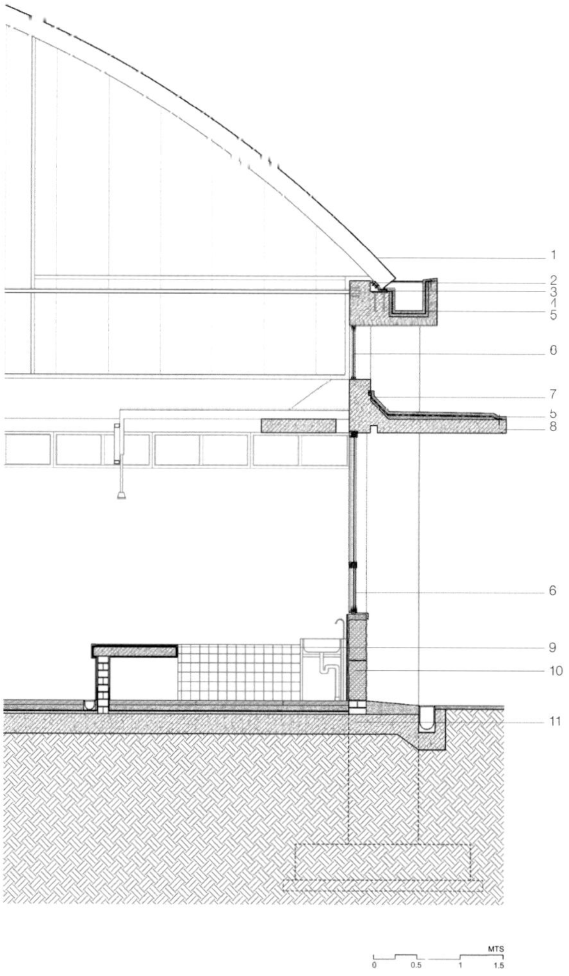

Scction of Block A's nothcrn wall

1. Arched corrugated steel roof
2. LJ1 full length layout
3. Φ20 mm steel string
4. Pre-buried steel panel
5. Modified bitumen WP membrane
6. Expansion web
7. Cement mortar filling
8. Reinforced-concrete roof slab
9. Jinyun stone bricks
10. Ceramic tile paving
11. Reinforced-concrete floor slab

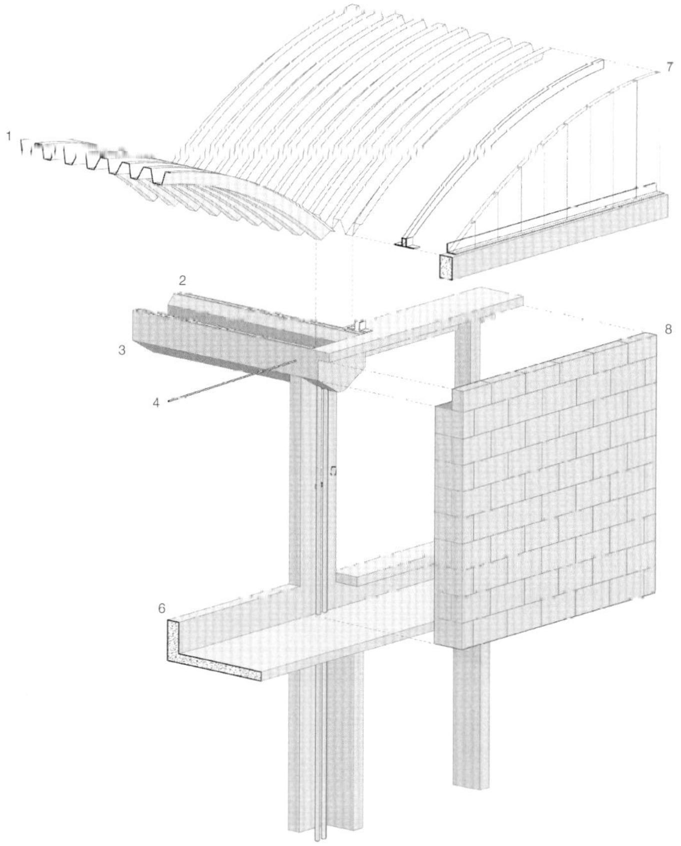

Block B joint assembly dctail

1. Arched corrugated steel roof
2. Pre-buried steel panel
3. Gutter beam
4. Φ20 mm steel string
5. Φ75 mm double steel drainage
6. Reinforced-concrete structural column
7. Translucent panels
8. Jinyun stone brick wall

XIANLIN SCHOOL

Location: Nanjing, Jiangsu Province, China
Lead architect: Shui Yanfei
Design team: Wang Haocheng, Xu Hanhua, Zou Yongjun, Qing Siyuan, Song Jingjing, Jian Shihan
Gross floor area: 64,000 square meters
Design period: April 2019–April 2021
Construction period: December 2022
Photography: Chen Hao, Su Shengliang, Yanfei Architects

Aerial view © Su Shengliang

Though it was originally planned as a forty-two-class junior high school, Xianlin School has been temporarily serving as an elementary school the past three years. Given that schools have highly restrictive structural and functional requirements, the team was conscious of rigidly adhering to conventions—such as the typical "fishbone" layout of classrooms joined by a single corridor—and not veering too far from tried and tested methods and accepted design aesthetics. To find a solution that was both practical and innovative, the shared characteristics of hundreds of sample schools serving elementary school students of the same two age groups as those in Xianlin School were carefully studied.

This project can be considered an unconventional response to the typical school design adopted in China today. It attempts to strike a balance between a series of interrelated factors: Large-group teaching and the scale of school buildings; layouts and rigid spacing requirements; class units and structural span regulations; the surface area of public spaces and economical construction; students' spatial perception and ease of movement; traffic congestion in surrounding areas caused by commuting to and from school; and interactivity and the sharing of spaces with the community. As many of these issues are implicit in a standard gross floor area ratio, the project was given the codename: FAR = 1.0.

Ultimately, a multilayered structure that blurs the boundaries between internal and exterior spaces, as well as corridors and platforms, was produced. The sides of the structure facing the city and the playground are open, while those facing the courtyard are closed, to allow discretion and tranquility.

1. Viewing platform © Chen Hao
2. Interior walkways © Chen Hao
3. Gymnasium © Chen Hao
4. Entrance © Chen Hao

The first and second floors accommodate the campus's shared spaces, such as gymnasium, lecture halls, and cafeteria, and the third to the fifth floors consist of standardized classrooms, laboratories, and offices. This layout produces a smooth and convenient transition between the school's public and private spaces.

A combination of single and double-span structures, supported by anti-buckling columns, create a degree of fluidity between internal and external environments. This fluidity accounts for the change in students' use of the spaces throughout the day. For example, the central courtyard serves not only as a space for holding assemblies, but also as a space for gathering, exercising, and eating. The outdoor platforms dispersed on the second and third floors are the most frequently used activity areas that are usually utilized during short breaks between classes. With their smaller scale and increased privacy, they're less likely to make young students feel overwhelmed. Some additional openings in the common classroom areas serve as drinking stations and study areas. There are also covered walkways provided for holding activities on a rainy day or adverse weather conditions. The building's open concept allows tremendous flexibility in terms of its use. Overall, this design aims to create a dynamic learning environment that caters to the diverse needs of students while promoting interaction, comfort, and adaptability.

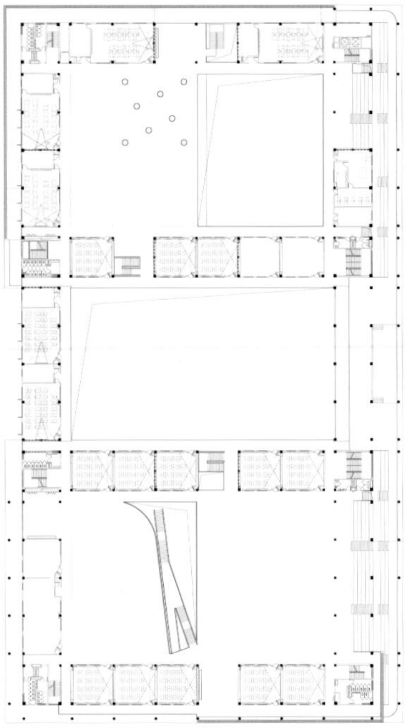

Third-floor plan

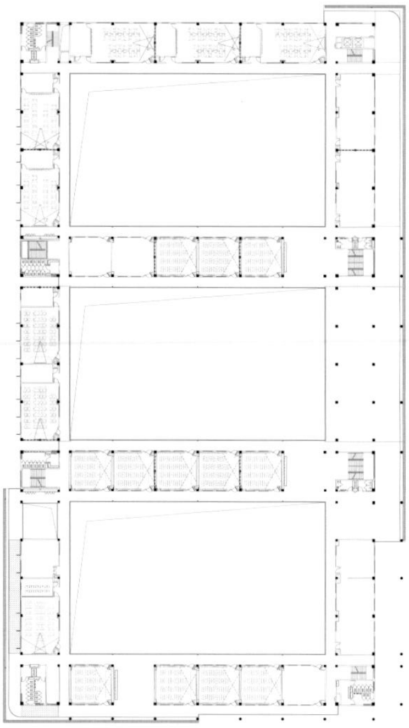

Fourth-floor plan

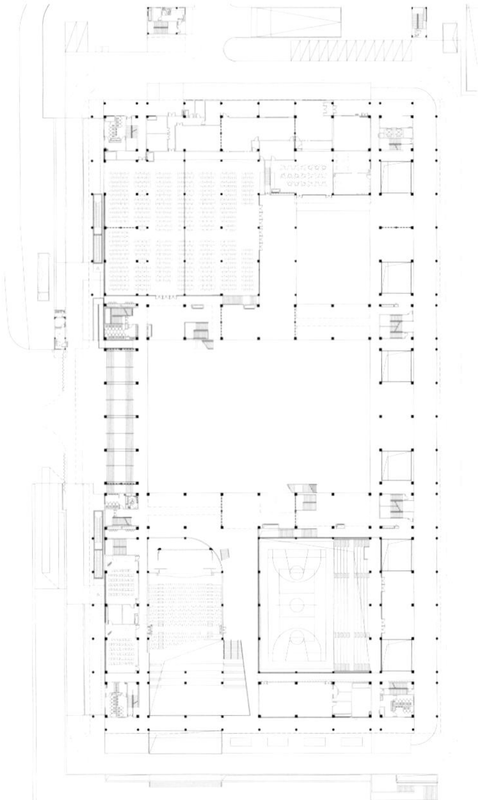

Ground-floor plan

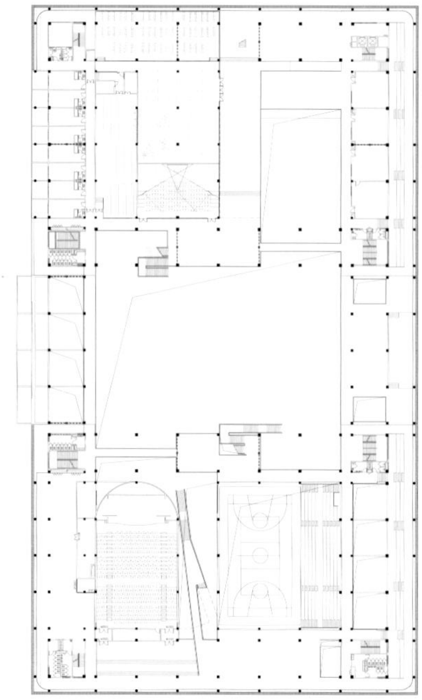

Second-floor plan

Street view © Yanfei Architects

Structural model © Yanfei Architects

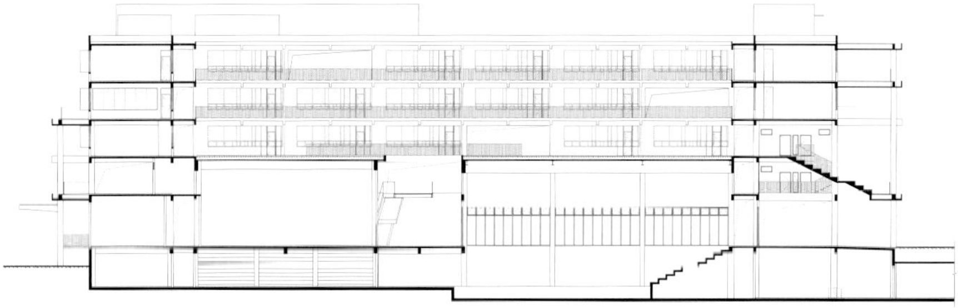

Section A-A

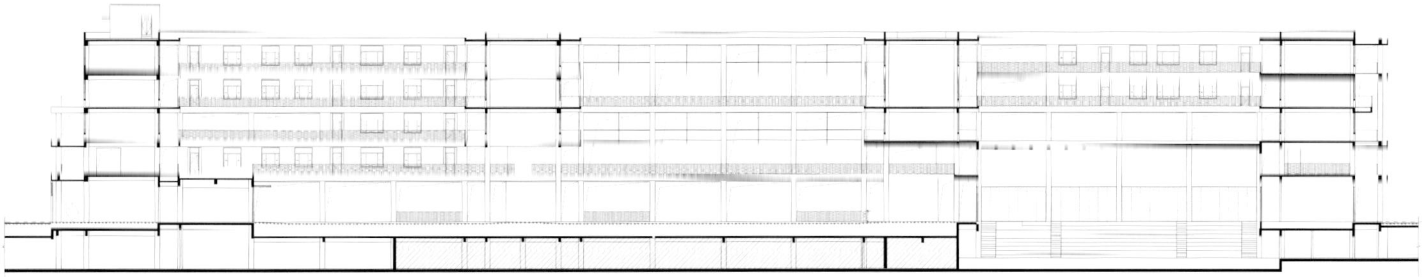

Section B-B

genarchitects (Fan Beilei, Kong Rui, Xue Zhe)

genarchitects

Fan Beilei:
Partner and Principal Architect
National First-class Registered Architect (PRC)
RIBA Chartered Architect
Visiting design instructor, Tongji University

Kong Rui:
Partner and Principal Architect
Member, Council of Institution of Vernacular Architecture, Architectural Society of China
RIBA Chartered Architect

Xue Zhe:
Partner and Principal Architect
RIBA Chartered Architect

genarchitects was founded in Shanghai in 2013. In the decade that followed since then, the studio has provided comprehensive architectural design solutions under the direction of its three lead architects. They have consistently upheld the importance of authenticity in design and construction, proposing practical solutions that consider both local characteristics and functional requirements. genarchitects' diverse body of work includes educational, cultural, and commercial buildings, with the scale of its practice varying from furniture to urban design.

The practice's flagship projects include Dingshu Vocational School of Pottery, Yitingting Cottage, and Youyi Bay Community at Aranya. These works have won awards in competitions like AIA Shanghai CDEA Awards, Building with Nature: Architecture China Award, the Iconic Awards, THE PLAN Awards, and WA Chinese Architecture Awards. genarchitects' practice and research have also been widely published in academic journals: *Architectural Journal*, *World Architecture*, and *Time+Architecture*, as well as in books published by Thames & Hudson Press, Birkhäuser, and other major publishers. The project Dingshu Vocational School of Pottery was featured on the cover of the May 2022 issue of *Architectural Journal*, which also published an article by the practice that reflected on the design process of the project. genarchitects has been invited to various exhibitions, such as Venice Biennale, the Sino-Europe Invitational Architectural Exhibition, and Towards a Critical Pragmatism: Contemporary Architecture in China, which was an exhibition held at Harvard Graduate School of Design in the United States.

The leading members of genarchitects currently act as guest lecturers at Tongji University, China, where they teach innovative design labs. They have also been previously invited to teach and evaluate drawings at Southeast University, Tianjin University, and the China Academy of Art, as well as take part in forums and give speeches at institutions like Harvard University, United States, the University of Hong Kong, Hong Kong, China, the University of Queensland, Australia, and Tongji, Southeast, and Shanghai Jiaotong Universities in China.

Selected Works

2021 **Dingshu Vocational School of Pottery, Yixing, Jiangsu Province, China**
2021 **Floral Pavilion at Horticulture Expo, Nanjing, Jiangsu Province, China**
2020 **Juanzong Books and Eureka! Touring Library at Aranya, Qinhuangdao, Hebei Province, China**
2019 **Yitingting Cottage, Tonglu, Zhejiang Province, China**
2018 **Jiaotong Warehouse Renovation, Shanghai, China**
2016 **Shangsian Cottage, Huzhou, Zhejiang Province, China**

Interviewer: *Architecture China*
Interviewee: genarchitects (g)
Editor: Wang Ying

Yitingting Cottage: view of the outer courtyard © Chen Hao

What is your understanding of the term "Building with Nature"?

g: First of all, I think "building with nature" is about letting things follow their natural course, while architecture is about mediating the relationship between humans and the environment. As intermediaries, architects identify aspects that are missing from an original site and introduce them with the aid of architectural methods.

What direction are you currently exploring in your practice?

g: At this stage, one of our main points of interest is the mutual influence between environments, on the one hand, and human behaviors and lifestyles on the other. Once a project is completed, we usually go back to visit it at a later date. On many occasions, we've noticed that the way a space is used by people is completely at odds with our initial expectations or intentions. That pushes us to ask ourselves: "Had we known this from the beginning, would we have designed the space differently?"

What we're particularly interested in at the moment are the type of conditions that lead people to adopt a space and adapt it to their needs, imbuing it with life that moves forward into the future.

How do you interpret the relationship between logical and intuitive construction?

g: Logic and intuition differ from one person to the next and are applied differently depending on the design brief at hand. Our interpretation of these two skills is: in every design project, it's necessary to make overall judgements that can be considered instinctive reactions. Logic allows you to build on these sensibilities and intuition to arrive at deeper conclusions.

What are the greatest challenges and opportunities faced by young architects today?

g: Today, we are at slightly over two decades since the year 2000, which was around the time that China joined the World Trade Organization and when independent architecture studios became possible in China. Our growth has followed that of China's construction and real estate industries. So really, the various obstacles we encountered throughout that process were relatively insignificant compared to that of today because architecture is heavily influenced by changes in the state of affairs from one period to another. I think the biggest challenge is really uncertainty regarding the future.

How can we interpret the relationship between architecture and sustainable construction?

g: I think that sustainability is one of architecture's oldest, most fundamental goals, because buildings have always needed to last a long time, and because our field has consistently strived to improve people's living environments. I think "sustainability" is used today as a kind of keyword or label that helps disseminate a concept that has always existed.

In the design process, every architect considers issues of sustainability to maximize the value and efficiency of a structure—especially when a lot of labor and resources are being invested in its construction. It's precisely for that reason that I don't think of sustainability as a new concept in architecture, but more as an inherent component that each architect needs to grapple with on their own terms.

Shangsian Cottage: view of the fifth courtyard after renovation—looking from the shed, toward the river and bridge © Hou Bowen

Dingshu Vocational School of Pottery © Su Shengliang

FLORAL PAVILION AT HORTICULTURE EXPO

Location: Nanjing, Jiangsu Province, China
Designers: genarchitects
Lead architects: Xue Zhe, Fan Beilei, Kong Rui
Design team: Liu Yang, Li Lanruo, Zang Min, Tao Shuting, Wang Shiyu, Chen Xi, Liu Jinghuan, Sun Haonan, Liu Weinan, Yang Tianyu
Design partners: Yangtze River Urban Architectural Design Co., Ltd., Suzhou Crownhomes Co., Ltd.
Site area: 4,275 square meters
Gross floor area: 2,050 square meters
Design period: December 2018–September 2019
Construction period: July 2019–April 2021
Photography: genarchitects

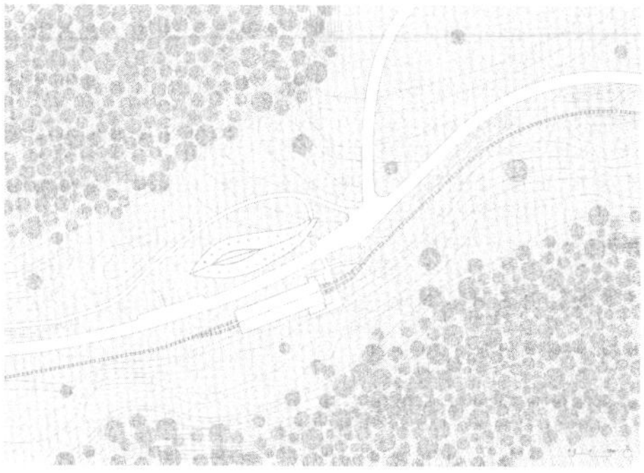

Site plan

Bird's-eye view of Floral Pavilion © genarchitects

Sitting in a valley wedged between two rolling mountain ranges, the Floral Pavilion serves as the main hall and café for the 11th Horticultural Exposition of Jiangsu Province. From the outset, equal importance was assigned to the natural scenery outdoors, as well as the ornamental plants inside. When visitors enter the Floral Pavilion from the outdoors, they are greeted by a space that is shielded from sunlight and noise, so that they may better appreciate the captivating natural landscapes that they've just strolled through, as they settle down high stools to rest their feet and enjoy some refreshments. Specifically selected, the high stools allow them to leisurely, and fully, take in their surroundings, both outside and inside, especially the expansive flower arrangement that runs from one end of the hall to the other. The scene is expertly sewn together by the lush hills in the distance that are still visible in the background imparting a sense of tranquility. In the master plan, the pavilion looks like a boat sailing through the hills. Upon reaching the pavilion's western-most point, visitors feel like they're standing at the prow, looking out to a "sea" of greenery.

The building is a combination of entirely prefabricated steel and wood components. The columns are placed toward the center of the space

Floral Pavilion © genarchitects

Interior of the Floral Pavilion © genarchitects

Interior of the Floral Pavilion © genarchitects

to prevent them from obstructing the panoramic views on either side of the pavilion. The weight of the roof largely rests on fusiform wooden pillars surrounding the flower bed. These pillars are joined by tie bars to the roof's wooden beams, which radiate outward and upward, like an upside-down umbrella.

To maintain the roof's balance, 4-centimeter-diameter steel tie bars are strategically positioned at 4-meter intervals along the exterior of the exhibition hall. These tie bars align with the gaps between the glass panels on the façade, and due to their inconspicuous nature, make the roof appear as if it's floating in the air. Inside the hall, a dark colour scheme has been adopted to create a calm atmosphere. Like in a theater, the dark ambiance draws visitors' attention to the flowers and outdoor scenery and creates an immersive experience, allowing these compelling subjects to hog the spotlight.

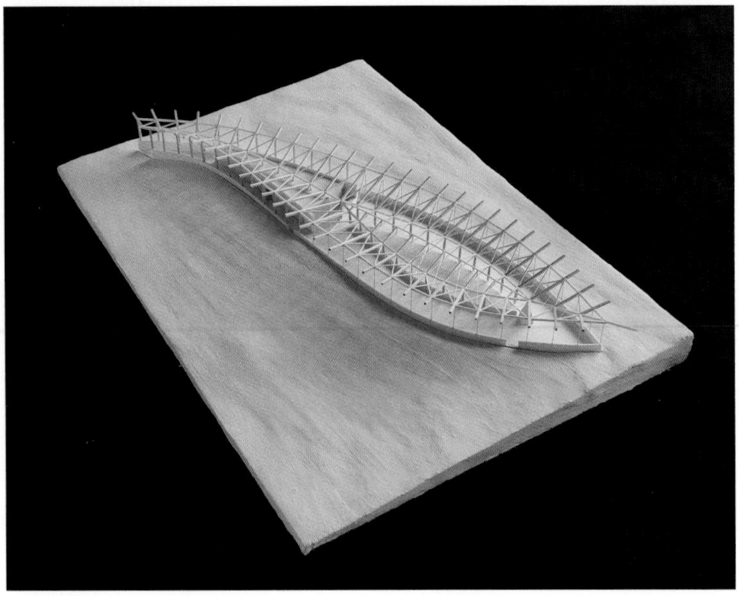

Structural model

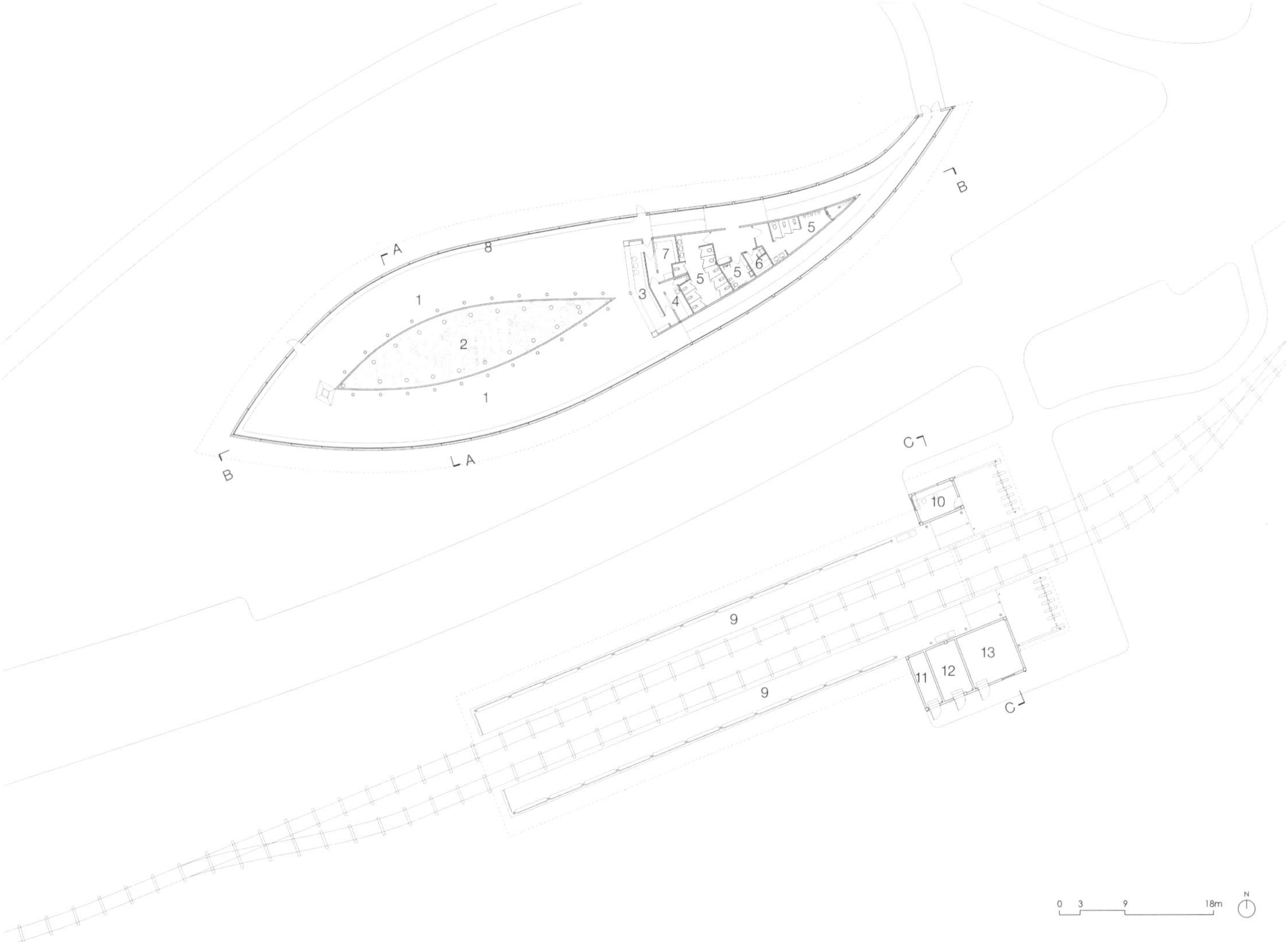

Pavilion and station plan

1. Exhibition area
2. Parterre
3. Information and bar
4. Pantry
5. Restrooms
6. Staff room
7. Manager's room
8. Bar table
9. Platform
10. Ticket office
11. Fire control room
12. Electrical room
13. Mechanical room

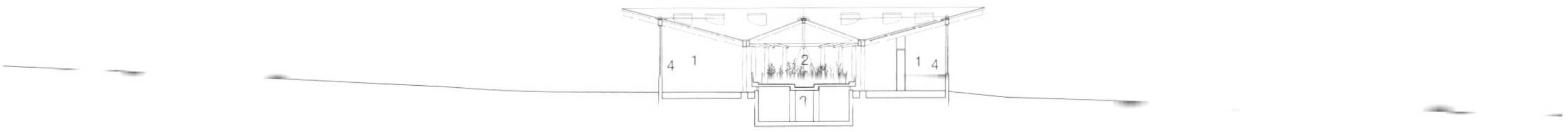

Section A-A

1. Exhibition hall
2. Parterre
3. Mechanical area
4. Bar table

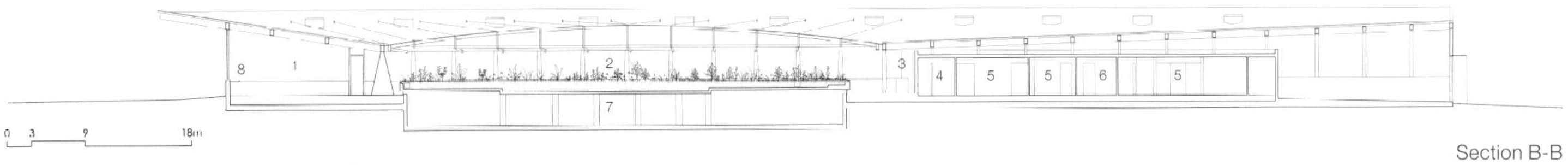

Section B-B

1. Exhibition hall
2. Parterre
3. Information and bar
4. Pantry
5. Restrooms
6. Staff room
7. Mechanical area
8. Bar table

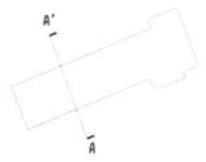

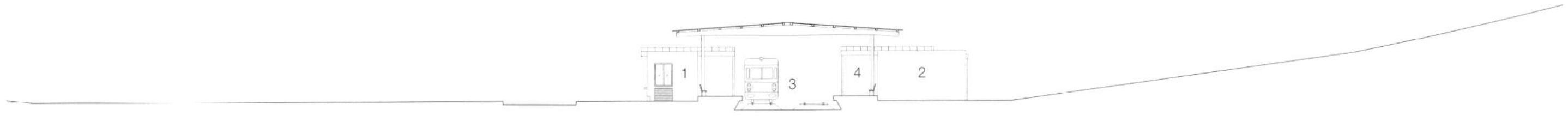

Section C-C

1. Mechanical room
2. Ticket office
3. Railroad
4. Platform

Detail

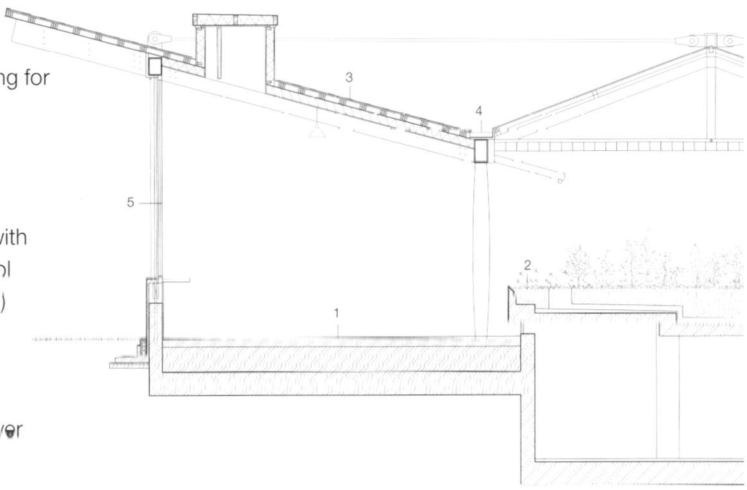

1. Black, cast-in-place terrazzo wear-resistant and anti-slip flooring layer
   Fine stone concrete protective layer
   Cement mortar
   Concrete bedding
   Rammed gravel or crushed brick
   Rammed soil
2. Plant soil overlay
   Geotextile filtration layer
   Plastic sheet drainage layer
   Cement mortar protective layer
   SBS modified asphalt water- and root-proof membrane
   Modified asphalt waterproofing membrane
   Cement mortar leveling and binding layer
   Reinforced-concrete structural slab
3. Specialized steel nail fixing for asphalt tiles
   EPDM waterproofing membrane
   OSB board
   Structural grating (filled with a compound mineral wool fireproof insulation board)
   PE membrane
   Fireproof gypsum board
   Glued timber beams
4. Perforated aluminum cover plate
   Metal gutter
   Metal guttering components
5. Glass
   Steel tie rods
   Decorative metal mesh

Xu Lang

CLAB Architects
Founder and Principal Architect, CLAB Architects
National First-class Registered Architect

Xu Lang was born in Chongqing, China, in 1982 and from 2000 to 2008, he studied at Chongqing University's School of Architecture, earning both a Bachelor of Architecture and Master of Architecture. In 2007, he won the JA Conceptual Architecture Award in Japan. In 2007, he co-founded NOffice, where he worked until 2009, at the same time also serving as Editor of *Urban China* magazine. In 2012, he worked as deputy chief architect at Hong Kong Huayi Design Consulting (Shenzhen) Co., Ltd. and in 2017 was certified a national first-class registered architect. He also founded CLAB Architects that year, thereby beginning his independent practice.

Since their inception in 2017, CLAB Architects have refused to limit themselves to one type of project or style. There are two keywords that can be applied to all their works: "construction" and "nature." Construction is the fundamental nature of their work, while nature is the value to which it subscribes. CLAB Architects attributes two layers of significance to "natural construction": construction that is in tune with the natural environment, and construction that is unpretentious, direct, and down-to-earth. The practice places emphasis on simple ingenuity and ingenious simplicity—the expression of clear concepts through the intuitive language of materials and structure. CLAB adopts an open attitude toward these two keywords, exploring their evolving connotations through their practice.

Selected Works

2023 The Nature Education Center of Tangjiahe Nature Reserve, Guangyuan, Sichuan Province, China
2022 Wildlife Observation Tower in Tangjiahe Nature Reserve, Guangyuan, Sichuan Province, China
2022 Exhibition Gallery of Local Specialties, Guangyuan, Sichuan Province, China
2021 Museum of Bamboo Weaving, Yibin, Sichuan Province, China
2020 Qionglai Liquor Museum and Wenjun Restaurant, Chengdu, Sichuan Province, China
2019 Christian Boltanski · The Heart Pavilion · WuLong, Chongqing, China
2019 Yinshanlan Garden in Yishala Village, Panzhihua, Sichuan Province, China
2018 House for Mother and Daughter in Mingyue Village, Pujiang, Chengdu Province, China
2018 Innovative Lab of Architecture and Art, Chengdu, Sichuan Province, China

Wildlife Observation Tower in Tangjiahe Nature Reserve © Xu Lang

Christian Boltanski The Heart Pavilion WuLong © Li Chibin

Exhibition Gallery of Local Specialties © Xu Lang

Interviewer: *Architecture China*
Interviewee: Xu Lang (XU)
Editor: Wang Ying

What is your understanding of the term "Building with Nature"?

XU: My understanding of "building with nature" is humility and simplicity as opposed to extravagance. When used as a noun, it can be understood as putting humans on equal standing with the environment; as a verb, I consider it to mean building less ostentatiously; more pared-down structures. I think that, as architects, we need to be more in sync with nature, whether it's in terms of emphasizing a harmonious coexistence with our natural surroundings or adopting a more natural approach to design. But, because we will never be able to fully understand the geometry of nature, establishing a connection between geometry and nature is a type of methodology that continually hones the architects' intuition and guides us toward nature.

What direction are you currently exploring in your practice?

XU: Our focus is perhaps on the structure of buildings—that is, their true essence. I tend to view the composition of buildings in hierarchical layers, such as structure, construction, and fenestration. What I find most inspiring is exploring different possibilities from the perspective of structure, because structure is architecture's most essential form of expression—it is the most fundamental condition to creating a space. Buildings can lack fenestration, but they can't lack structure. Structure is a building's underlying logic.

How do young architects take part in rural initiatives?

XU: There's currently no well defined set of strategies for rural architectural practice. It's a really new field. Much like how one hundred readers will each interpret a story in their own way, one hundred architects each have their own vision for China's countryside. I think that's a really interesting idea.

Based on our experience, I'd say that there are two key points. The first is to visit villages, build a rapport with their inhabitants, and mold the project around their community. This is something that our firm—and me in particular—don't excel at, so there are a lot of projects that came to an end before we could reach this step. But I think it's incredibly important because the structure of rural societies is very different from that of cities: in the countryside, relationships are based on blood ties and geographical affinities, whereas in the city, they tend to be more contractual.

Second, when working in rural villages, architects need to go back to our roots. Villages often have their own regional methods of construction. For instance, when building with concrete, some places make molds using papier-mâché or plastic, often with very satisfying results. I think that architects can explore different construction methods as they learn from rural communities. We should see it as an important learning process and an opportunity to study authentic building practices.

What are the greatest challenges and opportunities faced by young architects today?

XU: As the real estate market stagnates, there'll be more and more opportunities to realize the true power and value of design. But inherent in these opportunities are certain challenges, namely the overall reduction in the number of new construction initiatives.

INNOVATIVE LAB OF ARCHITECTURE AND ART

Location: Qiongyao Archaeological Park, Chengdu, Sichuan Province, China
Lead architect: Xu Lang
Design team: Xu Lang, Li Yunle, Chen Dongxu
Technical support for rammed earth: Wan Li, Chi Xin'an (One University, One Village team)
Gross floor area: 305 square meters
Design period: April 2017–August 2017
Construction period: May 2018
Photography: Xu Lang

Site plan

The Innovative Lab of Architecture and Art is surrounded by historic kilns © Xu Lang

Evening view of the outside space © Xu Lang

Architecture as a Form of Social Engagement

1. Project Story/Author's Self-introduction

In 2017, I got the chance to build a space for my studio in an archaeological park on the rural outskirts of Chengdu, Sichuan Province, China. This was my first experience of truly building something in rural China; my only source of labor was local farm workers who knew little of modern construction. I chose to name this space Innovative Lab of Architecture and Art. In the preparatory phase of the project, I identified a number of concepts that I wanted to explore.

- The first, was to construct the space using rammed earth.
- The second was that the rammed earth had to constitute the building's fundamental structure, rather than being an additional source of support.
- The third, was to organize training for local construction workers in ramming earth.
- Fourth, the building had to be compatible with modern equipment.

My insistence on using rammed earth in this way didn't derive from any aesthetic preference or a desire to return to tradition, but rather my personal theory that, perhaps, the skills involved in this material's production have the potential to reshape relations in rural China. I viewed the construction of this project as an experiment in applying architectural knowledge to social relations in the context of rural revitalization. Social engagement in rural construction is much more profound than simply building houses.

And because of point four, the traditional construction method of rammed earth had to be paired with advanced thermal design elements such as curtain walls with thermal breaks, as well as an inexpensive integrated roof system comprising both insulation and waterproofing capabilities. The curtain walls with thermal breaks were designed with manual construction techniques in mind, while the integrated roof was built with the help of a nearby building materials plant.

There was also a point five: I hate lamps and so wanted to integrate natural lighting into the building's structure.

Lecture hall within the site © Xu Lang

Workers installing steel structures on the rammed earth walls © Xu Lang

2. Earthquake Prevention: A Prototype of "Framed Tube Structures + Open Plane"

Ramming earth by hand is a traditional know-how that's deeply ingrained in the fiber of rural society. As architects participating in rural construction, our role is to enrich this know-how with our expertise to create a more durable, practical, and aesthetically pleasing material. In particular, durability (or safety) holds significant importance in rural areas where construction supervision and modern building systems are lacking. Another factor that contributes to the building's seismic resistance is structural ingenuity. The vast majority of its structural components have been designed as small framed tubes capable of resisting lateral forces from any direction. Between these framed tube structures is an open plane that serves as the building's public space. The wall panels in this space are connected to the shear-resistant framed tube structures by the steel frame of the roof and the foundation beams. This structural design of "framed tube structures + open plane" can be considered a prototype that can, in the future, be adapted to the construction of most rural public spaces.

3. Three Opportunities for Social Engagement through Rammed Earth

Cost-effectiveness: the affordability of rammed earth means that it can be applied as a construction method on a vast scale. However, this dissemination shouldn't come to be because of an order passed down from above, but rather, it should be a spontaneous choice that rural communities make based on their specific economic circumstances.

Handwork-based: Before the advent of contemporary construction techniques, building a house was viewed in rural China as a life skill rather than a type of professional expertise. Hand work–based construction methods are not only well-adapted to navigate the lack of technology in rural areas, they can also help to revive the collectivist spirit of these areas.

As a structure: Using rammed earth combined with structural expertise to ensure the integrity of a building is an effective solution to tackle the lack of technology in rural China. Unless this material is incorporated into the fundamental structure of the building, rural construction will still require other more technologically advanced forms of structural support. This may in turn hinder the material's ability to foster unity in rural societies. This project required local builders to receive training in ramming earth. Due to the tight-knit nature of rural acquaintances in such societies, I believe builders will continue to spread these skills they gained as they go about their day-to-day.

4. A Blend of Traditional and Modern Charm

Central air conditioning and a hot-water recirculation system were installed to give the building a more modern feel. This equipment needed to be paired with a similarly high-grade building maintenance system. However, certain limitations in rural construction meant that my original design for the curtain wall and integrated roof for heat insulation and rain protection was unviable and required adjustment.

For the updated structural curtain wall, I adopted a steel frame and set the thermal break at the structural level. The wall was, of course, designed to be compatible with manual construction techniques. Each steel column consists of two steel profiles filled with insulation material and the curtain wall's double panes were directly inserted into the profile grooves as part of the maintenance system. The indoor spaces are completely sealed off from the outdoors. Reducing the dimensions of the steel profiles made manual welding a possibility; it also meant that panes of equal width could be used to create a uniform look on the façade.

The design for the insulated and waterproof roof was adjusted based on the production capacity of a building materials plant located near the project site. Nano plates were chosen as the profile material, while layers of insulating mineral wool and waterproof material were fused together by the factory before being installed onto the roof's purlins. This type of integrated roof is only one-third as expensive as other similar products in the market with the same thermal performance.

The whole building was constructed manually by local workers.

Model

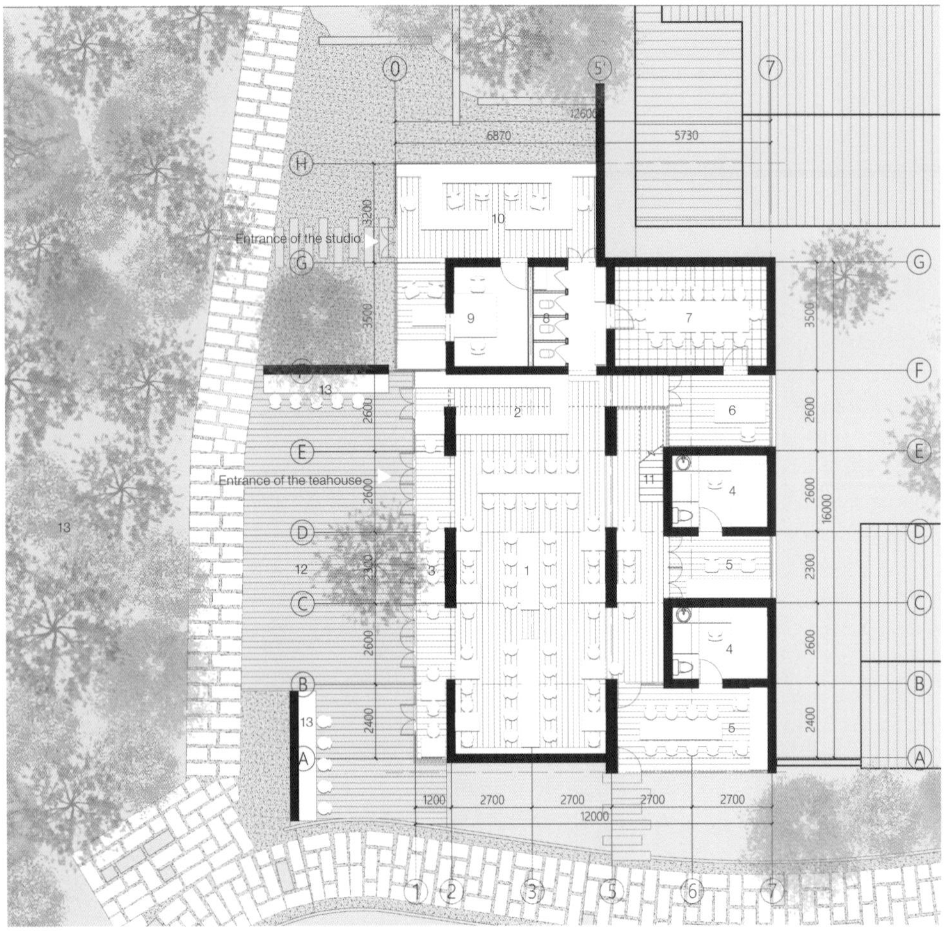

Ground-floor plan

1. Teahouse and salon
2. Operating bar
3. Veranda
4. Artists' residence
5. Artists' workshop
6. Office
7. Meeting room
8. Restrooms
9. 10-square-meter gallery
10. CLAB Architects' studio
11. Staircase
12. Terrace
13. Rammed-earth parapet

Section A-A

Section B-B

Structural installation of the lighting © Xu Lang

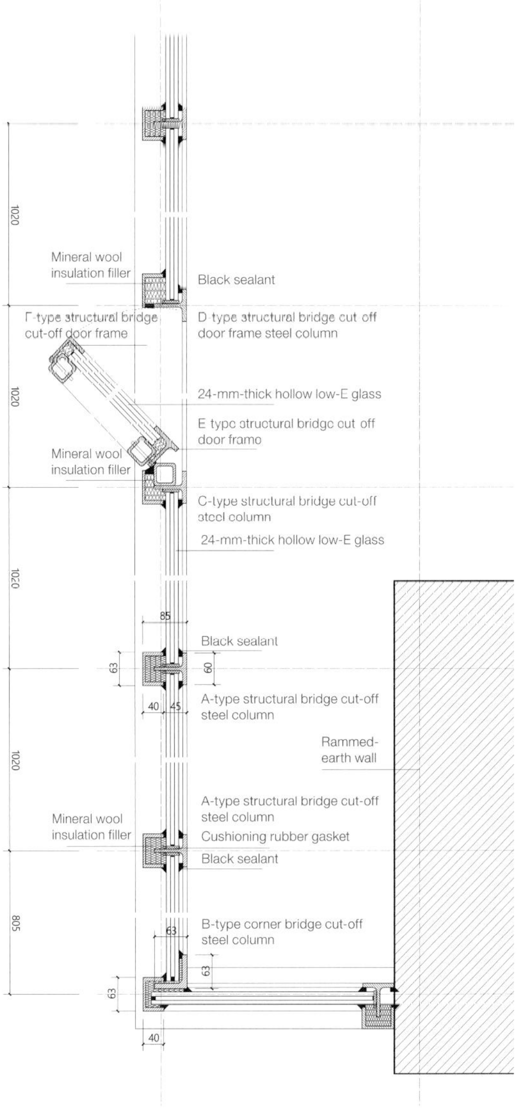

Detail

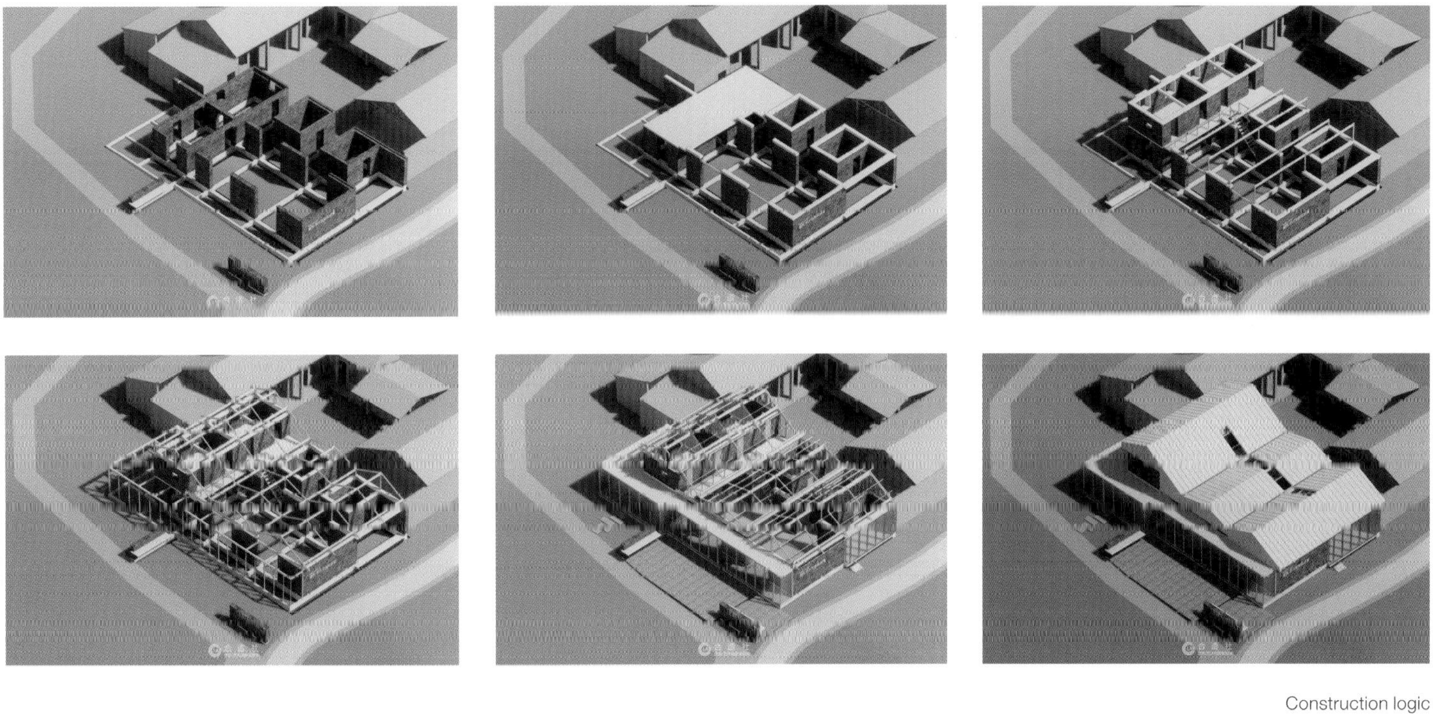

Construction logic

自然建造
ARCHITECTURE
CHINA
AWARD

SPECIAL PROJECT AWARD

The Special Project Award is given to high-quality architectural works completed in recent years that embody the *Building with Nature* concept, or similar concepts. The recipients are nominated and selected by the members of the jury.

Zeng Xiaolian Museum of Art
Elepheno Architects

Dingshu Vocational School of Pottery
genarchitects

Nanjing Qinhuai Bay Bridge
AND Office

Wind H Art Center
Thoughten Architects

ZENG XIAOLIAN MUSEUM OF ART

Yang Xiong
Elepheno Architects

Location: World Horticultural-Expo Garden (1999), Kunming, Yunnan Province, China
Lead architect: Yang Xiong
Design team: Yang Xiong, Nie Rongqing, Yang Mengya, Pu Han, Zhang Ling
Gross floor area: 661 square meters
Design period: June 2021
Construction period: October 2021
Photography: Wang Ce, Ono Studio, PrismImage

Site plan

1 | 2/3

1. Main façade of the Zeng Xiaolian Museum of Art © Wang Ce
2. Lateral view of the museum façade © Wang Ce
3. Outdoor garden © Ono Studio

The project is located on the north side of Expo Gardens Friendship Road, on the sites of the former Pakistan and Vietnam Gardens of the 1999 World Horticultural Expo Garden. The conception of the museum's layout began with a discussion on how to approach its "pre-existence." While expo architecture usually feels segregated from its surrounding natural and cultural context, the Pakistan and Vietnam Gardens presented quite a contrary impression. Weathered red bricks, cracks in marble surfaces, as well as the long shadows cast by the columns and trees under the sunlight gave the site a sense of history.

"Pre-existence" is defined as the preservation of old heritage amid new construction. Traces of history remain legible; rather than erasing them, new developments complement them and enrich their significance. The present is laid over the past like tracing paper on an old photo.

A steel structure facilitated the project's timely completion while minimizing its impact on the surrounding environment—not a single tree was felled during construction. The original open-air Pakistani Pavilion—with its stone plaque, marble banisters, wall niches, and stone benches—was also preserved in its entirety and integrated into the new museum.

While most walls rise from the floor, the walls of this museum are hung from the steel structure that stands overhead; the bottom of the walls just lightly kiss the floor. The curves and intersections of these lightweight suspended walls create rich interior and exterior spaces that showcase the museum's art while forming an intriguing contrast with the original site. The white museum and the red-brick Pakistan Garden coexist and embrace each other, forming a unique bond that connect the present and the past.

Pre-existing marble niches © Wang Ce

Sala I © PrismImage

Circular window in Sala III © PrismImage

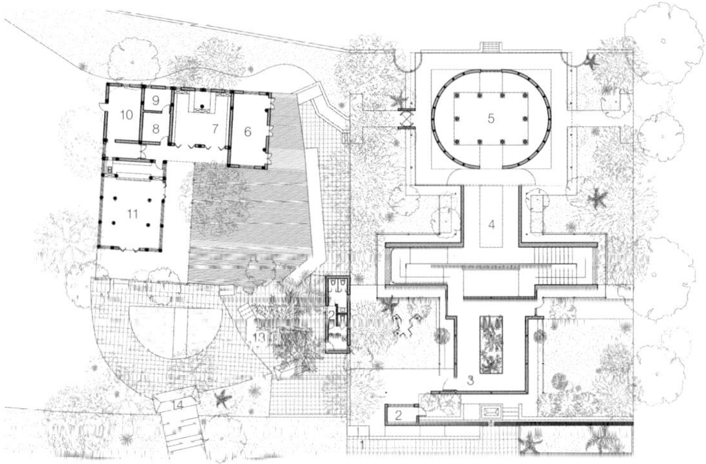

Ground-floor plan

1. Entry
2. Ticketing
3. Sala I
4. Sala II
5. Sala III
6. Artist studio
7. Bookstore
8. Office
9. Store
10. Kitchen
11. Café and bar
12. Restroom
13. Gazebo
14. Exit

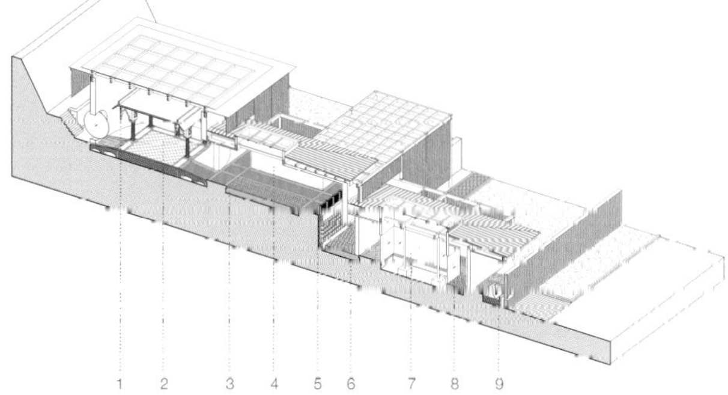

Longitudinal axonometric drawing

1. Existing gazebo
2. Sala III
3. Backfill pool
4. Sala II
5. Existing niche
6. Backfill pool
7. Greenhouse
8. Sala I
9. Existing stele

DINGSHU VOCATIONAL SCHOOL OF POTTERY

Xue Zhe, Fan Beilei, Kong Rui
genarchitects

Location: Dingshu, Yixing, Jiangsu Province, China
Architectural, interior, and landscape design: genarchitects
Lead architects: Xue Zhe, Fan Beilei, Kong Rui
Project architect: Wang Shiyu
Design team: Tao Shuting, Liu Yang, Xian Haohui, Xue Jun, Xiao Xinyu, Qian Jia, Li Lanruo, Guo Zhenghao, Liu Jinghuan, Huang Fanlang, Xie Rugui, Li Yunhong
Landscape architect: Chen Xi
Structural consultants: AND Office (Zhang Zhun, Zhang Chongchong, Chen Xuejian)
Site area: 29,542 square meters
Gross floor area: 10,905 square meters
Design period: December 2017–May 2019
Construction period: June 2019–April 2021
Photography: Chen Hao

Site plan

The new campus of Dingshu Vocational School of Pottery and the distant mountains near the town © Chen Hao

In today's industrialized world, — "handmade pottery"— has an undeniable allure and is still as captivating as ever before. The Dingshu Vocational School of Pottery recognizes the significance of craftsmanship in its curriculum, which is why— "artisanal workshops"— serve as the focal point of the campus's design. Each facility within the school showcases an architectural form that harmonizes with its function, and speaks for itself. The diverse array of buildings creates a variety of outdoor spaces that set the campus apart from the typical, large, mixed-use structures prevalent in traditional campus typologies. On this campus, people are invited to stroll comfortably between the architectural structures and experience the dynamic shifts in the physical landscape.

—genarchitects

Dingshu Pottery Culture and Vocational School

Situated in Yixing, Jiangsu Province, China, approximately 200 kilometers from Shanghai, Dingshu is a small town renowned for its thousand-year history of pottery manufacturing. The town's pottery heritage is particularly celebrated for its distinctive Zisha teapots crafted from zisha or purple clay. These refined teapots have long been coveted by Chinese literati and tea enthusiasts. Hence, over time, Dingshu emerged as a thriving hub for the manufacturing and trade of Zisha pottery in China, resulting in a deep-rooted connection between the local community and a pottery culture.

A comfortable, naturally lit environment inside the major workshop is created through windows and aluminum louvers © Chen Hao

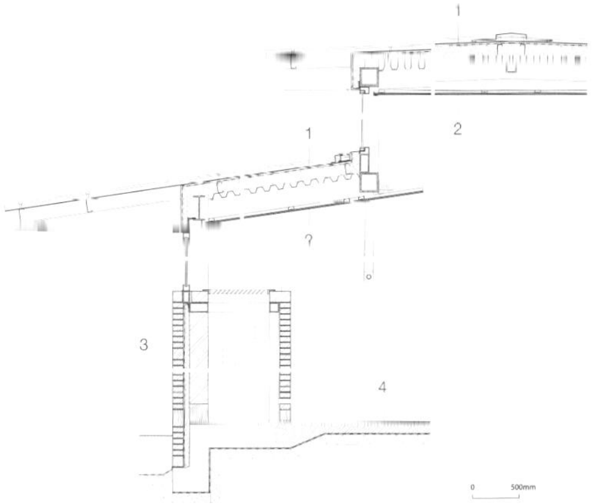

Detail

1. Standing seam metal roof
   EPDM waterproof
   Insulation
   Vapor barrier
   Steel purlin
   Steel beam
   Steel panel
2. Light steel keel
   Gypsum board
   Moisture-proof paint
   Putty leveling layer
   White paint
3. Brick
   Waterproof motar
   Anti-cracking mortar
   Alkali-resistant mesh fabric
   Foamed ceramic insulation panels
   Adhesives
   Aerated concrete blocks
4. Polished fine stone concrete floor
   Fine stone concrete slope-finding layer
   Cement slurry with construction adhesive
   C15 light concrete bedding
   Compacted earth

The pottery school stands as one of the few institutions within China's rural adult education system that focuses on pottery education and training. Its mission is twofold: to raise the income and enhance the livelihoods of local residents by providing academic education and skill-building opportunities, and to serve as a communal space for public education and events during after-school hours, catering to the rural community's lack of public facilities.

Workshop and Campus

By researching the history of local pottery culture and its workshops, genarchitects gained a broad understanding of the traditional apprenticeship model for nurturing pottery artisans. Through extensive consultations with the surrounding community, pottery practitioners, teachers, and craftspeople, the concept of an artisanal school with a low-density campus centered around pottery workshops gradually took shape.

Unlike a conventional campus layout characterized by large mixed-use buildings and expansive open squares, the Dingshu Vocational School of Pottery's campus embraces a more fragmented spatial arrangement reminiscent of traditional workshops. The four key structures—two workshops, a multifunction hall, and an exhibition hall—are strategically positioned at the heart of the campus, forming the central Beech Tree Plaza, which is conducive for hosting outdoor activities.

Parts of the Whole

Recognizing the specialized spatial requirements for each step in the pottery learning and manufacturing process, the priority was to optimize designs according to each function. This includes spacious and well-lit classrooms conducive to writing and painting, tranquil and lofty workshops tailored for shaping, painting, embossing, and sculpting pottery, and a showroom that exhibits the students' finest works within a hall adorned with expansive beams and columns. Each aspect of the school's diverse functions is accompanied by its own distinct space, structure, and equipment, forming a collection of independent architectural components that contribute to the greater whole.

The pottery school campus comprises over ten low-rise buildings, designed to maximize the benefits of abundant natural lighting and ventilation. The arrangement of these structures generates various outdoor spaces in between. The interplay of these diverse, internal and external spaces, complemented by canopied semi-outdoor porches, creates a dynamic and captivating environment. The pleasant campus landscape fosters open communication and interaction, while also cultivating creativity and inspiration.

Materials and Localization

Brick, concrete, and sandstone were selected as the primary materials as they aligned with the gene of manual craftsmanship inherent in pottery production. These materials also make it feasible for local workers to engage in the construction process. The use of ordinary materials alongside innovative construction techniques allows the campus to seamlessly blend into the fabric of the existing town, resulting in an instantly recognizable and familiar atmosphere that resonates with local residents.

As a provider of high-quality pottery training, the Dingshu Vocational School of Pottery annually equips thousands of students with the professional skills needed to improve their standards of living. As a recent addition to the local pottery culture, the school also actively contributes to the community through ongoing cultural exhibitions and exchanges, continuing the legacy of pottery making in Dingshu.

NANJING QINHUAI BAY BRIDGE

Zhang Zhun
AND Office

Location: Chengde Boulevard over Qinhuai River, Nanjing, Jiangsu Province, China
Designers: AND Office + NAN Architects
Span: 157 meters
Lead architects: (Structure) Zhang Zhun; (architecture) Nan Xu
Design team: Zhou Dingqi, Tang Huilian
Working drawings produced by: China Railway Engineering Design and Consulting Group
Photography: Liu Songkai, Tian Fangfang

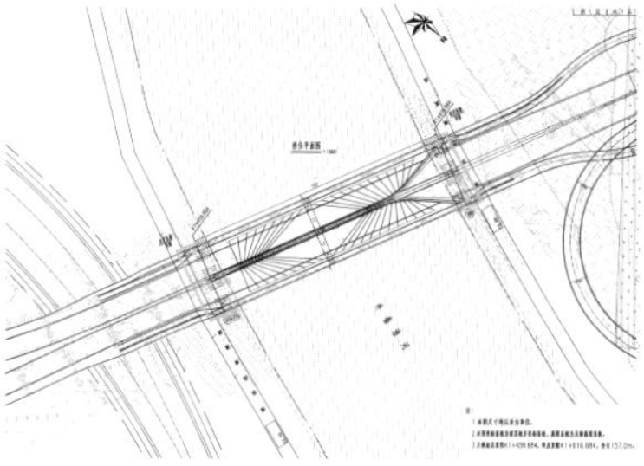

Site plan

Bird's-eye view of the Nanjing Qinhuai Bay Bridge © Liu Songkai

Aerial view of the Nanjing Qinhuai Bay Bridge © Liu Songkai

In the design of long-span vehicular bridges, structural rationality occupies a dominant position and this project explores a new beam configuration that breaks away from past conventions in bridge design. Different forms are arranged according to rigorous mechanical logic in order to produce an elegant design that showcases regional characteristics while taking into consideration users' actual needs.

The project's concepts were constrained by complex contextual factors and practical considerations, such as the clearance height for maritime traffic and the adjacent high-speed railway line. This provided little room for negotiation, in terms of the plane alignment and longitudinal slope of the road—and, by extension, crucial elements such as the height of the bridge's main girder structure. After a technical investigation, it was decided that the bridge had to be one of only two types: either tied-arch or single-tower cable-stayed.

Different possibilities were explored within designs for these two types of bridges, specifically focusing on structural variations that could express regional characteristics. Tied-arch bridges would recall the form of surrounding mountains, while a cable-stayed bridge would form a visual parallel with the nearby site of an abandoned airport. Ultimately, it was decided that the first of the two ideas had greater design potential.

In the early structural design process, independent triangular arches were combined to form a design element reminiscent of the mountains. However, a mechanical analysis revealed that these independent arches had poor stability. Eventually, following extensive research, the team arrived at a design that was both visually captivating and mechanically sound.

The arches of the tie-bridge and their cables are arranged in such a way as to produce a harmonious array of overlapping triangles of different sizes. Not only does this unique form create associations with the four surrounding mountains, Jiangjun, Fang, Qinglong, and Zijin, it also demonstrates ingenuity in terms of its load-bearing capacity.

The elegance and stability of the bridge are the fruit of its inherent geometric logic. Its intricate geometric relations are encapsulated within a stable rectangular shape. The main control point is the point from

View along the central axis of the Nanjing Qinhuai Bay Bridge © Tian Fangfang

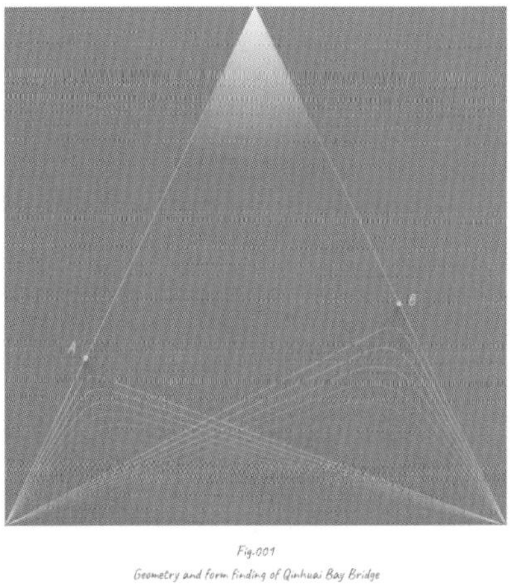

Geometry and form finding of Qinhuai Bay Bridge

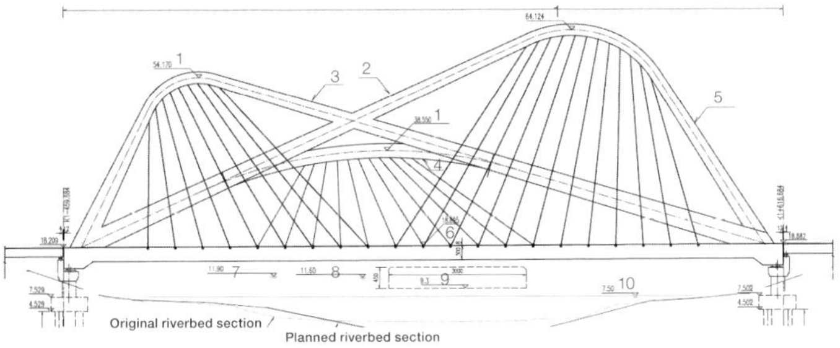

Elevation of the Nanjing Qinhuai Bay Bridge

1. Highest point
2. Arch rib A
3. Arch rib B
4. Arch rib C
5. Arch rib A1/A2
6. Center of the span
7. Nominal flood level P=0.5%
8. Nominal flood level P=0.1%
9. Maximum navigable water level
10. Normal water level

Structural analysis of the Nanjing Qinhuai Bay Bridge

1. Compression force
2. Tension force
3. Foundation reaction force

which the bridge's cables radiate outward act—thanks to which, a set of viable arch axes could be calculated. By contrast, the selection of curves was based on a combination of aesthetic and mechanical concerns.

The project's multiple cable surfaces and staggered tie-rod arch system are world-firsts. The triangular arches produce multiple surfaces to which cables can be attached, allowing for a greater dispersion of weight. The curved peaks of each arch not only add a sense of fluidity to the design, but [illegible] of cables, preventing stress from concentrating in a specific area.

The difference in height between the two arches creates a dynamic and captivating design. The higher arch forks into two separate beams at one end, increasing its stability by spreading its load. Meanwhile, in the interest of reducing its load, the lower arch is equipped with fewer cables.

In addition to its unique arches, the bridge is also characterized by its two-tiered pedestrian and non-motor vehicular pathways. This feature—which results in part from the bridge's restrictions—provides shelter for pedestrians crossing the bridge on rainy days, as well as makes their walk a more novel experience.

The iconic silhouette of the Nanjing Qinhuai Bay Bridge can be viewed as an extension of the dynamic South New City skyline. Its ingeniousness results not only from its artistic homage to its local setting, but also its innovative application of engineering logic to overcome practical concerns in bridge design.

Structural rigor is indispensable when it comes to designing long-span bridges like this, as veering from calculations in favor of ostentatious embellishments can come at the expense of safety. In the Nanjing Qinhuai Bay Bridge, this rigor has not only resulted in an entirely original system for guaranteeing the bridge's structural integrity, but has also produced a stunning visual effect. In addition to being mathematically sound, the overlapping triangular arches also form parallels with the bridge's natural backdrop. This fusion of aesthetic exploration and engineering logic has far-reaching appeal and will continue to be admired long into the future.

WIND H ART CENTER

Dong Yugan
Thoughten Architects

Location: 798 Art District, Beijing, China
Lead architect: Dong Yugan
Design team: Thoughten Architects
Gross floor area: 1,300 square meters
Design period: July 2019–July 2020
Construction period: July 2019–July 2020
Photography: Zhu Xi, Ke Yunfeng

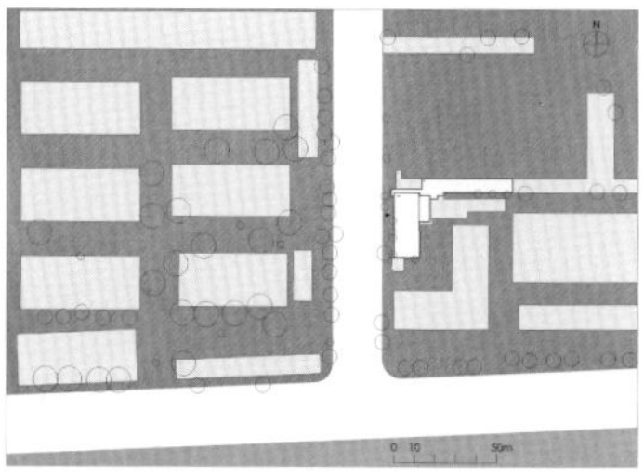

Site plan

First-floor exhibition hall © Zhu Xi

A wisteria "climbs up," trailing vines toward the attic from the plant pool on the ground floor © Ke Yunfeng

The Wind H Art Center underwent a comprehensive remodeling process by distinctly altering two parts. The first involved the transformation of an existing prefabricated concrete structure, which initially comprised seven rooms on two floors of a glass factory. Adjacent to this structure was also a two-story annex utilized as an office space. The second part entailed the conversion of a temporary warehouse with a steel structure. Situated in an alley between the factory and a two-story dormitory on the north side, the building had been repurposed as a noodle restaurant.

During the design phase of the first section, two significant challenges were addressed. First, was the landlord's request for an increased amount of usable floor space, especially so because of the high rental costs associated with the site. Second, the buildings displayed minimal natural elements, aside from a few mulberry trees on the western side. To address these issues, in three of the seven rooms on the first floor, the prefabricated floor slabs were selectively demolished—with the landlord's permission—and partially lowered to create self-contained spaces within the rooms using in-situ concrete. Additionally, an attic was incorporated on the second floor by repurposing the prefabricated steel beams that remained after removing the first-floor slabs. A mezzanine floor was also added between the ceiling of the newly constructed self-contained rooms on the first floor and the raised attic.

The additional rooms house the smaller museum facilities, such as the reception area, café, and offices, while the remaining four rooms form an interconnected, nearly unbroken two-story exhibition hall. To compensate for the lack of natural surroundings, the attic was designed to open toward the canopy of the mulberry trees. A large plant pool was also integrated into one of the sunken rooms; wisteria vines were planted along the staircase leading to the steel suspension bridge that connects the second-floor exhibition hall and the attic. The green element in the project is enhanced through several of such indoor plant pools that have been strategically placed in the gaps between the gallery and the annex, as well as within the existing and newly added wall niches.

View of the main building from the annex © Ke Yunfeng

The attic © Ke Yunfeng

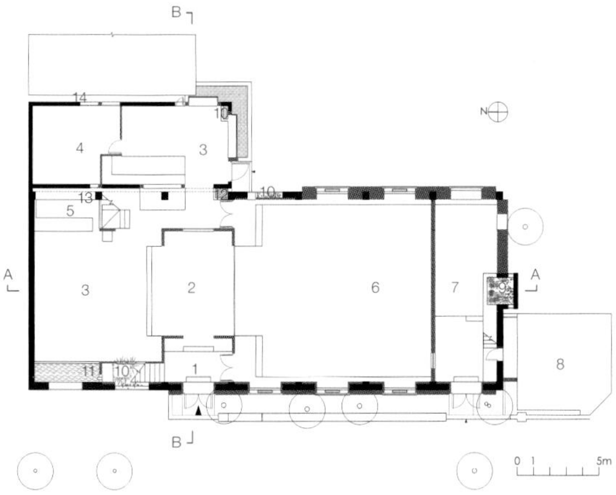

Ground-floor plan

1. Foyer
2. Reception
3. Café
4. Kitchen
5. Bar
6. Lecture and exhibition hall
7. Workshop
8. Restrooms
9. Pond
10. Plant pool
11. Shallow pool
12. Water plant pool
13. Slit
14. Crevice

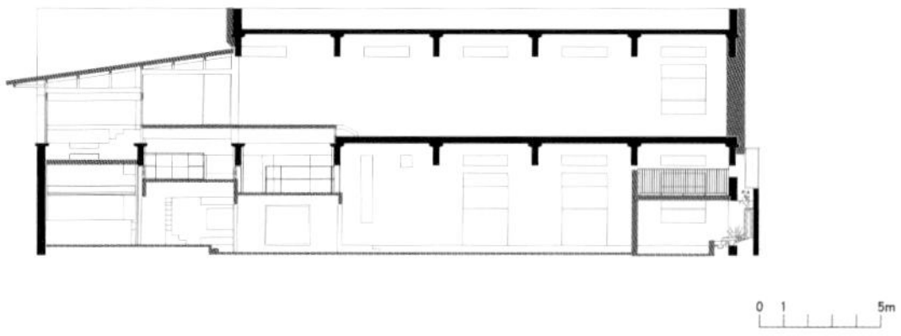

Section A-A

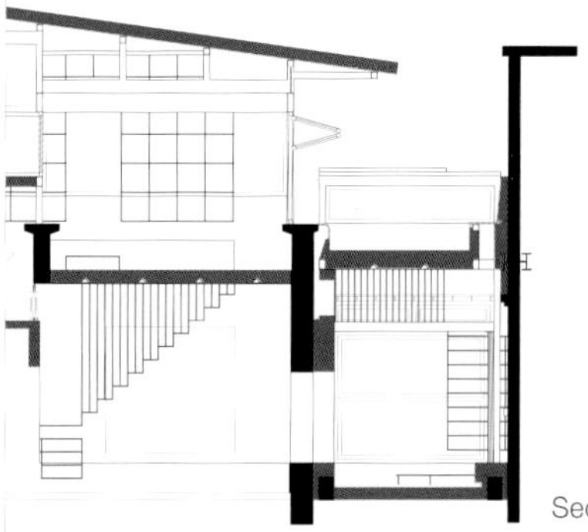

Section B-B

The remodeling of the second section faced certain challenges when it came to securing the landlord's approval. In order to minimize expenses associated with the front façade, as well as maintain the desired floor space, the landlord had decided to lease the rear portions of both the narrow noodle restaurant and the elongated dormitory building to the north. To infuse vitality into the depths of this elongated, Z-shaped space, the roof of the original noodle restaurant's kitchen, situated in one corner, was removed, and the space was transformed into a courtyard. This reduced available space and did not sit well with the landlord. However, compensatory measures were implemented, which includes the addition of a loft at the entrance and the installation of a glass roof above the newly created courtyard. To maintain an aesthetic cohesion, a vine trellis has been positioned beneath the glass roof, effectively concealing the fact that the courtyard retains a semi-indoor character.

View from the entrance toward the attic © Zhu Xi

自然建造2023
ARCHITECTURE
CHINA
AWARD 2023

ARCHITECTURE
CHINA

Trophy design by Qin Xiaowan and Li Hongkai